T0138005

Empirical Studies on the Development
of Executable Business Processes

Daniel Lübke • Cesare Pautasso

Editors

Empirical Studies on the Development of Executable Business Processes

 Springer

Editors
Daniel Lübke
Fachgebiet Software Engineering
Leibniz Universität Hannover
Hannover, Germany

Cesare Pautasso
Faculty of Informatics
Università della Svizzera italiana (USI)
Lugano, Switzerland

ISBN 978-3-030-17668-6   ISBN 978-3-030-17666-2   (eBook)
https://doi.org/10.1007/978-3-030-17666-2

This Springer imprint is published by the registered company Springer Nature Switzerland AG.
The registered company address is: Gewerbestrasse 11, 6330 Cham, Switzerland

To my family and my friends. Without them none of this would be possible. I am very glad to be surrounded by people who are that nice and support me every day. Thank you!

– Daniel

To my Hope for the future

– Cesare

Foreword

Executable business processes. At first sight, the topic may sound trivial to some people used to model business processes on a regular basis, yet I feel it is not. Getting from a graphical model to software (or a configuration thereof) that is able to automatically orchestrate other software components, such as web services or generic web APIs, or to coordinate people performing different business activities, requires not only familiarity with the chosen modeling notation but also intimate knowledge of the target runtime environment and of the model's execution semantics. Let's be frank: while it is relatively easy to draw some form of understandable process model on paper, for example, using Business Process Model and Notation (BPMN), how many of us have the necessary knowledge and skills to also deploy that model on a given business process engine and to successfully run it at the first attempt? I don't. At least, not any longer.

I first got in touch with business process modeling and execution during my PhD in the early 2000s, where I worked as teaching assistant of a course on workgroup and workflow management systems at Politecnico di Milano. I adopted model- and process-driven paradigms in my research since, e.g., to enable end users to model own process logics or to specify complex crowdsourcing processes. I used them in the research papers written together with other PhD students and colleagues, collecting lots of comments and criticism from reviewers. As senior PC member and PC chair of the International Conference on Business Process Management (BPM), I then had the chance to look behind the curtain and to review (and criticize) myself the work of others—an activity that also allowed me to get to know and appreciate the editors of this volume. Both Cesare and Daniel are known for their sensibility toward well-designed business processes and concrete practices. No frills.

This concreteness is evident in this volume. In fact, it brings together contributions that all provide some form of empirical perspective on or evidence of state-of-the-art business process management challenges. The first part of the volume looks into architectural aspects and covers the implementation of process-driven applications and the analysis of how data flow logics are supported. The second part proposes a set of case studies and experiments on the suitability of process modeling notations for the collection of requirements and on the implementation of process support in both manufacturing and services industries—two sectors with contrasting business process requirements, ranging from very fine grained and repetitive to coarse grained and case based. The third and last part concerns quality, quality in terms of engine performance and process model correctness. The volume is the result of the joint work of authors from all over the world, and evidence itself of the significance and widespread acknowledgment of the problem of correct process execution and the need for concrete and repeatable results.

As researchers, teachers, and practitioners, how many times have we seen process models containing gateway nodes testing conditions without any prior activity producing the necessary data for the evaluation of the condition? How many times have we seen models where it was impossible to understand who was supposed to execute a given activity, sometimes not even being able to tell whether the executor was a software or a human agent? And how many times was it evident that a given model, although formally correct, would not meet expected running times?

Well, this volume will not teach you how to model your business processes or how to do so better. For this, lots of other books already exist. This volume provides you with a reasoned snapshot of empirical evidence showing that your impressions are right and of actionable results that you may want to know to prevent your concerns from coming true. That is, this volume shows you what other people like you actually learned in their projects, case studies, and experiments and how they solved their problems, in practice.

I am confident that, as a reader, you will find in this volume both practical hints and research stimuli, just like I did, and that you will appreciate the thoughtful selection of content as well as the meticulous work by the contributing authors.

Associate Professor   Florian Daniel
Politecnico di Milano, Milano, Italy
January 2019

Preface

Thank you for your interest in the topic of empirical research in the domain of executable business processes! We want to take you on an interesting tour on how technologies in this domain can be applied in practice and what obstacles and benefits projects actually encounter and how they can overcome the former and achieve the latter.

Executable business processes are one of the success stories of model-driven engineering (MDE) at the intersection of software engineering (SE) and business process management (BPM). On the one hand, an executable model is formally and precisely defined so that a computer is able to interpret it and execute it. On the other hand, models are visualized so that humans can describe, document, and optimize business processes at a higher level of abstraction than with traditional textual programming languages. While these important research areas have been long separated from each other, this book is an attempt at cross-fertilization, driven by the understanding that business processes are the software running today's digital organizations and that achieving a precise representation of such processes so that they can be reliably executed requires to adopt rigorous software engineering practices.

With the rising importance of digitalization and fully end-to-end automated or at least software-supported business processes, we expect the interest in executable business processes to rise and software technology supporting business processes to become ever more important in organizations across all domains and all sizes.

While research into executable business processes has been ongoing for a few decades, as witnessed, for example, by the significant efforts put into applying process technology within service-oriented architectures, our focus in this book is on empirical research. We wanted to compile an up-to-date snapshot featuring empirical case studies in order to assess and give visibility to examples of practical impact of BPM within the industry.

To lay some groundwork before starting on this book, we realized that empirical studies were hard to compare and that researchers lacked in their design concerning the collection of metadata of the analyzed processes, since such metadata is lacking from plain process model collections. Therefore, our first step toward this book was the development of a template that allows an easy overview of the business process models used in a publication and gives researchers a template for collecting general metadata. You will find this template used in every chapter of this book, where it adds value to the chapter. A description of the contents of this template and how it was derived can be found in Chap. 2 in this book.

In the second half of 2017, we advertised a call looking for chapters that investigate questions of interests to both academia (e.g., identifying challenges for which no solution exists, new insights into how existing approaches are really used) and industry (e.g., guidelines for using certain technologies, guidelines for modeling understandable executable processes).

Our open call was answered with proposals by many interested potential contributors, spanning across both industry and academia, out of which we selected based on their relevance and quality the chapters in the book you are currently reading.

As a result, the book collects valuable real-world experience on the development and practical usage of executable business processes in software architectures, e.g., model-driven solutions that are built with languages such as BPEL or BPMN for the support and automation of digital business processes. This experience was acquired within different application domains (e.g., healthcare, high-tech manufacturing, software development), and it covers most phases of the software engineering life cycle (from requirements analysis to testing). We are also grateful to our chapter authors for explicitly featuring insights and takeaway messages directed to practitioners as well as to researchers.

Hannover, Germany   Daniel Lübke
Lugano, Switzerland   Cesare Pautasso
January 2019

How to Read This Book

Besides the background chapters found in Part I, this book presents research results and industry experience on a variety of topics related with executable business processes. Part II is concerned with architectural implications: what do we need to think about when implementing executable business process solutions. In Part III, two case studies and one experiment are presented. The case studies deal with how to successfully implement executable business processes in different domains, while the experiment is concerned with analyzing the effect of complementing use cases with BPMN process models. The two chapters of Part IV are concerned with extra-functional quality attributes (i.e., performance benchmarking and testability) of the solutions implemented with executable BPM.

You can read and skip ahead and back the different chapters as you like. All chapters close with takeaways for both researchers and practitioners. Researchers can find open challenges and new ideas for their research, while practitioners can read how to apply in their projects the valuable insights shared by the authors.

Book Chapters Overview

Part I. Background

Chapter 1, **Empirical Research in Executable Process Models**. Perhaps one of the reasons BPM research concentrates on analytical modeling of business processes is that BPMN is standardized fully in this regard and modeling tools support the notation very well. In this book, we focus instead on empirical research in executable process models. This requires a complete and precise specification of process models, which graduate from "PowerPoint slide" into an executable artifact running inside a workflow engine in the Cloud. In this chapter, we introduce fundamental background concepts defining executable business processes, discussing empirical research methods suitable for business process management, and presenting different architectural options for process execution and close with a brief history leading toward executable BPMN.

Chapter 2, **A Template for Categorizing Business Processes in Empirical Research**. Empirical research is becoming increasingly important for understanding the practical uses of and problems with business process technology in the field. However, no standardization on how to report observations and findings exists. This sometimes leads to research outcomes which report partial or incomplete data and makes published results of replicated studies on different data sets hard to compare. In order to help the research community improve reporting on business process models and collections and their characteristics, this chapter defines a modular template with the aim of reports' standardization, which could also facilitate the creation of shared business process repositories to foster further empirical research in the future. The template has been positively evaluated by representatives from both BPM research and industry. The survey feedback has been incorporated in the template. We have applied the template to describe a real-world executable WS-BPEL process collection, measured from a static and dynamic perspective.

Part II. Solution Architecture

Chapter 3, **Effectively and Efficiently Implementing Complex Business Processes: A Case Study**. The implementation of business processes has been neglected for many years in research. It seemed to be that only hard coding was the appropriate solution for business process implementations. As a consequence in classical literature about business process management (BPM), the focus was mainly on the management aspects of BPM, less on aspects regarding an effective and efficient implementation methodology. This has changed significantly since the advent of BPMN 2.0 (Business Process Model and Notation) in early 2011. BPMN is a graphical notation for modeling business processes in an easy to understand manner. Because the BPMN standard had the process execution in mind when it was designed, it allows for a new way of implementing business processes, on which the process-driven approach (PDA) is based. This approach has been applied in a huge project at SAP SE since 2015 comprising more than 200 business-critical processes. In order to get an impression about the power of the process-driven approach for really complex business process implementation scenarios, this chapter explains the basics about the process-driven approach and shares experiences made during the execution of the project.

Chapter 4, **Analysis of Data-Flow Complexity and Architectural Implications**. Service orchestrations are frequently used to assemble software components along business processes. Despite much research and empirical studies into the use of control flow structures of these specialized languages, like BPEL and BPMN2, no empirical evaluation of data flow structures and languages, like XPath, XSLT, and XQuery, has been made yet. This paper presents a case study on the use of data transformation languages in industry projects in different companies and across different domains, thereby showing that data flow is an important and complex property of such orchestrations. The results also show that proprietary extensions are used frequently and that the design favors the use of modules, which allows for reusing and testing code. This case study is a starting point for further research into the data flow dimension of service orchestrations and gives insights into practical problems that future standards and theories can rely on.

Part III. Case Studies and Experiments

Chapter 5, **Requirements Comprehension Using BPMN: An Empirical Study**. The Business Process Model and Notation (BPMN) has become the de facto standard for process modeling. Currently, BPMN models can be (1) analyzed or simulated using specialized tools, (2) executed using business process management systems (BPMSs), or (3) used for requirements elicitation. Although there are many studies comparing BPMN to other modeling techniques for analyzing and executing processes, there are few showing the suitability of BPMN models as a source for requirements comprehension in projects where process-aware software is built without using BPMSs. This chapter presents a study aimed at comparing the comprehension of software requirements regarding a business process using either BPMN or traditional techniques, such as use cases. In our study, we analyzed responses of 120 undergraduate and graduate students regarding the requirements comprehension achieved when using only BPMN models, only use cases, or both. The results do not show significant impact of the artifacts on the comprehension level. However, when the understanding of the requirement involves sequence of activities, using the BPMN shows better results on the comprehension time.

Chapter 6, **Developing Process Execution Support for High-Tech Manufacturing Processes**. This chapter describes the development of an information system to control the execution of high-tech manufacturing processes from the business process level, based on executable process models. The development is described from process analysis to requirements elicitation to the definition of executable business process, for three pilot cases in our recent HORSE project. The HORSE project aims to develop technologies for smart factories, making end-to-end high-tech manufacturing processes, in which robots and humans collaborate, more flexible, more efficient, and more effective to produce small batches of customized products. This is done through the use of Internet of Things, Industry 4.0, collaborative robot technology, dynamic manufacturing process management, and flexible task allocation between robots and humans. The result is a manufacturing process management system (MPMS) that orchestrates the manufacturing process across work cells and production lines and operates based on executable business process models defined in BPMN.

Chapter 7, **Developing a Platform for Supporting Clinical Pathways**. Hospitals are facing high pressure to be profitable with decreasing funds in a stressed healthcare sector. This situation calls for methods to enable process management and intelligent methods in their daily work. However, traditional process intelligence systems work with logs of execution data that is generated by workflow engines controlling the execution of a process. But the nature of the treatment processes requires the doctors to work with a high freedom of action, rendering workflow engines unusable in this context. In this chapter, we describe a process intelligence approach to develop a platform for clinical pathways for hospitals without using workflow engines. Our approach is explained using a case in liver transplantation, but is generalizable on other clinical pathways as well.

Part IV. Quality

Chapter 8, **IT-Centric Process Automation: Study About the Performance of BPMN 2.0 Engines**. Workflow management systems (WfMSs) are broadly used in enterprise to design, deploy, execute, monitor, and analyze automated business processes. Current state-of-the-art WfMSs evolved into platforms delivering complex service-oriented applications that need to satisfy enterprise-grade performance requirements. With the ever growing number of WfMSs that are available in the market, companies are called to choose which product is optimal for their requirements and business models. Factors that WfMSs' vendors use to differentiate their products are mainly related to functionality and integration with other systems and frameworks. They usually do not differentiate their systems in terms of performance in handling the workload they are subject to or in terms of hardware resource consumption. Recent trend saw WfMSs deployed on environments where performance in handling the workload really matters, because they are subject to handling millions of workflow instances per day, as does the efficiency in terms of resource consumption, e.g., if they are deployed in the Cloud. Benchmarking is an established practice to compare alternative products, which helps to drive the continuous improvement of technology by setting a clear target in measuring and assessing its performance. In particular for WfMSs, there is not yet a standard accepted benchmark, even if standard workflow modeling and execution languages such as BPMN 2.0 have recently appeared. In this chapter, we present the challenges of establishing the first standard benchmark for assessing and comparing the performance of WfMSs in a way that is compliant to the main requirements of a benchmark: portability, scalability, simplicity, vendor neutrality, repeatability, efficiency, representativeness, relevance, accessibility, and affordability. A possible solution is also discussed, together with a use case of micro-benchmarking of open-source production WfMSs. The use case demonstrates the relevance of benchmarking the performance of WfMSs by showing relevant differences in terms of performance and resource consumption among the benchmarked WfMSs.

Chapter 9, **Effectiveness of Combinatorial Test Design with Executable Business Processes**. Executable business processes contain complex business rules, control flow, and data transformations, which makes designing good tests difficult and, in current practice, requires extensive expert knowledge. In order to reduce the time and errors in manual test design, we investigated using automatic combinatorial test design (CTD) instead. CTD is a test selection method that aims at covering all interactions of a few input parameters. For this investigation, we integrated CTD algorithms with an existing framework that combines equivalence class partitioning with automatic BPELUnit test generation. Based on several industrial cases, we evaluated the effectiveness and efficiency of test suites selected via CTD algorithms against those selected by an expert and random tests. The experiments show that CTD tests are not more efficient than tests designed by experts, but that they are a sufficiently effective automatic alternative.

Acknowledgements

We are grateful to all of our authors for their efforts in contributing to the book, their time dedicated to the cross-review and revision of their chapters, and most of all their patience with the long publication process.

We would also like to thank our external reviewers very much for their constructive feedback. Without them, such a book would have not been possible. Therefore, we like to offer warmful thanks to (in alphabetical order):

- Dieter Burger
- Peter Fasler
- Tammo van Lessen
- Kai Niklas
- Kurt Schneider
- Barbara Ulrich

Contents

Part II   Solution Architecture

Part III Case Studies and Experiments

Part IV   Quality

Contributors

Panagiotis Bouklis European Dynamics, Athens, Greece

George Boultadakis European Dynamics, Athens, Greece

Jaime Chavarriaga Universidad de los Andes, Bogotá, Colombia

Marcus Danei SAP SE, Walldorf, Germany

Remco Dijkman School of Industrial Engineering, Eindhoven University of Technology, Eindhoven, Netherlands

Juliet Elliott SAP SE, Walldorf, Germany

Jonnro Erasmus School of Industrial Engineering, Eindhoven University of Technology, Eindhoven, Netherlands

Vincenzo Ferme Software Institute, Faculty of Informatics, USI, Lugano, Switzerland

Anastasia Garbi European Dynamics, Athens, Greece

Joel Greenyer Leibniz Universität Hannover, Fachgebiet Software Engineering, Hannover, Germany

Paul Grefen School of Industrial Engineering, Eindhoven University of Technology, Eindhoven, Netherlands

Matthias Heiler SAP SE, Walldorf, Germany

Nico Herzberg SAP SE, Dresden, Germany

Ana Ivanchikj Software Institute, Faculty of Informatics, USI, Lugano, Switzerland

Torsten Kerwien itelligence AG, Bielefeld, Germany

Kathrin Kirchner Technical University of Denmark, Kgs. Lyngby, Denmark

Frank Leymann Institute of Architecture of Application Systems (IAAS), University of Stuttgart, Stuttgart, Germany

Mario Linares-Vásquez Universidad de los Andes, Bogotá, Colombia

Daniel Lübke Leibniz Universität Hannover, Fachgebiet Software Engineering, Hannover, Germany

Cesare Pautasso Software Institute, Faculty of Informatics, USI, Lugano, Switzerland

Mario Sánchez Universidad de los Andes, Bogotá, Colombia

Marigianna Skouradaki Institute of Architecture of Application Systems (IAAS), University of Stuttgart, Stuttgart, Germany

Volker Stiehl Faculty of Electrical Engineering and Computer Science, Technische Hochschule Ingolstadt (THI), Ingolstadt, Germany

Konstantinos Traganos School of Industrial Engineering, Eindhoven University of Technology, Eindhoven, Netherlands

Tobias Unger Opitz Consulting Deutschland GmbH, Nordrhein-Westfalen, Germany

Irene Vanderfeesten School of Industrial Engineering, Eindhoven University of Technology, Eindhoven, Netherlands

David Vatlin Leibniz Universität Hannover, Fachgebiet Software Engineering, Hannover, Germany

Olga Lucero Vega-Márquez Universidad de los Andes, Bogotá, Colombia
Universidad de los Llanos, Villavicencio, Colombia

Daniel Wutke W&W Informatik GmbH, Ludwigsburg, Germany

Part I
Introduction and Background

Chapter 1
Empirical Research in Executable Process Models

Daniel Lübke and Cesare Pautasso

Abstract Perhaps one of the reasons BPM research concentrates on analytical modeling of business processes is that BPMN is standardized fully in this regard and modeling tools support the notation very well. In this book, we focus instead on empirical research in executable process models. This requires a complete and precise specification of process models, which graduate from "PowerPoint slide" into an executable artifact running inside a workflow engine in the Cloud. In this chapter, we introduce fundamental background concepts defining executable business processes, discussing empirical research methods suitable for business process management, and presenting different architectural options for process execution and close with a brief history leading toward executable BPMN.

1.1 Executable Business Processes

Modeling executable business processes requires domain knowledge from business process management (BPM) combined with software engineering (SE) skills. Executable models are at the foundation of model-driven engineering (MDE), where running software systems are generated from formally specified, sufficiently detailed, and precisely defined representations of processes [14]. These specify the behavior of software compositions, both in terms of the control flow and data flow connecting different types of tasks, which when successfully executed together allows to achieve a given goal [20]. Is executable process modeling a refined form of visual programming? Or why are traditional developers skeptical when approaching

D. Lübke (✉)
Leibniz Universität Hannover, Fachgebiet Software Engineering, Hannover, Germany
e-mail: daniel.luebke@inf.uni-hannover.de

C. Pautasso
Software Institute, Faculty of Informatics, USI, Lugano, Switzerland
e-mail: c.pautasso@ieee.org

© Springer Nature Switzerland AG 2019
D. Lübke, C. Pautasso (eds.), *Empirical Studies on the Development of Executable Business Processes*, https://doi.org/10.1007/978-3-030-17666-2_1

BPMN modeling tools and execution engines? And should business analysts, thanks to executable process models, be the ones driving the integration of large and complex IT information systems?

These and many other questions have been investigated [16, 24, 26], sometimes independently and sometimes in an interdisciplinary way, across software engineering and business process management. For example, in the area of quality assurance, the BPM community has focused much on model verification [34, 36], while SE has developed its own set of model checking methods and a depth of further resources concerned with testing (e.g., Myers [22]) and test coverage metrics (e.g., Malaiya et al. [21]). This has also led to combining techniques from both domains for executable processes, e.g., by Foster et al. [7]. Another overlapping activity is the elicitation of requirements as SE puts it, or process analysis as BPM names it. Interestingly, a whole workshop series called REBPM (https://www.rebpm.org/) is concerned with the application of methodologies of each domain in this intersection. Considering the empirical results we have collected in this book, the two disciplines can still learn much from one another.

In this chapter, we provide an overview over the main topics covered by this book—Empirical Research in Business Process Management (Sect. 1.2), Architectures for Process Execution (Sect. 1.3), and Executable BPMN (Sect. 1.4).

1.2 Empirical Research in Business Process Management

Empirical research tries to find and explain effects in real life by observing the application of technologies (or other objects in research domains). While computer science was very theory- and technology-driven in its beginnings, the whole research area concerned with software engineering has built up a tremendous amount of empirical studies especially over the last years. The Journal of Empirical Software Engineering is one of the premiere journals to publish and is highly regarded in the academic world. The same is also true for BPM, which is conducting intensive research in the application of defined methodologies, notations, and tools. However, empirical research is limited by the amount of access to primary sources. In this regard, SE benefits from the availability of open-source platforms and projects [41], while empirical—especially experimental—BPM research is mostly concerned with analytical, i.e., non-executable, process modeling across industry and public administration [9].

While the theoretical foundations in computer science and BPM are very valuable and necessary, in the end, going into the "wild," i.e., trying things out and gathering feedback from and in practice, is the only way for improving our understanding of the application of novel technologies. Many software, BPM, and digitalization projects are not as successful as we want them to be. If we only look at developers' resistance in adopting workflow languages, we can already see the huge need for empirical research.

There are three main research designs researchers can choose from and combine in order to answer their research questions:

- **Experiments** try to control the environment as much as possible and induce wanted, controlled effects. Thus, usually two groups are involved, which are differing in the aspects to be understood. Examples for experiments include studying modeling practices [18], notations [32], visual metaphors [39], or layout strategies (e.g., in UML [33] and BPMN [5]). However, because the environment in an experiment needs to be controlled, it is usually only possible to study the impact of small changes. The replication of whole (industrial) projects, which are differing in only some aspects, is an impossible task. For example, it is impossible as a researcher to conduct an experiment that focuses on two different architectural styles. The (realistic, industrial) software solution requires many professional developers for several months. Because an experiment needs a large data set in order to derive statistical conclusions, such an experiment would need to fund a large number of project teams for a nontrivial time span. More information about experiments can be found in [40].
- **Case studies** are somewhat complementary to experiments: researchers analyze real projects, try to gather data, and interview people. While therefore they can research in the most realistic environment possible, in real projects, they lose the control about the environment and influencing variables. Therefore, usually many case studies need to be made, or findings of case studies need to be validated by other research methods in order to improve them. However, case studies are very valuable for being done in real environments which cannot be simulated in experiments. Further information about case studies can be found in [31].
- **Surveys** are the third option for empirical inquiries. By letting people answer questionnaires, one can gather insights, get to know the target population, and even find very interesting problems to solve (e.g., [10, 30]). However, surveys or focus groups could be affected by sampling bias and are limited in what can be achieved with them. They are usually a very good starting point in finding or validating your research questions and hypotheses, which then can be followed up with case studies or experiments.

Another empirical research stream, which is becoming more popular, is repository mining. A whole conference called *IEEE International Working Conference on Mining Software Repositories* is concerned with mining existing software repositories (http://www.msrconf.org/). However, it is not clear whether open repositories, e.g., those found on GitHub, necessarily resemble or can be considered representative of typical industry code repositories [13].

But not only public repositories face the risk of lacking generalizability so that the observed effects hold true or the achieved results can be applied within other domains; all empirical research methods share this limitation—even if the research was done perfectly [6].

Researchers need to be aware of typical industry practices and constraints in order to judge what can and what cannot be generalized into other contexts. In the domain of executable business processes, there can be different generalizability questions, e.g., Does notation understandability generalize between different stakeholder groups? Do findings generalize to different business process modeling languages? Are results applicable to other BPM tool suites? This list can continue, and every research project must be careful not to be overconfident and—as a result— wrongly overstate the generality of its results. Good empirical reports therefore state their threats to validity in which possible errors in the research design and limitations of their sources with regard to the data and its interpretation are discussed [23].

Empirical research allows to gain insight into how business users and IT developers are applying certain technologies (languages, notations, modeling tools, execution engines), which is important because both SE and BPM are not purely technical nor theoretical disciplines. Instead, they also consider the broader socio-technical context in which projects are carried out. Human nature, and the degree of understanding, mastery, and experience with technologies, is likely to influence a project outcome. For example, the theoretical expressiveness of a business process modeling language, e.g., evaluated by using workflow patterns [29], is only half the equation when comparing different languages. The other half is how *comprehensible* they are by process modelers or process readers. The latter question has been subject to ongoing research, most of which is compiled by Figl [5].

Statistical methods are required to evaluate effects in empirical studies. However, this book will not introduce hypothesis testing, correlation, and other statistical concepts. There is a wide range of literature on this topic available. One practical introduction is written by Crawley [3].

1.3 Architectures for Process Execution

Business processes together with software are part of any organization which claims being digital or undergoing a digital transformation. However, the alignment between those two is a critical property, which makes successfully supporting processes with software possible [19]. While in general software can support parts of business processes in isolation, an organization is more efficient if the software is integrated along the process flow, i.e., data is exchanged between systems so that (human) tasks can access and process it from all relevant software systems.

Integration architecture is concerned with how systems communicate with each other and which technologies should be used within an organization [2]. Choices range (including old standards) from CORBA, SOAP, and REST to different messaging protocols [28]. These technologies build the technical foundation on which business contents are exchanged between the heterogeneous, autonomous, and distributed software systems, which can be internal (owned by the same organization) or external (owned by somebody else.). The main two architectural choices for organizing the control flow and data flow between systems are *orchestration* and *choreography* [1].

Orchestrations are centralized, hub-and-spoke, or star-like architectures in which a central orchestrator calls other systems (often via its service interfaces or API) and

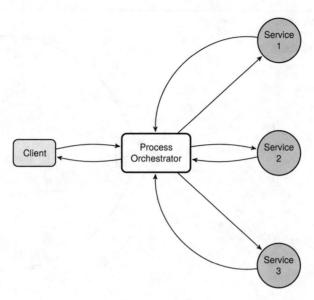

Fig. 1.1 Orchestration: process models drive the behavior of the process orchestrator used to implement a composite service out of three services

waits for their answers, which in turn trigger the next actions until the process is completed (Fig. 1.1). Orchestrations can be programmed with standard executable business process languages like BPEL and BPMN. Such a programming-in-the-large implementation has the advantage of a clear mapping of analytical business processes to executable ones and thus an easy way to measure key performance indicators when analyzing the behavior of running process instances. Alternatively, orchestrations can be manually implemented using general-purpose programming language, but this would require a significant effort to map the original business-level flow into code and then at run-time to reverse engineer (or mine) low-level event logs back into process models.

With *choreographies*, all systems exchange messages directly as they make their (service) calls in a peer-to-peer-like manner without going through the centralized orchestration hub (Fig. 1.2). The advantage of this approach is that there is no central point of failure and the orchestrator does not become a scalability bottleneck. The rise of event-based architectures nowadays can be seen as a form of choreographies in which every service consumes and produces events to be asynchronously processed by other services. Thanks to events, systems are even more decoupled

Fig. 1.2 Choreography:
direct, peer-to-peer,
event-driven service
interaction

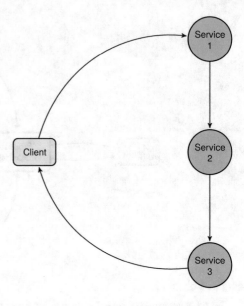

because a system emitting an event does not know which system or systems might respond to it [27]. This improved decoupling is achieved while running the risk of losing oversight about how a business process is executed by which system and which system is involved in which process, especially if messages do not carry along any form of correlation identifier.

As opposed to hard-coding assumptions about a business process into the architecture of an integrated information system (e.g., the choreography approach), having an explicit description of the orchestration process has several advantages:

1. A process model represents the high-level procedural aspect of a business process. It can be used as documentation for business analysts and internal auditors while retaining a formal, executable semantics that can be automatically enforced by a workflow engine.
2. Explicit workflow models make it possible to directly track the progress of running processes and perform off-line analysis of the executions which can provide useful feedback for improving the performance of the processes and contribute to the efficiency of an organization.
3. In addition to information and data, also business processes, i.e., the connection of tasks in a value chain, are valuable assets of an organization. Thus, similar to database management systems, which are normally used for the safekeeping and management of an organization's data, also process management tools should be used to model, analyze, and execute its business processes.

1.4   Executable BPMN

Process modeling languages go beyond classical architectural description languages as in addition to providing information on which components need to be assembled, they explicitly describe the behavior of the composition. To do so, processes use representations (e.g., control and data flow graphs [26], Petri nets [35, 37], XML document trees [15]) which are meant to be independent of the specific integration technology used to access individual services, thus abstracting away technical details which need to be provided if the model should become executable. With some standards, e.g., Web Services Business Process Execution Languages (WS-BPEL), this independence was lost, making the process model (represented in XML) tightly coupled with the service invocation technology (also XML based). While initially this was expected to make it easier and cheaper to connect processes with services [25], as service APIs evolved toward more lightweight messaging formats such as JSON/YAML, the language needed to be heavily extended [17].

In this book, we include chapters featuring both processes modeled using BPEL and BPMN. These are both very rich and sophisticated languages [42], for which this book can only introduce the relevant features in order for readers to follow each chapter's research questions and findings. For interested readers looking for a gentle introduction into each of those modeling languages, we recommend [38] for BPEL and [8] for BPMN.

Following several standardization attempts for representing executable work-flows such as XPDL and BPML, the Web Services Business Process Execution Languages (WS-BPEL [12]) was probably the first standard language emphasizing the fully executable aspect of process models represented using it. It was the result of merging Microsoft's structured XLANG (the standard born out of the BizTalk integration tool) and IBM's unstructured WSFL (derived from the FlowMark engine). However, the BPEL standard lacked a graphical notation as it was intended purely for technical users, as modelers were expected to describe processes using the XML syntax. A visual syntax was provided instead by BPMN 1.0, frequently used for the analytical models of the business level. These visual processes would be manually or semiautomatically translated to BPEL for execution [29].

BPMN 1.0 (standardized in May 2004)—defining only the visual syntax of the notation—evolved into BPMN 2.0 (released in January 2011 [11]). This was a significant progress with the inclusion of a token-based executable semantics as well as an XML serialization. The former would lead to a new generation of process engines which could directly (or indirectly, via model translation) execute BPMN; the latter would ensure the portability of models across graphical modeling tools.

Other execution attributes, e.g., which service to use for a service task, which code to execute in a script task, and how to configure a human task, are specified by attributes to the corresponding BPMN model elements which are not visible in BPMN's graphical notation. While BPMN 2.0 defines, e.g., how to specify which service to call in a service task, BPMN 2.0 does not define a standard technology mapping. While BPEL is clearly using WSDL descriptions for defining the offered and consumed services, BPMN 2.0 does not directly support any integration technology. Vendors have to define their mapping to WSDL/SOAP, HTTP/REST, and/or Java/JavaScript code and other options for providing the implementation of tasks as they see fit. While the BPMN 2.0 specification specifically mentions WS-HumanTask, most vendors also have opted to use other standards for human task management. Consequently, vendors and their products differ very much in this regard. Some are offering SOAP-based BPMN execution environments, which allow easy integration in large SOA-based enterprise architectures using services as building blocks for processes. Other vendors provide the opportunity for tasks to call into arbitrary Java code, which then can do anything the developers want it to, thus fulfilling the old vision of combining programming in the large (with executable process models) with programming in the small (with tasks implemented using traditional programming languages) [4].

References

1. G. Alonso, F. Casati, H. Kuno, V. Machiraju, *Web Services: Concepts, Architectures and Applications* (Springer, Berlin, 2004)
2. C. Bussler, *B2B Integration: Concepts and Architecture* (Springer, Berlin, 2003)
3. M.J. Crawley, *Statistics: An Introduction Using R* (Wiley, Hoboken, 2014)
4. F. DeRemer, H.H. Kron, Programming-in-the-large versus programming-in-the-small. IEEE Trans. Softw. Eng. **SE-2**(2), 80–86 (1976)
5. K. Figl, Comprehension of procedural visual business process models. Bus. Inf. Syst. Eng. **59**(1), 41–67 (2017)
6. R. Fisher, Statistical methods and scientific induction. J. R. Stat. Soc. Ser. B Methodol. **17**, 69–78 (1955)
7. H. Foster, S. Uchitel, J. Magee, J. Kramer, LTSA-WS: a tool for model-based verification of web service compositions and choreography, in *Proceedings of the 28th International Conference on Software Engineering*, ICSE '06 (ACM, New York, 2006), pp. 771–774
8. J. Freund, B. Rücker, *Real-Life BPMN: With Introductions to CMMN and DMN* (CreateSpace, Scotts Valley, 2016)
9. C. Houy, P. Fettke, P. Loos, Empirical research in business process management–analysis of an emerging field of research. Bus. Process. Manag. J. **16**(4), 619–661 (2010)
10. A. Ivanchikj, C. Pautasso, S. Schreier, Visual modeling of restful conversations with restalk. Softw. Syst. Model. **17**(3), 1031–1051 (2018)
11. D. Jordan, J. Evdemon, *Business Process Model and Notation (BPMN) Version 2.0* (Object Management Group, Inc., Needham, 2011). http://www.omg.org/spec/BPMN/2.0/
12. D. Jordan, J. Evdemon et al., Web Services Business Process Execution Language (WS-BPEL) Version 2.0 OASIS standard, Burlington, April 2007, pp. 1–264
13. E. Kalliamvakou, G. Gousios, K. Blincoe, L. Singer, D.M. German, D. Damian, The promises and perils of mining github, in *Proceedings of the 11th Working Conference on Mining Software Repositories, MSR 2014* (ACM, New York, 2014), pp. 92–101
14. S. Kent, Model driven engineering, in *International Conference on Integrated Formal Methods* (Springer, Basel, 2002), pp. 286–298
15. R.K.L. Ko, S.S.G. Lee, E.W. Lee, Business process management (bpm) standards: a survey. Bus. Process. Manag. J. **15**(5), 744–791 (2009)
16. J. Koehler, R. Hauser, J. Küster, K. Ryndina, J. vanhatalo, M. Wahler, The role of visual modeling and model transformations in business-driven development. Electron. Notes Theor. Comput. Sci. **211**, 5–15 (2008)

17. O. Kopp, K. Görlach, D. Karastoyanova, F. Leymann, M. Reiter, D. Schumm, M. Sonntag, S. Strauch, T. Unger, M. Wieland et al., A classification of bpel extensions. J. Syst. Integr. **2**(4), 3–28 (2011)
18. M. Kunze, A. Luebbe, M. Weidlich, M. Weske, Towards understanding process modeling – the case of the BPM academic initiative, in *Business Process Model and Notation (BPMN 2011)*, ed. by R. Dijkman, J. Hofstetter, J. Koehler, vol. 95 (Springer, Berlin, 2011), pp. 44–58
19. F. Leymann, Managing business processes via workflow technology, in *Proceedings of the 27th International Conference on Very Large Data Bases (VLDB 2001), VLDB 2001* (2001), p. 729
20. F. Leymann, D. Roller, M.-T. Schmidt, Web services and business process management. IBM Syst. J. **41**(2), 198–211 (2002)
21. Y.K. Malaiya, M.N. Li, J.M. Bieman, R. Karcich, Software reliability growth with test coverage. IEEE Trans. Reliab. **51**(4), 420–426 (2002)
22. G.J. Myers, *The Art of Software Testing* (Wiley, Hoboken, 1979)
23. A.J. Onwuegbuzie, N.L. Leech, Validity and qualitative research: an oxymoron? Qual. Quant. **41**(2), 233–249 (2007)
24. C. Ouyang, M. Dumas, W.M.P. van der Aalst, A.H.M. ter Hofstede, J. Mendling, From business process models to process-oriented software systems. ACM Trans. Softw. Eng. Methodol. **19**(1), 2 (2009)
25. J. Pasley, How BPEL and SOA are changing web services development. IEEE Internet Comput. **9**(3), 60–67 (2005)
26. C. Pautasso, G. Alonso, Visual composition of web services, in *Proceedings of the 2003 IEEE Symposium on Human Centric Computing Languages and Environments (VL/HCC2003)* (IEEE, Piscataway, 2003), pp. 92–99
27. C. Pautasso, E. Wilde, Why is the web loosely coupled?: a multi-faceted metric for service design, in *Proceedings of the 18th International Conference on World Wide Web* (ACM, New York, 2009), pp. 911–920
28. C. Pautasso, O. Zimmermann, The web as a software connector. IEEE Softw. **35**(1), 93–98 (2018)
29. J. Recker, J. Mendling, On the translation between BPMN and BPEL: conceptual mismatch between process modeling languages, in *Proceedings of Workshops and Doctoral Consortium of the 18th International Conference on Advanced Information Systems Engineering (CAISE)* (2006), pp. 521–532
30. H.A. Reijers, J. Mendling, A study into the factors that influence the understandability of business process models. IEEE Trans. Syst. Man Cybern. Part A Syst. Humans **41**(3), 449–462 (2011)
31. P. Runeson, M. Höst, A. Rainer, B. Regnell, *Case Study Research in Software Engineeering – Guidelines and Examples* (Wiley, Hoboken, 2012)
32. K. Sarshar, P. Loos, Comparing the control-flow of epc and petri net from the end-user perspective, in *Business Process Management*, ed. by W.M.P. van der Aalst, B. Benatallah, F. Casati, F. Curbera (Springer, Berlin, 2005), pp. 434–439
33. H. Störrle, On the impact of layout quality to understanding uml diagrams: diagram type and expertise, in *Proceedings of the 2012 IEEE Symposium on Visual Languages and Human-Centric Computing (VL/HCC)* (IEEE, Piscataway, 2012), pp. 49–56
34. W.M.P. van der Aalst, Verification of workflow nets, in *International Conference on Application and Theory of Petri Nets* (Springer, Berlin, 1997), pp. 407–426
35. W.M.P. van der Aalst, The application of petri nets to workflow management. J. Circuits Syst. Comput. **8**(1), 21–66 (1998)
36. W.M.P. van der Aalst, Formalization and verification of event-driven process chains. Inf. Softw. Technol. **41**(10), 639–650 (1999)
37. W.M.P. van der Aalst et al., Three good reasons for using a petri-net-based workflow management system, in *Proceedings of the International Working Conference on Information and Process Integration in Enterprises (IPIC'6)*. Citeseer (1996), pp. 179–201
38. S. Weerawarana, F. Curbera, F. Leymann, T. Storey, D.F. Ferguson, *Web Services Platform Architecture: SOAP, WSDL, WS-Policy, WS-Addressing, WS-BPEL, WS-Reliable Messaging, and More* (Prentice Hall, Upper Saddle River, 2005)

39. R. Wettel, M. Lanza, R. Robbes, Software systems as cities: a controlled experiment, in *33rd International Conference on Software Engineering (ICSE), 2011* (IEEE, Piscataway, 2011), pp. 551–560
40. C. Wohlin, P. Runeson, M. Höst, M.C. Ohlsson, B. Regnell, A. Wesslén, *Experimentation in Software Engineering* (Springer, Berlin, 2012)
41. L. Zhang, J.-H. Tian, J. Jiang, Y.-J. Liu, M.-Y. Pu, T. Yue, Empirical research in software engineering—a literature survey. J. Comput. Sci. Technol. **33**(5), 876–899 (2018)
42. M. zur Muehlen, J. Recker, How much language is enough? Theoretical and practical use of the business process modeling notation, in *Proceedings of the 20th International Conference on Advanced Information Systems Engineering (CAiSE 2008), CAiSE 2008* (Springer, Berlin, 2008), pp. 465–479

Chapter 2
A Template for Categorizing Business Processes in Empirical Research

Daniel Lübke, Ana Ivanchikj, and Cesare Pautasso

Abstract Empirical research is becoming increasingly important for understanding the practical uses of and problems with business processes technology in the field. However, no standardization on how to report observations and findings exists. This sometimes leads to research outcomes which report partial or incomplete data and makes published results of replicated studies on different data sets hard to compare. In order to help the research community improve reporting on business process models and collections and their characteristics, this chapter defines a modular template with the aim of reports' standardization, which could also facilitate the creation of shared business process repositories to foster further empirical research in the future. The template has been positively evaluated by representatives from both BPM research and industry. The survey feedback has been incorporated in the template. We have applied the template to describe a real-world executable WS-BPEL process collection, measured from a static and dynamic perspective.

2.1 Introduction

Empirical research in the field of business process management follows the increasingly wide adoption of business process modeling practices and business process execution technologies [9, 18]. The validation of theoretical research, the transfer between academia and industry, and the quest for new research perspectives are all supported by empirical research, e.g., experiments, case studies, and surveys.

This chapter was originally published as part of the BPM Forum 2017 [12].

D. Lübke (✉)
FG Software Engineering, Leibniz Universität Hannover, Hannover, Germany
e-mail: daniel.luebke@inf.uni-hannover.de

A. Ivanchikj · C. Pautasso
Software Institute, Faculty of Informatics, USI, Lugano, Switzerland
e-mail: ana.ivanchikj@usi.ch; cesare.pautasso@usi.ch

© Springer Nature Switzerland AG 2019
D. Lübke, C. Pautasso (eds.), *Empirical Studies on the Development of Executable Business Processes*, https://doi.org/10.1007/978-3-030-17666-2_2

The goal of empirical research is to find repeatable results, i.e., observations that can be replicated, thus providing results that can be combined and built upon. The more data points are available, the higher the significance of a study. One way to increase the number of data points is to perform meta-studies that combine results from multiple researchers (e.g., [15]). While this is common in other disciplines, such as ecology or medicine, business process-related data is usually not published in a comparable nor reusable way.

Additionally, the access to industry data is often restricted due to confidentiality requirements. Thus, publication of data sets must be done in an aggregated and/or anonymized manner.

To improve the reporting of empirical research concerning business processes, we propose a template that can be used to characterize processes in terms of their metadata and (if applicable) their static and dynamic properties, without revealing confidential details. For example, business process models are used for different modeling purposes such as discussion, analysis, simulation, or execution. Processes are modeled using different languages (e.g., BPMN, BPEL, EPC). Process models also vary in terms of their size and structural complexity, which can be determined depending on the actual modeling language used to represent them.

The goal of the proposed template is to (a) give readers the opportunity to "get a feeling" of a process (collection) and (b) allow researchers to build on top of existing research by ensuring the presence of metadata with well-defined semantics. Since, to the best of our knowledge, no such classification exists, in this chapter we make an initial top-down proposal, intended as a starting point for extending and refining the template together with the research community.

In order to improve the reporting of research related to business process model collections (e.g., [6, 21] as a starting point), we propose a set of metadata described in tabular form. The metadata template can be extended with other tables. For such extensions, we initially propose static metrics for BPEL processes and some dynamic metrics, although further extensions for other modeling languages are welcomed.

We validate the metadata template by a survey gathering the feedback of academic and industry professionals. Additionally, we apply the template in an industry case study to describe a large process collection.

The remainder of this chapter is structured as follows: In Sect. 2.2, we motivate the need for such template, which we describe in Sect. 2.3. Section 2.4 depicts how we validated the template with a survey and a case study. Section 2.5 presents related work before concluding in Sect. 2.6.

2.2   Motivation

Models describing business processes contain sensitive information, making it difficult for companies to reveal how they use standard languages and tools and rendering it challenging for empirical researchers to further improve the state of the art. As one of our survey respondents emphasized, much of the "research stops at the toy example level."

It is possible to anonymize process models, thereby limiting the understandability of what the processes do and hiding their purposes and sources. Anonymized processes retain their entire control and data flow structure (which would be available for static analysis) while losing important metadata (which would limit the types of analyses that can be performed).

For example, Hertis and Juric published a large study with a set of over 1000 BPEL processes [8]. However, they stated that they "were unable to classify the processes into application domains since plain BPEL processes do not contain required information." This shows that researchers have to be aware when collecting the processes that they also need to collect associated metadata.

Thus, whether or not a complete or anonymized process model is present, it is necessary to accompany it with a given set of metadata. The metadata has to be carefully selected and placed in a template to ensure that readers and other researchers can get an overall understanding of the discussed processes. Such a template needs to support the following goals:

1. Help researchers to collect data about processes that is relevant to others.
2. Help researchers to publish meaningful results by knowing which properties of the business processes can be anonymized and which should not.
3. Help researchers to report the important properties of business processes in their publications, so that their audience has sufficient details to evaluate the quality of the reported research.
4. Foster empirical research about business processes so that a body of knowledge can be accumulated based upon multiple, comparable works.
5. Enable meta-studies that combine, aggregate, and detect trends over existing and future empirical research about practical use of business processes.

2.3   Template

Business process models can be created in many languages and can serve many purposes. Thus, it makes sense to report only values that have been actually measured in the specific usage context and are related to the conducted research. The templates are defined in a tabular format with a key/value presentation in order to allow quick digestion and comparison of reports. We understand that research publications need to present their results in a compact form. When space does not allow to use the tabular format, the tabular templates can be published together with the data, e.g., in technical reports and research data repositories.

The template we propose is built in a modular fashion. It consists of a required metadata template that describes general, technology-independent properties of the process. The metadata part can be extended by standardized templates for reporting different properties that have been analyzed. Researchers should reuse existing templates as much as possible in order to provide results that can be compared to previous works.

For instance, in this chapter, two additional templates for executable BPEL processes are presented. The list of static and dynamic metrics proposed in the additional templates is not exhaustive and can be extended depending on the research needs. BPEL was chosen for convenience, as the case study in Sect. 2.4.2 uses BPEL processes. Support for other languages can be easily defined in additional templates.

2.3.1   Metadata Template

The metadata template, as shown in Table 2.1, is the only required part. It is designed to be applicable to any process model regardless of the modeling language used. This template contains the basic information necessary to obtain general understanding about a process model and the most important properties that can be of interest to filter and classify such process model. Its content has been updated with the feedback received during the survey described in Sect. 2.4.1. The following is a more detailed description of the categories and the classes included in the table:

Process name: The process name as used in the organization. If the real name cannot be published, this field can be anonymized by providing an ID that can be used to reference the process from the text.
Version: If available, the name can be augmented with process versioning metadata.
Domain: The business domain which this process is taken from. Existing ontologies like [7] can be used.
Geography: The geographical location where the process is used.
Time: The time period the process data refers to.

Table 2.1 The metadata template for describing business process models

Process name	Name or anonymous identifier of the process
Version	Process version (if available)
Domain	Business domain of the process
Geography	Location of the processes
Time	Period of data collection
Boundaries	Cross-organizational/intraorganizational/within department
Relationship	Calls another/is being called/no call/event triggered
Scope	Business scope: core, auxiliary, or technical scope
Process model purpose	Descriptive/simulation/execution
People involvement	None/partly/no automation
Process language	For example, WS-BPEL 2.0/EPC/BPMN1/BPMN2 / ...
Execution engine	Engine used for running the process model if the model is executable
Model maturity	Illustrative/reference/prototypical/reviewed/productive/retired

Boundaries: The organizational scope of the process: *cross-organizational* for processes that span across multiple legal entities, *intraorganizational* for processes that are conducted within one legal entity but across different departments/units in it, and *within department* for processes that are narrowed to a single organizational unit within one legal entity.

Relationship: The structural dependencies of the process with other processes: *calls another*, *is being called*, *no call*, and *event triggered*.

Scope: The process model can have a horizontal, business scope or a technical scope. In the business scope, we can distinguish between *end-to-end* processes for fully end-to-end descriptions like order to cash and *auxiliary* processes for processes that do not contribute directly to the business purpose. Processes can have a pure technical scope instead, e.g., an event handling process that propagates permissions in the infrastructure.

Process model purpose: The purpose of a process model can be description, simulation, or execution. A *descriptive* process is a model from a business point of view, which is more abstract in order to facilitate discussion and analysis among stakeholders and also to prescribe how operations are carried out in an organization; a *simulative* process contains further details regarding resources, costs, duration, frequency, etc.; and an *executable* process contains sufficient details to enable the automation of the process. Because a model can serve multiple purposes, this field is a list. The main purpose should be the first item in this list.

People involvement: Classification of how much manual/human work is to be done. Ranges from *none* (fully automated) to *partly* to *no automation* (people involvement in each task).

Process language: The process language used to create the process model. If a standard process language, such as BPEL, BPMN, etc., has been extended, that should be specified in the metadata.

Execution engine: The execution engine(s) used to run the process model (if executable), including the exact version, if available.

Model maturity: *Illustrative* for models which are not intended for industry use but to showcase certain modeling situations for educational purposes, *reference* for generic models which prescribe best practices and are used as starting point for creating other types of models, *prototypical* for models that are under discussion or are technical prototypes, *reviewed* for models that have been reviewed but are not yet in productive use, *productive* for models that are used productively in a real-world organization with or without systems to enact them automatically, and *retired* for models which had been productive previously but have been replaced with other models.

The metadata template is the main template that describes process characteristics regardless of the context and used technologies. In order to report details, additional templates should be used which often need to be language specific. Within this chapter, we define additional templates that describe different viewpoints of business processes, especially for those modeled in executable WS-BPEL.

2.3.2 BPEL Element and Activity Count Template

One of the interesting properties of processes are the various "size" metrics, with "size" being defined by Mendling [14] as "often related to the number of nodes N of the process model." Since every process language provides different ways to express nodes and arcs for defining the control flow, such template must be process language specific. Thus, in this paper, we define the template for measuring the size of BPEL processes by using activity and element counts, since BPEL is used in the case study that is presented in Sect. 2.4.2.

The template for reporting BPEL element counts is shown in the case study in Table 2.3. The values are merely the counts of different BPEL constructs as defined by the WS-BPEL 2.0 standard [10]. In addition, the total count of basic activities and structured activities is given because these are often used to judge the size of a process model. In the literature, they are also called number of activities (NOA) and number of activities complex (NOAC) [5]. In addition to activities, this table also contains the number of links, number of different sub-activity constructs (e.g., pick branches, if branches), and the number of partner links (service partners). To distinguish between the different BPEL constructs, basic activities are marked with a (B), and structured activities are marked with an (S) in Table 2.3.

2.3.3 BPEL Extensions Template

Although BPEL is a standardized language, it offers support for extensions. These extension points are used to extend the BPEL standard, e.g., the standardized extension BPEL4People to support human tasks or to enable vendors to offer unique features that distinguish their products from their competitors'. BPEL defines a general facility to register extensions globally and the extension activity that can contain activities that are not defined in the core standard or to use additional query and expression languages that are referenced by a nonstandard URI. In contrast to [16], we think that the use of extensions is common. Also, the case study has shown a high use of both vendor-specific and standardized extensions.

When reporting on BPEL processes, researchers can use the template as shown in the case study in Table 2.4 that contains all declared extensions in the BPEL process and the extension activities used together with their activity counts.

2.3.4 Process Runtime Performance Template

For executable processes, it becomes possible to report their runtime performance. While a large number of metrics have been proposed (e.g., [19]), for space reasons, in this chapter, we propose to focus on reporting the number of process instances and their duration. These metrics can be described for each process instance or aggregated among multiple instances.

Counting the total number of process instances for a given process model gives an idea of its usage frequency relative to other process models.

Capturing the performance of individual process instances amounts to measuring their execution time (T (finish) $- T$ (start)). Since the execution time of every process instance is usually not of interest, we suggest to give statistical information about the distribution of the process instance duration for all process instances of a given process model as shown in Table 2.5.

2.4 Validation

To validate the usefulness of the proposed templates, we combine an exploratory survey with researchers and industry experts (Sect. 2.4.1) and a case study of real-world BPEL business processes (Sect. 2.4.2).

2.4.1 Survey with Researchers and Industry Experts

To validate whether the proposed template fulfills the goals presented in Sect. 2.2, we have conducted an exploratory survey [20, Chap. 2].[1] The intention of this survey was not statistical inference of the results, but rather getting a deeper understanding of the surveyed field. We targeted audience from both academia and industry, i.e., both producers and consumers of empirical research. Thus, we used different social media channels and private connections to disseminate the survey.

Survey Design We organized the questions in five sections: Background, Metadata Template, Template Remarks, Template Extensions, and Empirical Research in BPM. While the Background questions were mandatory to enable further classification in the analysis of the results, the remaining questions were optional to incentivize greater survey participation. In the Metadata Template section, we showed the metadata presented in Table 2.1 and asked the respondents to rate the importance of each of the proposed metadata classes. In the Template Remarks section, we focused on the perceived need of standardized reporting and asked suggestions for the appropriateness and completeness of the proposed process classification and metadata. In the Template Extensions section, we inquired about the relevance of reporting structure and performance metrics on process level, as well as on the usefulness of using the metadata and metrics for describing entire

---

[1]The questionnaire is available at http://benchflow.inf.usi.ch/bpm-forum-2017/.

collections of process models. Last but not least, in the Empirical Research in BPM
section, we asked for personal opinions on the state of the empirical BPM research.

Survey Sample Since we were not aiming at inferring statistical conclusions from
the conducted survey, we closed the survey as soon as we considered the obtained
feedback sufficient for improving the proposed templates. This has resulted in 24
respondents with diversified background. To obtain more insights into respondents'
professional background, they could select multiple options between experience in
academia (further divided into IT or business process management) and in industry
(further divided into IT or business). While most of the respondents, i.e., 46%, have
experience only in academia, 21% have experience only in industry and 33% in both
academia and industry. Most of them, i.e., 88%, have IT background (16 respondents
in academia and 12 in industry), and 63% have been dealing with the business
perspective of process management (12 respondents in academia and 3 in industry).

Respondents participate in different phases of the business process life cycle
and/or simply conduct empirical research in BPM. When asked what type of
experience they have with business processes, the majority, i.e., 83%, marked
analyzing, while 79% marked defining, 75% implementing, and 29% researching.
These results could already indicate some lack of empirical research in this area.

All the respondents have more than 1 year of experience in working with business
processes with 50% having up to 5 years and other 33% over 10 years of experience.
Figure 2.1 shows the years of experience vs. the business process life cycle experience of the survey participants. It is noticeable that people with longer experience
have been more exposed to different phases of the business process life cycle.

Survey Results We have presented the metadata and process classifications as
shown in Sect. 2.3.1 to the respondents, which in addition included the Modeling
Tool category that we removed from the updated table as per respondents' feedback.
We asked them to evaluate each proposed category on a scale of 1 (not important)
to 5 (very important). As per the average score, the Process Model Purpose
was considered the most important with 4.38 points to be followed by People
Involvement with 4.13 points. As mentioned previously, the Modeling Tool was
considered as the least valuable with 3.17 points together with the Execution Engine

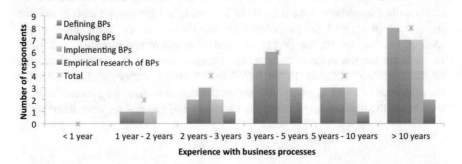

Fig. 2.1 Survey respondents: years of experience vs. expertise in business process areas

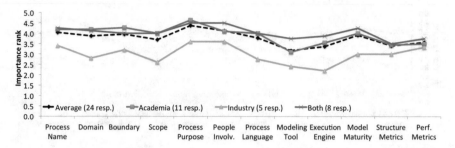

Fig. 2.2 Process metadata template validation (mean importance)

with 3.38 points. Indeed in an ideal world, where the standards are correctly implemented, these two categories would not add to the understanding of the process model. In Fig. 2.2, we stratify the importance rating of each proposed category per sector (industry, academia, or both). It is interesting to notice that, even if those having experience only in industry allocate less importance to the metadata on average, similar importance trends are evident between the different sectors. If stratified per years of experience, the highest ratings are provided by respondents with 1–2 years of experience to be followed by those with over 10 years of experience.

Encouraging ratings were also obtained on the helpfulness of the standardized reporting approach for "getting a feeling" about the studied process (4.08 points on average) and for comparing different empirical reports (4.29 points on average). Based on the feedback on missing metadata, we have added the Version, Geography, Time, and Relationship categories to Table 2.1 as well as the Reference and Retired classes in the Model Maturity category.

In the next section of the survey, we focused on the extended tables presented in Sects. 2.3.2 and 2.3.4. Always on the same scale of 1–5, the respondents found the presentation of structure metrics and performance metrics sufficiently relevant, with average points of 3.40 and 3.57, respectively. We were curious to see whether priorities and interests change when using the metadata and extended data presented in Sect. 2.3 on a collection of business processes. Thus, we asked respondents to rate them. While on process level, as mentioned earlier, Process Model Purpose and People Involvement were considered the most important, at collection level the Aggregated Structure Metrics (4.11 points) and the Domain (3.84 points) were considered the most important. As on process level, on collection level as well, the least important remained the Modeling Tool (3.11 points) and the Execution Engine (2.68 points).

As for the processes, also with the collections, the responses followed similar trends among different sectoral experiences (academia, industry, or both) evident from Fig. 2.3, with industry always providing lower average scores than academia, while people with experience in both sectors tending to have opinions more aligned with academia. The greatest differences in opinions between industry and academia refer to the Model Maturity and Process Name where average academia's

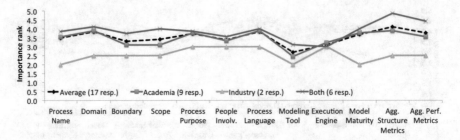

Fig. 2.3 Process collection metadata template validation (mean importance)

importance rating is around 4, while industry's importance rating is around 3 on process level and 2 on collection level. Significant differences in opinion are also noticed on collection level regarding the importance of the Structure Metrics which is rated at 2.5 by industry, 3.9 by academia, and 4.9 by respondents with experience in both sectors. However, when aggregating among the importance ratings of all proposed metadata and extended data categories, the opinions are relatively positive with an average of 3.77 out of 5 points for data on process level and 3.53 out of 5 points for data on collection level.

We asked for additional properties that respondents would like to have in the template. Two recommendations, the connectedness of the model and a link to a process map, were made. However, connectedness is hard to define without requiring a special modeling language, while without standardized process maps, we think that the links are not helpful.

Last but not least, when asked whether they consider the existing empirical research in business process management (surveys, experiments, case studies) sufficient, out of the 16 respondents to this question, only 4 answered positively.

2.4.2   Case Study with Industry Processes

We use the Terravis project as a case study for reporting process metadata and metrics in a standardized fashion. Terravis [2] is a large-scale process integration project in Switzerland that coordinates between land registries, banks, notaries, and other business processes concerning mortgages. In contrast to previous reporting of metrics [11], in this chapter, we apply our template and all additional templates as defined in this chapter.

The research questions addressed by this case study are the following:

- Can the template be applied without problems? Especially are all category values clearly defined and applicable?
- Can all categories be measured? Which measurements can be automated?
- Is the categorization in the metadata template beneficial when evaluating the process metrics?

Table 2.2   The metadata template for a Terravis process

Process name	Transfer register mortgage certificate to trustee
Version	26.0
Domain	Land registry transactions
Geography	Switzerland
Time	08-30-2016
Boundaries	Cross-organizational
Relationship	Calls another/is being called
Scope	Core
Process model purpose	Executable
People involvement	None
Process language	WS-BPEL 2.0 plus vendor extensions
Execution engine	Informatica ActiveVOS 9.2
Model maturity	Productive

The set contains 62 executable BPEL models that are executed on ActiveVOS 9.2. We acquired a total of 918 versions of the process models and information for 435,093 process instances executed in Switzerland in the period between 2012 and 2016. To apply the templates, we conducted the following steps:

- For each process, we assigned a value to each category of the general metadata template, automating the assignment where possible.
- We automatically measured the static metrics for the models.
- We validated the People Involvement assignment by cross-checking the value of the count of human activities in the static metrics.
- We automatically collected the used BPEL extensions.
- We calculated the runtime metrics from the process logs.

In the first step, we manually classified each process as per our metadata template. In the People Involvement category, we initially chose to offer more fine-grained values (partly, mostly). However, it was impossible to find a meaningful and objective threshold for these values. Thus, we opted to offer only one intermediate value, i.e., partly. To showcase the application of the metadata template, the metadata of one process model is shown in Table 2.2.

Many static metrics, e.g., the static element counts [3, 13], have been proposed; and some tools have been developed for calculating them [1, 8]. However, to our knowledge, no working tool is freely available to calculate element counts and extract extension information from BPEL process models. Thus, we have built an open-source implementation[2] to automatically calculate the data for the BPEL element and activity count template (Tables 2.3 and 2.4).

---

[2] Available at https://github.com/dluebke/bpelstats.

Table 2.3 BPEL element and activity counts for a Terravis process

Transfer register mortgage certificate to trustee (version 26.0)

BPEL element	Count	BPEL element	Count
Assign (B)	79	OnAlarm (pick)	0
Catch	4	OnAlarm (handler)	0
CatchAll	2	OnMessage (pick)	6
Compensate (B)	0	OnEvent (handler)	0
Compensate scope	0	Partner link	15
Compensation handler	0	Pick (S)	3
Else	13	Receive (B)	13
Else if	3	Repeat until (S)	0
Empty (B)	42	Reply (B)	18
Exit (B)	9	Rethrow (B)	0
Extension activity	1	Scope	74
Flow (S)	1	Sequence (S)	90
ForEach (S)	4	Throw (B)	0
If (S)	13	Validate (B)	0
Invoke (B)	37	Wait (B)	0
Link	2		
Derived metrics			
Basic activities (B)	198	Structured activities (S)	185

Table 2.4 BPEL extensions for a Terravis process

Extensions	http://www.activebpel.org/2006/09/bpel/extension/activity	
	http://www.activebpel.org/2009/06/bpel/extension/links	
	http://www.activebpel.org/2006/09/bpel/extension/query_handling	
	http://www.activebpel.org/2009/02/bpel/extension/ignorable	
	http://www.omg.org/spec/BPMN/20100524/DI	
Activities	Type	Count
	ActiveVOS continue	1
	Total	1

To calculate the runtime metrics, the process logs were extracted and processed automatically. However, not all executable processes were configured with persistence and logging enabled. Thus, for some models, we could not calculate any runtime metrics. Process instance runtime metrics are shown in Table 2.5.

After successfully applying the templates to all process models, an aggregation over the whole collection can be made. The results are shown in templated form in Table 2.6 with information on the percentage of models belonging to each class.

If the categorization in the metadata template is meaningful, there should be no overlapping between classes in the same category, and preferably each class should have some processes which pertain to it. We grouped the static metrics and process duration metrics of the latest version of every process model according

Table 2.5 Template for capturing runtime performance metrics of process instances

Transfer register mortgage certificate to trustee (version 26.0)	
Number of process instances	13
Execution time (min)	00 h:00 min:01 s
Execution time (med)	02 h:33 min:00 s
Execution time (mean)	12 h:34 min:39 s
Execution time (max)	64 h:24 min:14 s
Execution time (total)	163 h:30 min:32 s

Table 2.6 Aggregated metadata for the Terravis process collection

Collection name	Terravis
Process count	62 models with 918 versions
Domain	Land registry transactions
Geography	Switzerland
Time	03-09-2012–08-30-2016
Boundaries	Cross-organizational 37%, intraorganizational 13%, within system 50%
Relationship	Is being called 31%, calls another 26%
	is being called/calls another 8%, event triggered 24%
	no call 11%
Scope	Technical 52%, core 39%, auxiliary 10%
Process model purpose	Executable
People involvement	None 79%, partly 21%
Process language	WS-BPEL 2.0 plus vendor extensions
Execution engine	Informatica ActiveVOS 9.2
Model maturity	51 productive, 11 retired models
	51 productive, 867 retired model versions

to the different categories and their classes. The results are shown in Table 2.7. As can be seen, the distribution of the number of process models in the classes is different than the distribution of the number of activities. For example, only 37% of the process models describe cross-organizational processes, but they contain 71% of the activities. This means that on average the cross-organizational models are larger than those in the different classes of the Boundaries category and the within-system processes are the smallest on average. The distribution of the number of process instances and the distribution of the accumulated process duration among all executed process instances also differ. Only 14% of the process instances are cross-organizational but account for 68% of the overall process time spent. This means that cross-organizational and intraorganizational processes on average take longer to complete than within-system processes. Also, technical process models have a very different distribution.

The results support the classification categories because based on these values different characteristics of the processes in this collection are exhibited.

Table 2.7 Distribution of Terravis process models and instances by category

	#Models	#Activities	#Instances[a]	#Duration
Total	62	10,132	86,035	2,238,583 h
Boundaries				
Cross-organizational	37%	71%	14%	68%
Intraorganizational	13%	19%	8%	32%
Within system	50%	10%	78%	0.1%
Relationship				
Is being called	31%	22%	19%	71%
Calls another	26%	55%	62%	9%
Is being called, calls another	8%	12%	2%	20%
Event triggered	24%	3%	15%	0%
No call	11%	9%	2%	1%
Scope				
Technical	52%	10%	85%	0.2%
Core	39%	85%	13%	99%
Auxiliary	10%	5%	2%	1%
People involvement				
None	79%	66%	86%	10%
Partly	21%	34%	14%	90%
Model maturity				
Production	82%	84%	100%	96%
Retired	18%	16%	0.2%	4%

[a]Only for latest process model version

2.5 Related Work

The extensions to the metadata template (Sects. 2.3.2–2.3.4) are language specific, and their aim is emphasizing the need of including structure and performance metrics while not trying to be exhaustive in the list of metrics. Defining such metrics is out of the scope of this chapter and has already been addressed in existing work [4, 5, 14, 19]. The main goal of this chapter is standardizing the metadata on process level and/or collection level. Thus, the related work we survey in this section refers to current availability and definition of such metadata.

The need of extracting knowledge from business processes has been identified in literature and has led to the creation of business process repositories. Yan et al. [21] propose a repository management model as a list of functionalities that can be provided by such repositories and survey which of them are offered by existing repositories. Since what they propose is a framework, they emphasize the need of metadata for indexing the processes, but do not define which metadata should accompany each process. They have found that only 5 out of 16 repositories use a classification scheme based on part-whole and generalization-specialization relations. Vanhatalo et al. [17] built a repository for storing BPEL processes with the related metadata, which in their usage scenario referred to the number of activities, degree of concurrency, execution duration, and correctness. Their flexible repository architecture could be used to store the templates proposed in our paper. The MIT Process Handbook Project focuses on classifying the process activities and on knowledge sharing.[3] We focus on standardization of the reporting of such acquired knowledge.

The BPM Academic Initiative [6] is a popular process repository offering an open process analysis platform, aimed at fostering empirical research on multiple process collections. The metadata required when importing processes refers to the process title, the collection it belongs to, the process file format, and the modeling language. Even though the data to be stored is not restricted only to these fields, no further standardization of the process classification is offered. In their survey on empirical research in BPM, Houy et al. [9] define a meta-perspective, a content-based and a methodological perspective for classifying the surveyed articles. Their content-based perspective refers to context (industry or public) and orientation (technological, organizational, or interorganizational). The standard metadata we propose can offer a richer classification for meta-studies like [9, 15] and more in-depth analysis performed using platforms like [6].

2.6   Conclusions and Future Work

Empirical research in BPM helps to close the feedback loop between theory and practice, enabling the shift from assumptions to facts and fostering real-world evaluation of so far untested theories. While the process mining research has benefited from the availability of large event log collections, the same cannot be claimed concerning process model collections [6]. As process models clearly represent trade secrets for the companies using them productively, in this chapter, we have proposed a language-independent template for describing them by focusing on key properties (classification metadata, size, and instance duration) which are useful for empirical analysis by the academic research community without revealing proprietary information. The template has been validated with an exploratory survey among 24 experts from industry and academia, who have positively commented on the choice of properties (no negative score was reported) and also made constructive suggestions that have already been incorporated in the template described in this chapter. We have also demonstrated the applicability of the template in an industrial case study by using it to report on the Terravis collection of 62 BPEL processes and a subset of their 435,093 process instances executed across multiple Swiss financial and governmental institutions in the period between 2012 and 2016.

While the metadata template presented in this chapter is language independent, the extensions concerning static metrics are BPEL specific. Therefore, we plan to

---

[3] http://process.mit.edu/Info/Contents.asp.

work on similar templates for other modeling languages in the future. Additionally, we plan to collaborate with modeling tool vendors to enable the automated collection of the metadata described in this chapter. The long-term plan is to grow the amount of available and well-classified process models to the empirical BPM community. One way to increase the number of classified processes is to auto-classify existing model collections. Future work will elaborate which properties can be inferred from existing data.

Most of the respondents of our survey said that there is not enough empirical research in the field of BPM. We hope that more empirical research will be conducted and that the metadata presented in this chapter will help researchers to improve the classifications of data collections and make them easier to compare and reuse across different publications.

Acknowledgements The authors would like to thank all of the participants in the survey for their time and valuable feedback.

References

1. E. Alemneh et al., A static analysis tool for BPEL source codes. Int. J. Comput. Sci. Mob. Comput. **3**(2), 659–665 (2014)
2. W. Berli, D. Lübke, W. Möckli, Terravis – large scale business process integration between public and private partners, in *Lecture Notes in Informatics (LNI)*, vol. P-232, ed. by E. Plödereder, L. Grunske, E. Schneider, D. Ull (Gesellschaft für Informatik e.V., Bonn, 2014), pp. 1075–1090
3. J. Cardoso, Complexity analysis of BPEL web processes. Softw. Process Improv. Pract. J., **12**, 35–49 (2006)
4. J. Cardoso, Business process control-flow complexity: metric, evaluation, and validation. Int. J. Web Serv. Res. **5**(2), 49–76 (2008)
5. J. Cardoso, J. Mendling, G. Neumann, H.A Reijers, A discourse on complexity of process models, in *International Conference on Business Process Management* (Springer, Berlin, 2006), pp. 117–128
6. R.-H. Eid-Sabbagh, M. Kunze, A. Meyer, M. Weske, A platform for research on process model collections, in *International Workshop on Business Process Modeling Notation* (Springer, Berlin, 2012), pp. 8–22
7. Executive Office of the President – Office of Management and Budget, North American Industry Classification System (2017)
8. M. Hertis, M.B. Juric, An empirical analysis of business process execution language usage. IEEE Trans. Softw. Eng. **40**(08), 738–757 (2014)
9. C. Houy, P. Fettke, P. Loos, Empirical research in business process management-analysis of an emerging field of research. Bus. Process Manag. J. **16**(4), 619–661 (2010)
10. D. Jordan et al., Web Services Business Process Execution Language Version 2.0. OASIS (2007)
11. D. Lübke, Using metric time lines for identifying architecture shortcomings in process execution architectures, in *2015 IEEE/ACM 2nd International Workshop on Software Architecture and Metrics (SAM)* (IEEE, Florence, 2015), pp. 55–58
12. D. Lübke, A. Ivanchikj, C. Pautasso, A template for categorizing business processes in empirical research, in *Proceedings of the Business Process Management Forum (BPM 2017)*, vol. 297, ed. by J. Carmona, G. Engels, A. Kumar. LNBIP (Springer, Cham, 2017), pp. 36–52

13. C. Mao, Control and data complexity metrics for web service compositions, in *Proceedings of the 10th International Conference on Quality Software* (2010)
14. J. Mendling, *Metrics for Process Models: Empirical Foundations of Verification, Error Prediction, and Guidelines for Correctness*, 1st edn. (Springer, Berlin, 2008)
15. J. Mendling, Empirical studies in process model verification, in *Transactions on Petri Nets and Other Models of Concurrency II* (Springer, Berlin, 2009), pp. 208–224
16. M. Skouradaki, D. Roller, C. Pautasso, F. Leymann, "bpelanon": anonymizing bpel processes, in *ZEUS* (2014), pp. 1–7. Citeseer
17. J. Vanhatalo, J. Koehler, F. Leymann, Repository for business processes and arbitrary associated metadata, in *Proceedings of the Demo Session of the 4th International Conference on Business Process Management* (2006)
18. B. Weber, B. Mutschler, M. Reichert, Investigating the effort of using business process management technology: results from a controlled experiment. Sci. Comput. Program. **75**(5), 292–310 (2010)
19. B. Wetzstein, S. Strauch, F. Leymann, Measuring performance metrics of WS-BPEL service compositions, in *Proceedings of ICNS* (2009), pp. 49–56
20. C. Wohlin, P. Runeson, M. Höst, M.C. Ohlsson, B. Regnell, A. Wesslén, *Experimentation in Software Engineering* (Springer, Berlin, 2012)
21. Z. Yan, R. Dijkman, P. Grefen, Business process model repositories–framework and survey. Inf. Softw. Technol. **54**(4), 380–395 (2012)

Part II
Solution Architecture

Chapter 3
Effectively and Efficiently Implementing Complex Business Processes: A Case Study

Volker Stiehl, Marcus Danei, Juliet Elliott, Matthias Heiler, and Torsten Kerwien

Abstract The implementation of business processes has been neglected for many years in research. It seemed to be that only hard coding was the appropriate solution for business process implementations. As a consequence in classical literature about business process management (BPM), the focus was mainly on the management aspects of BPM, less on aspects regarding an effective and efficient implementation methodology. This has changed significantly since the advent of BPMN 2.0 (Business Process Model and Notation) in early 2011. BPMN is a graphical notation for modeling business processes in an easy to understand manner. Because the BPMN standard had the process execution in mind when it was designed, it allows for a new way of implementing business processes, on which the process-driven approach (PDA) is based. This approach has been applied in a huge project at SAP SE since 2015 comprising more than 200 business-critical processes. In order to get an impression about the power of the process-driven approach for really complex business process implementation scenarios, this chapter explains the basics about the process-driven approach and shares experiences made during the execution of the project.

V. Stiehl (✉)
Faculty of Electrical Engineering and Computer Science, Technische Hochschule Ingolstadt (THI), Ingolstadt, Germany
e-mail: volker.stiehl@thi.de

M. Danei · J. Elliott · M. Heiler
SAP SE, Walldorf, Germany
e-mail: m.danei@sap.com; juliet.elliott@sap.com; matthias.heiler@sap.com

T. Kerwien
itelligence AG, Bielefeld, Germany
e-mail: torsten.kerwien@itelligence.de

© Springer Nature Switzerland AG 2019
D. Lübke, C. Pautasso (eds.), *Empirical Studies on the Development of Executable Business Processes*, https://doi.org/10.1007/978-3-030-17666-2_3

3.1   Introduction

Business process management (BPM) in general has been explored over many years covering a variety of topics such as strategic BPM, process organization, process planning, process controlling, process evaluation, risk management for processes, process performance analysis, process optimization, process mining, and change management when introducing BPM in organizations. These areas are well researched, and many improvements have been achieved for all of these topics over time. However, in the authors' view, one area in this whole process universe seems somewhat neglected by comparison: the model-driven implementation of complex business processes. There have been several standards in the past like BPEL which tried to give answers to the topic. However, due to a range of issues, from missing standardized notations to an almost exclusively technical focus, companies were not able on a large scale to use them to implement software to meet the needs of complex, real-life scenarios. Precisely this implementation of complex business processes is what companies need to do when they want to address differentiating business processes which cannot be covered by standard processes delivered by standard software (e.g., SAP S/4HANA) due to their uniqueness for a company. But what options do we have at our disposal for implementing differentiating business processes? For many years, the only option seemed to be hard coding the processes using an appropriate development environment of choice, e.g., environments based on widespread programming languages such as Java/C#/JavaScript or proprietary environments like SAP's development environment based on the ABAP programming language. Experience has shown though that this approach has some weaknesses. Issues that companies have experienced include the following:

- Development speed and ease of maintenance.
- Making changes is usually cumbersome.
- Transparency in running or finished process instances is not innately given.
- Changes in market conditions can require extensive recoding.

Since differentiating business processes are a key factor in gaining or keeping a competitive advantage, we can see that finding more effective ways to address these issues could be vital to a company's success.

Maintaining that competitive advantage is more crucial than ever before, given the ever-increasing pace of change brought on by the pressure to innovate as a result of global digitalization. If companies miss new trends, they might be out of business very soon. In this dynamic environment, the need to address the challenges arising out of the business/IT alignment problem becomes ever more acute: in most cases, process experts in operating departments work out the to-be business processes using graphical notations such as EPC (Event-Driven Process Chain) or BPMN (Business Process Model and Notation). As part of the software specification, process models are exchanged with the developers who have to implement the new solution based on the process models. Experience at several companies has shown though that changes made to the models during implementation mean the original models are outdated by the time the implementation is complete and they are rarely updated to reflect the reality of the implementation. This rather limits the usefulness of the models, and consequently they become "shelf-ware." This is highly frustrating considering the effort which has been spent on these models.

In order to gain transparency into running/finished processes, companies often then invest in additional software for process mining and process analysis. Process mining, for example, helps to determine which paths the finished processes followed during their execution. It sounds illogical that additional software is necessary to derive a process model out of the logged data, although originally the processes were implemented using process models.

Experience therefore shows that this approach has its shortcomings, and it is valid to search for alternative approaches which address all or at least some of the mentioned limitations—ideally without introducing new limitations at the same time. With the introduction of BPMN, we now have new options at our disposal, especially with version 2.0 of the BPMN specification because it explicitly contains execution semantics for business process engines which can now execute BPMN-based process models. The approach of developing business processes using a standardized notation and running the models on a process engine would seem to offer some potential for addressing the limitations mentioned. Model-based development is not in itself new, but the development of software based on models is seen critically by experts due to the fact that models get quite complicated and unmanageable when it comes to complex real-life business scenarios. One method of addressing this challenge is introduced in the book Process-Driven Applications with BPMN [4] published in 2014. It introduces a holistic approach for implementing complex real-life business processes based on BPMN models. The presented solution is named the "process-driven approach (PDA)" and describes precisely what needs to be done to successfully implement differentiating core business processes. The process-driven approach comprises the following:

- A collaboration model between business and IT called "BizDevs" to overcome the business/IT alignment problem (see Sect. 3.2.2)
- A new way of thinking about BPMN-based business process implementations (process-driven thinking; see Sect. 3.2.3)
- A new methodology for business process implementation projects (process-driven methodology; see Sect. 3.2.4)
- A specific software architecture recommendation for process-driven applications (process-driven architecture) and a suggested development approach (process-driven development; see Sect. 3.2.5)
- A recommendation for a technology stack which supports process-driven applications best (process-driven technology; see Sect. 3.2.6)

The feasibility of the approach in theory was proven in the book itself. Using a small example, the basic architectural and development details were explained. However, what remained open was the applicability of the approach for real-life scenarios.

The arguments in favor of the process-driven approach led SAP Language Services to decide to use this approach for a major project to fulfill their core business requirement: providing services for translations (in 40 languages) of a variety of items for SAP products, such as user interfaces, business reports, marketing materials, videos, and handbooks. The requirements for running the business processes supporting these services were so unique that no standard off-the-shelf translation management software could meet them. So the SAP Language Services team decided, after an intensive evaluation phase, to build their differentiating business processes following the PDA methodology. As part of this chapter, we will describe the project and will summarize the experiences made with the process-driven approach applied to a real-life scenario. It addresses in particular the following questions:

- Is it possible to use the model-based approach to build applications that fulfill complex, real-life business needs? What needs to be done to achieve this goal?
- Is it possible to preserve BPMN process models developed in operating departments following the BizDevs collaboration model during implementation?
- One of the main attributes of PDA is the separation of business process and technical artifacts. Is it possible to keep the obvious technical and business complexities under control if the process-driven approach is applied? What needs to be considered?
- Which benefits do companies gain by applying the process-driven approach, and which of the aforementioned shortcomings are being addressed by it?
- Finally, how does the BizDevs collaboration model contribute to overcoming the business/IT alignment problem?

The remainder of this chapter is structured as follows. In Sect. 3.2, we explain briefly the ideas behind the process-driven approach. Section 3.3 describes the project at SAP SE in more detail, and Sect. 3.4 summarizes the results for researchers as well as for practitioners and gives an outlook on further research topics.

3.2   The Process-Driven Approach

The spark for the process-driven approach came from the release of the BPMN 2.0 specification in January 2011[2]. For the first time, execution semantics were defined for a graphical process notation by a standards organization (OMG—Object Management Group). This created a clear definition of how a process should behave if executed by a process engine that complied with the BPMN 2.0 standard. Software vendors immediately started implementing the new process modeling standard, providing process engines that executed BPMN process diagrams. This was a big step forward and laid the foundation on which process-driven applications could prosper. The question was: How can this idea of running BPMN-based models using an engine be transferred into real-life projects? The research carried out for the book on process-driven applications established that several aspects are required, which must work hand in hand for it to be successful. Although it is impossible to repeat all the details of the process-driven approach described in the book, in the forthcoming paragraphs, we will summarize the main ideas. More details can be found in [4].

3.2.1 Definition of a Process-Driven Application

The definition of a process-driven application is as follows [4, p.19]:

Process-driven applications are business-oriented applications that support differentiating end-to-end business processes spanning functional, system, and organizational boundaries by reusing data and functionality from platforms and applications.

The definition stresses already the importance of business requirements and process logic as the main driver for all decisions that need to be made while developing the application. The process-driven application is the result of applying the process-driven approach. If we take a closer look at business processes, we can distinguish between standard business processes and unique, company-specific, differentiating business processes. Standard processes are well covered by standard products, and it doesn't make too much sense for companies to implement these themselves. However, companies cannot do much to differentiate themselves from the competition by using standard processes, so the next question we have to answer is this: How can companies quickly and sustainably build, run, and monitor differentiating business processes? This is exactly where the process-driven approach fits into the picture by providing an effective and efficient implementation methodology. Key criteria for a process-driven application are independence from the IT landscape and process flexibility in regard to changing market conditions and competition. These criteria will be mainly supported by the process-driven architecture which will be discussed in Sect. 3.2.5.

3.2.2 Process-Driven Collaboration (BizDevs)

The main idea behind process-driven collaboration is overcoming the alignment problem between business and IT, with both sharing common responsibility for *one* BPMN model right from the beginning of a project. The traditional development process was very much dictated by business folks handing over software specifications which had to be implemented by their IT colleagues. Because of the potential misunderstandings caused by software specifications formulated using mainly prose, the results of the implementations rarely fulfilled the original requirements immediately. The typical ping-pong game between business and IT started, consisting of implementation (by developers) and review phases (by business colleagues) until the final result was eventually reached. This "procedure" is time-consuming, error prone, and highly frustrating for both parties.

The process-driven approach targets those shortcomings, changing the collaboration between business and IT by stipulating that a well-defined notation (BPMN) must be used to depict the process logic precisely. In addition, the modeling of the business processes is done together right from the start of an implementation project. Both sides enter into a partnership of equals. Because both sides work together on one BPMN model, chances are very high that the implementation immediately fits the expectations, and that increases development productivity. This raises the question of whether a roundtrip of one BPMN model between the business and IT teams is possible or not. However, BPMN as the common language between business and IT allows work on new levels. The new collaboration model is based on collaborative work on *one* BPMN model, which is then executed, as it is, by a BPMN engine. The BizDevs collaboration model simply does not permit changes to the BPMN process model just to make it executable. Although this may sound challenging to achieve in practice, the goal can be reached if organizations are willing to follow the new collaboration model, where both sides are equally responsible for one BPMN model and where the focus is on the preservation of this model throughout the transition to execution. This preservation of one BPMN model is also supported by the process-driven architecture which will be discussed in more detail in Sect. 3.2.5. The responsibility for the executed processes is now extended to the business side, so there can be no more finger-pointing between the two camps. For this new kind of collaboration, the term BizDevs has been coined to describe the collaboration between business and development. The term is influenced by the term "DevOps," which describes the collaboration between development and operations.

BizDevs means that business people become an integral part of the process development cycle—a new accountability that the business folks have to get used to. In addition to defining how the process should ideally run, it is also important from the start to define exceptions—what should happen if an expected outcome is not reached. For example, if it is critical that a process participant responds within a certain time frame, what should happen if they fail to do so? Another example could be a technical error that prevents the process from moving on. Here again, the value of business-IT collaboration becomes obvious. Without this collaboration model, the implementation of BPMN-based process models becomes questionable at best. Hence, BizDevs is an indispensable prerequisite for successful PDA implementations.

3.2.3 Process-Driven Thinking

BPMN is not just another modeling notation for business processes. Unfortunately, many authors of books about business process management see it this way: they only describe BPMN alongside other modeling notations, reducing the comparison between them to just the different shapes supported by the notations. Process-driven thinking uses the full shape set of the BPMN palette. For a thorough understanding of BPMN, it is crucial to consider the semantics of all shapes in the palette in order to apply them correctly in process models that can then be correctly interpreted by BPMN process engines at runtime. BPMN process engines in the end implement the semantics described in the BPMN specification. So thinking in "process engines" is a new challenge for modelers, business people, and developers, who have to design for execution right from the start. Process models need a new level of precision as engines require detailed information to make models executable. Because of this precision, there is no room for misunderstandings or ambiguities left. To increase this level of precision, modeling guidelines such as the ones described in Bruce Silver's book [3] are highly recommended. Together, modeling guidelines and the awareness that process engines rely on precise process models result in high-quality process models which can be understood from the diagrams alone.

Another aspect of process-driven thinking puts the business processes in the center of gravity. Every decision to be made during a project's lifetime always asks for the business requirements first. It is also at the heart of our next section, the process-driven methodology.

3.2.4 Process-Driven Methodology

Because of the importance of the business processes, one central question is: How should a process-driven project be started? Should we start with an actual analysis of the current (process) situation and derive the to-be processes from there (bottom-up)? Or should we start with the new to-be processes right away, without considering the current situation at all (top-down)? The answer for the process-driven approach is pretty clear: it's the second option. The problem with the bottom-up approach is the following: you will most probably spend a lot of time and money on the documentation of processes that you already know don't work satisfactorily and for very little benefit. If you try to improve the current process, you are working on symptoms, not on an overall process improvement that takes advantage of the latest technology options. Starting with the to-be processes gives you the freedom to innovate, both in terms of the business logic itself and of harnessing technical innovations.

One core rule of the process-driven methodology is not to let yourself be restricted by the current process implementation or by other technical or organizational constraints, such as the existing IT landscape, external systems, partners, suppliers or customers. The key question for decision-making in the process-driven methodology is always: What does the business logic require? From this point of view, it is possible to derive the business objects (e.g., a purchase order, an account, an employee) and their properties, the required services and their interfaces, user interfaces, decision rules, events, process steps, etc.—everything that is necessary to make a business process model executable. Applying the process-driven methodology sounds easy at first, but is sometimes hard to follow because people tend to always think about their IT landscapes and the restrictions they imply. The clear recommendation is not to think too much about IT landscapes and systems because they are changing anyway, especially in times like these where the trend to cloud-based systems is increasing, where mergers and acquisitions happen, all contributing to an even more fragmented IT landscape. You simply cannot afford to depend on such a brittle foundation. It is better to abstract from specific systems and stay independent from them. Following this approach allows much shorter time to market cycles from concept to implementation. Remember that it is one of the major goals of a process-driven application to be as independent as possible from a company's IT landscape, and the process-driven methodology contributes to that goal. It is further strengthened by the process-driven architecture which will be discussed next.

3.2.5   *Process-Driven Architecture and Process-Driven Development*

In order to fulfill the promises of independence and flexibility for the process-driven application as described in Sects. 3.2.2 and 3.2.3 as well as the promise of preserving a BPMN model throughout the transition from the original model to execution, an architectural blueprint is required: the process-driven architecture. An architectural blueprint is needed because the usage of BPMN alone neither ensures a successful development project nor a sophisticated architecture for the resulting applications. The problems known from normal programming apply for BPMN-based developments as well and can best be explained using an example which is taken from [4, pp. 67–74]. Compare Fig. 3.1, the result of the traditional approach, with Fig. 3.2 which uses the process-driven architecture.

You can see from the model how the core processes that are so critical to the success of the company (the upper process in Fig. 3.2) are not obscured by the technical details because these are put into a separate layer: the service contract implementation layer (SCIL). The valuable business process stays intact and, most importantly, remains under the control of the business department. However, the process can be easily adapted for use in other regions; you simply need to adapt the service contract implementation layer (the lower BPMN model in Fig. 3.2). Of course, this adaptation does involve some effort, but applying this approach will be of benefit in the long term, as it releases you from the complex web of connections between back-end systems. Business processes (e.g., the upper BPMN model in Fig. 3.2) and technical processes (e.g., the lower BPMN model in Fig. 3.2) can be developed and modified independently, but remain connected by the service contract (e.g., the message flow between the two BPMN models). This architecture also helps you to keep the business processes in their original form as conceived by the business departments. The key question in an implementation project will be to determine exactly which activities belong in which layer, in other words, which

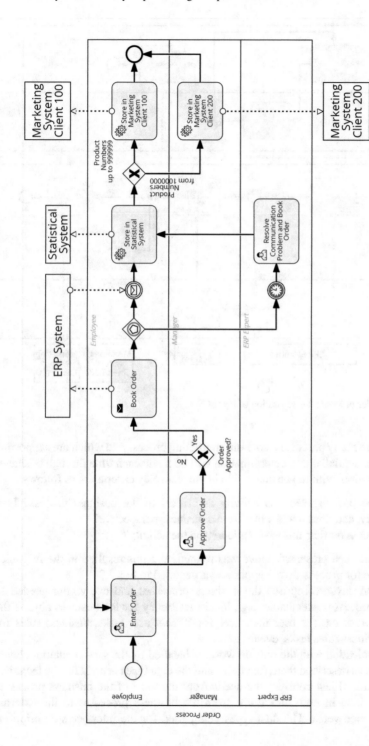

Fig. 3.1 Order process after processing by developer

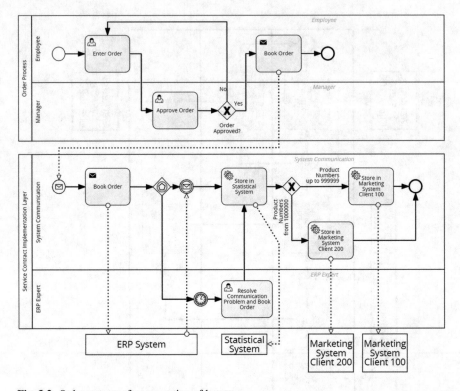

Fig. 3.2 Order process after separation of layers

activities are really part of the core differentiating process and which are supporting activities. Essentially, this determination will be made each time through business-IT collaboration, with the business side in the lead. Key criteria are as follows:

- Does the business see this activity as critical to the business process? Is it necessary, and does it add value from a business perspective?
- Can process participants easily understand the activity?

The basic idea presented above was refined, and this resulted in the reference architecture for process-driven applications depicted in Fig. 3.3.

The PDA layer comprises the business processes and everything needed to make the processes executable, e.g., local persistency for the business objects the processes work on, the user interfaces for BPMN user tasks, business rules for BPMN business rules tasks, events, etc.

Communication with the outside world is handled by the service contract layer. The interfaces described there (the fields and the data types needed for the technical implementation) just consider the needs from the view of the business processes and are defined in both directions: from the business processes to the external world and vice versa. The data types being used for the interface's descriptions

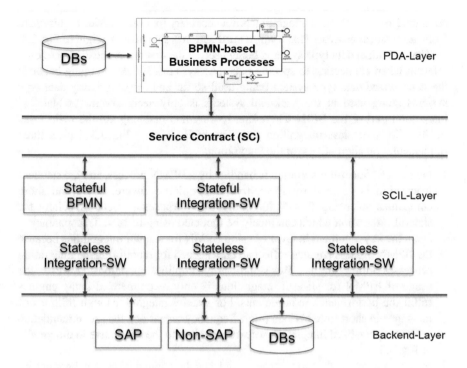

Fig. 3.3 Reference architecture for process-driven applications

are identical to the ones being used within the business process itself, avoiding mappings between different data types. The service contract layer is an abstraction from the specific back-end systems and shields the process-driven application from the IT landscape with its proprietary data types, interfaces, and technologies. A process-driven application never connects to one of the back-end systems directly. This is a typical pitfall in many BPMN models. They contain direct connections to back-end systems, and therefore a change in the system landscape makes a change in the process models necessary. The abstraction of the business model from the IT landscape is no longer given and makes adapting the model to new requirements unnecessarily complicated.

The actual implementation for each service contract is summarized in the service contract implementation layer (SCIL) which, for sure, looks different for each IT landscape the business processes should run on. It takes over the integration part of a process-driven application. As can been seen from Fig. 3.3, the SCIL differentiates between stateful and stateless integration. Stateful integration means the handling of wait states during integration. This is, for example, the case if an aggregation of several messages is necessary before finally sending the collection to a target system, e.g., a combined bank transfer. Stateful integration still relies on a harmonized data type system as it is used in the business process and the service contract. However, stateful integration is not necessary for every service requirement from the business process. That's why a third option is shown on the right of Fig. 3.3.

The individual data type systems being used in the diverse applications are only relevant when connecting to specific back-end systems. Hence, mapping between the harmonized data type system being used so far and the proprietary data type systems being used in the back-end systems is only necessary in the stateless integration part of the SCIL. Therefore, routing and mapping are the main tasks of the SCIL's stateless integration part. The SCIL layer in Fig. 3.3 depicts three implementation alternatives for the integration:

1. On the left: Stateful integration is handled by a BPMN process, and the stateless integration is covered by specialized integration software. More and more companies are using BPMN for integration purposes as well, especially for stateful integration which can nicely be modeled using BPMN. Transparency is again the key argument in favor of using BPMN for stateful integrations because the BPMN process engines collect all data needed for monitoring the integration processes during runtime. This significantly simplifies operations. However, the usage of BPMN for stateful integrations is only recommended if the engines fulfill the performance requirements. For stateful integrations with millions of messages in short time periods (high-frequency scenarios), the recommendation is to use specialized integration software, leading to the alternative in the middle of Fig. 3.3.
2. In the middle: Both parts, stateful and stateless integration, are handled by specialized integration software. This is recommended for high-performance scenarios where an optimized integration engine is capable of managing the load.
3. On the right: As outlined above, a stateful integration part is not necessary in all cases. A simple transfer of a message (including routing) to the right target system(s) and mapping between data types is all that is required in this scenario. This is best covered by specialized integration software. It is not recommended to use BPMN engines for these use cases as BPMN software is optimized for executing business processes and not for integration. Even though vendors of BPMN engines claim to integrate with many systems out of BPMN processes, it is definitely not recommended to use this functionality. BPMN engines cannot connect to as many systems as specialized integration software can, and they (BPMN engines) are also not optimized for executing complex mappings between data types. Leave those tasks to optimized integration software.

We can conclude that a process-driven architecture relies on the "separation of concerns" principle allowing for a maximum of parallelism during development which increases development efficiency. This is the key principle of *process-driven development*. We gain process flexibility because we can easily adapt the BPMN process models in the PDA layer to changing market conditions and new competitors as the BPMN models are not polluted with technical integration flows. Hence, they are less complex and easier to maintain. The adaptability to changing IT landscapes is ensured by the service contract together with the service contract implementation layer. If there is a change in interfaces or systems, this can be adjusted locally using the specialized integration software. And finally, we preserved the BPMN model during development—exactly what we wanted to achieve.

3.2.6 Process-Driven Technologies

In order to implement a full-fledged process-driven application, it is recommended to use the following technologies:

1. BPMN engines for the execution of the business processes as well as the stateful integration part of the SCIL. As was outlined in Sect. 3.2.5, the usage of BPMN engines for integration purposes is only recommended if the performance requirements for handling the message volume are met.
2. Business rules engines (or decision management systems (DMSs) as they are also known) complement process engines. BPMN engines concentrate on the execution of process logic, whereas a DMS executes decision logic and/or calculations.
3. Enterprise service bus for integrations—both stateful (e.g., aggregator pattern) and stateless (e.g., routing/mapping) integrations.
4. Although not discussed in detail in this chapter, event stream processing (ESP) software is recommended for new IoT (Internet of Things) scenarios with a multitude of sensors sending signals about, e.g., temperature, pressure, humidity, etc. which need to be filtered and analyzed for business-relevant information. The ESP solution is responsible for signaling business-critical events to the business processes. They are typically not directly connected with BPMN-based processes in the PDA layer of Fig. 3.3; instead, they send the business events to the SCIL which is then in charge of handing them over to the responsible processes. This is mentioned here for the sake of completeness—while not directly relevant to this case study, it gives an indication of potential further use cases for process-driven applications.

This setup ensures a very flexible environment for process-driven applications which is prepared for fast adaptability to changing conditions for a long time to come.

In this section, we've covered the basic ideas of the process-driven approach and proposed theoretical answers to the following questions raised at the beginning of this chapter:

- Is it possible to preserve BPMN process models developed in operating departments following the BizDevs collaboration model during implementation?
- Is it possible to keep the obvious technical and business complexities under control if the process-driven approach is applied? What needs to be considered?
- Which benefits do companies gain by applying the process-driven approach, and which of the aforementioned shortcomings are being addressed by it?

3.3 Implementation Project at SAP Language Services Using the Process-Driven Approach

In Sect. 3.2, we've described the main ideas behind the process-driven approach in reasonable detail because it is the foundation for the ongoing project at SAP Language Services. All the aspects discussed in Sect. 3.2 were completely applied during this project. We will now continue with a closer look at the situation at SAP Language Services before the project and how it was improved using the process-driven approach. The remaining part of this section is based on an article by Matthias Heiler, which was first published in the January-February-March 2016 issue of SAPinsider [1]. It was updated with latest numbers and slightly enhanced.

The SAP Language Services (SLS) department provides translation services (in 40 languages) for a variety of items for SAP products, such as user interfaces, business reports, marketing materials, videos, handbooks, and documentation. SAP Language Services collaborates with several translation agencies across the world and coordinates more than 2800 native speakers in order to achieve high-quality translations, even taking into account the local culture of the respective country for which a translation is needed. Just to give you an impression about the volume that needs to be translated, in 2016 more than 700 million words were translated (one Harry Potter book contains roughly one million words). The business requirements for running the processes supporting these services were so unique that no standard off-the-shelf translation management software could deliver what SAP needed. There are two main aspects that make this process so unique and differentiating: Firstly, the ability to simultaneously ship localized versions of software products and features in a high number of languages is a key competitive advantage for SAP. Secondly, in order to meet this goal and maintain that advantage over time and in changing market conditions, SAP Language Services has developed a range of approaches and processes that are fairly unique in the localization industry. So the SAP Language Services team decided after an intensive evaluation phase to build their differentiating business processes following the PDA methodology and to run them using an SAP product called SAP Process Orchestration.

The first step was to design an overall framework for the business processes. There were several factors to consider in building the business process framework. The services the SLS team has to deliver depend on specific translation scenarios. The process inputs can vary widely, as can the requirements of the process outputs, and the process must be able to produce the required result from these different inputs. There can also be variations within one project. For example, very high linguistic quality is required for the Japanese version—so in this case, machine translation will need to be reviewed by language experts. The Italian version however is only needed for test purposes; the quality need not be perfect, but it is needed much sooner—so here, just using machine translation without expert review would meet the goal better. The source text might be in German, so for Japanese it would make sense to produce an English version first and then translate into Japanese from English, as this will considerably lower the cost of translation into Japanese

(German-Japanese translators are much rarer and consequently significantly more expensive). In addition, every translation project must consider different types of text sources (there are a wide variety of formats and system types that need to be processed, such as typical software file formats, ABAP systems, Microsoft Office files, video files, etc.) as well as different types of texts, such as user interfaces for software, marketing materials, texts for internal communication, and even official financial statements. As a result, each translation process must factor in those requirements by variants in their execution—this was a key influencing factor in the design of the business process framework. In addition, the primary goals of the project included achieving a high degree of automation to improve operational efficiency and allowing for flexible adjustments of the services to accommodate new or changed requirements.

This difficult constellation, consisting of a multitude of different translation requirements, an overly complex IT landscape with several hundred systems to be integrated, and inefficient process implementations with many redundant manual tasks, caused the valuable and highly skilled people at SAP Language Services to spend the majority of their time just to keep the processes alive and running ("keeping the lights on"). Their capacity was obviously not available for innovations (compare Fig. 3.4, left side).

Therefore, one of the key goals of the project is to relieve the team from time-consuming, inefficient, redundant tasks and give them more room for business innovations in new language technologies such as neural and statistical machine translation and other natural language processing technologies (compare Fig. 3.4, right side). Optimizing the IT landscape by consolidating systems, high reuse of linguistic assets, and, last but not least, process automation are the main measures that support this goal.

During many workshops, a list of requirements for the new solution was collaboratively worked out and consisted of the following three main items:

- Best practices, which have been established over many years through cooperation with partners and customers, have to be considered in the new application as

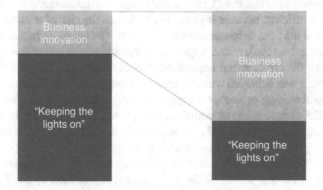

Fig. 3.4 Key goal of the SLS project: freeing capacity for business innovations

well. It requires the right balance between standardization and flexibility without compromising high service levels.

- Agile and sustainable process adaptations must be possible (e.g., adding new translation technologies to a process), even on short notice.
- Process documentation must always be up-to-date and must not be a separate step in a project's life cycle: process documentation must correspond 1:1 to the running processes. The goal is, on the one hand, to minimize effort and, on the other hand, to facilitate the exchange of best practices.

With so much complexity, easily understandable process models were essential to the project. Hence, it was decided to implement the business processes using the process-driven approach including the BizDevs collaboration model. Figure 3.5 shows, for example, the result of the collaboration between business and IT in a BPMN model that could be created using any business-friendly BPMN modeler, and Fig. 3.6 shows the resulting executable BPMN model in SAP Process Orchestration. Note that the two models are identical—exactly what we wanted to achieve using the process-driven approach.

The process-driven approach is generic and independent from specific tools and environments, so it works with any BPMN-based modeling tool. The PDA methodology, with its uncluttered and collaborative approach to process modeling, is an ideal fit for the SAP Language Services project, enabling business users, BPMN specialists, developers, and user interface designers to discuss process logic, business functionality, user interfaces, and services very precisely. The project took the approach of educating business users both in BPMN 2.0 and the PDA methodology. As a result, the business users quickly became BPMN specialists in their own right, capable of using the full BPMN palette. The only restrictions on shape sets used were those imposed by the process engine itself, where the palette was not completely implemented. For those cases, the business users were able to use the implemented shapes to achieve the same outcome, but of course a full implementation would eliminate the need for such workarounds.

As a result, the executable process is truly business driven; and thanks to the early, intensive involvement of key users, acceptance of the model is very high. Communication between the IT and business units is standardized through BPMN and is highly efficient because it virtually eliminates the risk of misunderstandings and decreases the time between concept and implementation. In fact, although this project required a standardized approach to handling multiple different language technologies, the creation and implementation of 65 process models following the PDA approach was achieved within 9 months. Compared to traditional methodologies for implementing processes using programming languages such as ABAP and Java, the PDA approach has an implementation time savings of roughly 75% (status in January 2016). One additional time accelerator in the project was to start directly with the design of to-be processes instead of struggling with legacy as-is processes. In theory, it would have been possible, following the bottom-up approach, to first create process models to reflect the as-is processes and then to use those as the basis for improvement. The team rejected this approach, as it was seen as very

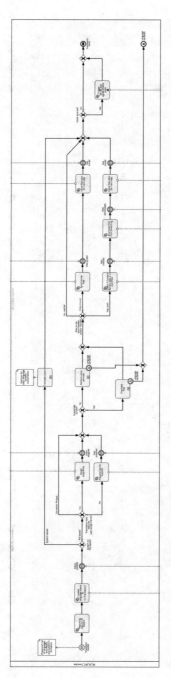

Fig. 3.5 The BPMN-based process model from the business perspective

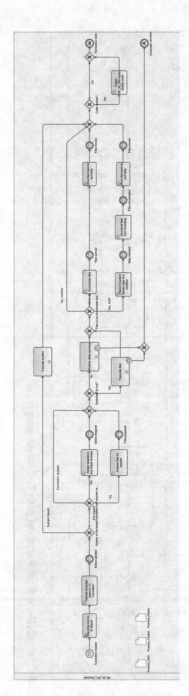

Fig. 3.6 The executable BPMN model in SAP Process Orchestration is identical to the structure of the business process model which was defined before

effort intensive with little to no benefit. Since the business experts were directly involved, they were already perfectly aware of the shortcomings of the existing processes, even without well-defined models or in-depth analysis. The consensus was also that spending time and effort to create those models would have a negative impact on their ability to define to-be processes and that they would risk carrying over undesirable elements and patterns from the as-is processes for the sake of expediency. Therefore, the approach selected was to start with the to-be processes and then to use those as the basis for further optimizations. The team found that they also faced the fairly common difficulty of abstracting from the given infrastructure and translation tools. From the first iteration, while it was relatively easy to define generic processes that could be used for all translation types for aspects such as project management, it was significantly harder to do so for the parts dealing with the actual translation itself in all the different tools. In fact for these processes, the first iteration did not succeed in completely separating the business process from the systems used. However, after gaining some experience in the practical application of the methodology, the team was able to achieve this goal, so that now changes can be made in either the business or the technical layer, without impacting the other layer. For example, it is possible to add or replace translation tools without changing the business process. Where changes need to be made that impact both layers (e.g., a new business activity is added and requires a new system), these changes can be implemented in parallel, increasing development efficiency.

The project is still ongoing and has evolved since then. The latest numbers after a total implementation time of 33 months are impressive (December 2017): 206 really complex nontrivial business processes, 169 integration processes (SCIL implementations), and 126 user interfaces speak for themselves. Process execution times have also been noticeably reduced: for example, the execution time for the end-to-end order process for marketing materials was reduced to one-third of the original execution time. As microservice architectures have become more common, SLS has also seen additional benefits to the PDA approach. On the one hand, it is easy and efficient to integrate new microservices into the process as they become available. On the other hand, the process-driven approach provides a highly effective framework for orchestrating diverse microservices to create business value in a range of different scenarios. Overall, SLS achieved the following:

- Improved efficiency in process execution
- Improved user experience
- Higher automation rate
- Increased flexibility and adaptability
- Increased transparency in operational business

Besides that, two more goals have been reached:

1. SLS took a major step toward active process management, where business and IT work closely together and can adjust their processes more quickly and consistently.
2. This in turn gives the team opportunities to expand the services offered and to develop and even commercialize business models relevant to the digital era.

Table 3.1 Aggregated metadata for the SLS process collection

Collection name	SLS
Process count	206 models, up to 3 versions/model
Domain	Managing of translation projects
Geography	Worldwide
Time	03-2015–12-2017 (ongoing)
Boundaries	Cross-organizational 26%, intraorganizational 24%, within department 50%
Relationship	Is being called/calls another 100%
Scope	Core 206, technical 169
Process model purpose	Executable
People involvement	None 45%, partly 55%
Process language	BPMN 2.0
Execution engine	SAP Process Orchestration 7.5
Model maturity	206 productive

Table 3.1 gives an overview of the implemented processes using the process collection template for categorizing business processes described in Chap. 2.

It should be noted that the process version count does not reflect the number or frequency of changes to the models. A new version is only created when this is technically necessary, e.g., in case of interface changes. Managing version compatibility can be a challenge—in addition to keeping the number of versions low, the team has developed mechanisms to automatically upgrade running process instances to the latest version on a new feature release (e.g., at key points, the process checks if it is running in the latest available version; if not, it cancels itself and restarts at the same process point in the latest version, with the same data). In terms of assessing maintainability or sustainability, the number of process instances is perhaps the more telling figure. For business processes alone, there have been a total of almost three million instances, with on average around 16,500 instances running at any given time. The figures for technical processes are significantly higher. Application support is facilitated by a dedicated process that provides support staff with relevant error data in the form of a human task in case of technical or business errors. One team role has dedicated responsibility for operations/maintenance, mainly in terms of oversight on tickets/tasks; remaining operations activities are carried out by all team roles on the fly—a BizDevOps model.

One further insight that the team has gained is that it seems much easier to manage this kind of implementation project using agile methodologies. A new team was set up for the project, consisting of business and IT specialists from SAP Language Services, supplemented with PDA and BPM experts from consulting partner itelligence AG. Initially, a hybrid development management approach was selected; however, as the team has matured and gained experience, this has evolved over time to an adapted version of agile development methodologies. While some elements (e.g., teams of ten) are not practical for our purposes, clearly defined user stories, sprints, and feature-based deliveries have proven valuable. The team has found it helpful to describe how they work in detail using a process model. Overall, requirements from stakeholders are continuously added to the concept backlog. After prioritization, they are grouped into user stories that form coherent units of business value. Part of the concept work includes carefully examining dependencies (both business and technical) between the user stories—failure to do this early on can block deliveries of features that are in themselves complete, but cannot be deployed separately from parallel developments. In addition to creating process models and UI prototypes, the concept team (consisting of business and IT specialists) also prepares backlog items for implementation. Developers attach effort estimates to the backlog items; and these, together with the known dependencies, are the basis for development sprint planning. This approach has provided a great deal of flexibility in terms of delivering features as soon as they are ready, as well as providing greater transparency for all team members around the status. Delivery frequency is weekly, with larger updates reaching production on average approximately every 2 months.

In summary, therefore, we find that we have now been able to answer our five questions:

- Complex real-life scenarios can be completely covered using a model-based approach.
- BPMN models developed by business departments using the BizDevs collaboration model can be preserved 1:1 during implementation.
- The process-driven approach provides an effective methodology for mastering complexity, both business and technical.
- The benefits are listed above.
- The BizDevs collaboration model has proved to be a vital tool in addressing alignment issues, and the benefits proposed in theory are observed in practice.

3.4 Conclusions and Outlook

3.4.1 Conclusions for Researchers and Practitioners

This chapter of the book has outlined the fundamentals of the process-driven approach (PDA). As result of applying the process-driven approach, you get process-driven applications. These are defined as business-oriented applications that support differentiating end-to-end business processes spanning functional, system, and organizational boundaries by reusing data and functionality from platforms and applications. We can summarize the key aspects of the process-driven approach as follows:

- Process-driven *collaboration* between business and IT (BizDevs)
- Process-driven *thinking* that considers shape semantics and the process engine while modeling

- Process-driven *methodology* that develops process models top-down without considering restrictions—no analysis of the current process implementations
- Process-driven *architecture* including a reference architecture for process-driven applications
- Process-driven *development* that rigorously applies the "separation of concerns" principle to achieve a maximum of parallelism during development
- Process-driven *technologies* comprising a BPMN engine, business rules engine (or decision management system), integration software such as an ESB, and ESP software for scenarios relying on events

The approach is being applied in a complex project at SAP SE. SAP Language Services (SLS), part of the Globalization Services department at SAP, has to solve the challenge of standardizing their differentiating end-to-end language production processes while retaining broad flexibility to meet a wide range of changing requirements. So far, a total of 206 complex processes have been implemented within 33 months. The advantages gained to date by the application of the process-driven approach for this project can be summarized as follows:

- Time

  - Shorter development time due to parallel independent development
  - Shorter innovation cycle and faster time to market
  - Shorter strategy-to-reality cycle

- Money

  - No additional documentation necessary (modeled process = documented process = executed process)
  - Cost benefits during development *and* maintenance
  - No need to buy additional software for process mining or business activity monitoring if the process engine collects comparable data and provides relevant analytical tooling (depends on the engine used)

- Higher-quality implementation output (more precise, gets it right the first time)
- Increased flexibility on both sides: business process flexibility and flexibility regarding the integration of various IT landscapes
- Increased implementation efficiency as the first implementation is immediately fitting requirements due to early end user involvement resulting in an increased acceptance
- Transparency

  - Increased transparency during process execution
  - Increased transparency by analyzing automatically collected process execution data (via BPMN execution engine)

- Ability to act: PDA offering the best-possible management support in driving a company's strategy

It is advisable to use the process-driven approach in the following cases:

- Alignment of business and implementation requirements in a single BPMN model is important (only one common BPMN model for both sides, business and IT).
- Independence from the system landscape is critical for the resulting application.
- More than one system needs to be integrated.
- The system landscape on which the processes of the solution must run is not stable.
- The solution is complex and justifies the effort involved.
- The solution will provide a competitive advantage.
- The processes in the solution are expected to change frequently.
- The processes in the solution will be used in other organizational units, areas, regions, or other subsidiaries or companies.

However, if none of these statements apply to a development project, it is certainly worthwhile to consider alternatives. The application of the process-driven approach has proven (at least for the SLS project) the following:

- Real-life, complex business processes can be completely modeled and executed using a graphical notation (BPMN).
- BPMN-modeled business processes can really be executed as they were initially planned by the business (preservation of the business BPMN model during implementation).
- Business and technical complexities can be controlled using the right methodology and just one notation (BPMN).
- The BizDevs collaboration model achieves unprecedented efficiency and eliminates misunderstandings. (Thinking in process engines executing business processes forces a new level of precision as it requires that all details have to be made explicit. As a result, companies understand much better how they really work).
- The BizDevs collaboration model requires a thorough understanding of the complete BPMN shape set on both sides—both business and IT. Experience at SLS has shown that while this does require a learning effort especially on the business side, this investment more than pays off in terms of the results. The process-driven project has been invaluable in providing practical experience of the kind of lifelong learning that is fundamental to success in the digital era.

3.4.2 Outlook

The process-driven approach is still in its early stages. However, the results achieved in a first really complex real-life project are more than promising. It seems as if implementation efficiency can be significantly increased compared to common programming approaches. Additionally, the process-driven approach is not only a solution for the first implementation. Due to its modular design, it also helps to reduce the maintenance effort after going productive. The transparencies gained during process execution and after finalization are further key arguments in favor of the approach. For sure, the results have to be confirmed in more projects of this complexity, and both aspects need to be analyzed in more detail: the initial development effort/efficiency and the maintenance effort/efficiency. Besides the mentioned aspects which are worth more research effort, the following list summarizes some ideas for further research questions:

- How suitable are current BPMN engines and their development environments for the development of applications following the process-driven approach?
- What does the ideal development environment for the process-driven approach look like?
- Which additional development guidelines can be given to PDA developers?
- Can the promises of the process-driven approach be confirmed by further projects?
- Can the BizDevs collaboration model be further detailed?
- Are BPMN choreography diagrams useful in the process-driven approach?
- Can BPMN collaboration diagrams be utilized to explicitly visualize the vertical process collaboration between the layers?
- What are the influences of latest IT trends (e.g., in-memory DBs, big data, cloud computing, mobile, Internet of Things, machine learning, NoSQL DBs) on the process-driven approach?
- How can the extensibility of process-driven applications be achieved (e.g., by extension points which are also applied if a new version of a process-driven application is shipped by a vendor)?
- Which prerequisites must be fulfilled for a roundtrip of BPMN models between business-oriented modeling environments and developer-oriented IDEs?
- How can customizing of process-driven applications be achieved?
- The process-driven approach involves a learning effort on the part of project team members that is representative of the type of lifelong learning needed to succeed in the digital era. How can organizations best harness the experience from process-driven projects as they seek to establish a culture and methodology of lifelong learning that fits their unique situation and needs?
- Successful process-driven projects result in substantial efficiency gains for an organization, creating room for further innovation and new business models. New business models will likely require then new process-driven projects to implement them, which the organization is now equipped to do. How can organizations structure these innovation cycles to maximum benefit?
- How can the PDA approach best be combined with agile software development techniques?

Obviously, there is more to explore in the domain of the process-driven approach. We hope that the publication of the results gained by the complex SAP Language Services project and the application of the process-driven approach for differentiating business processes has provided interesting insights for researchers and practitioners alike and motivates them to invest more into this promising approach. It can be a starting point for a new wave of business process implementations helping companies to prepare themselves for the digitalization era.

References

1. M. Heiler, Managing modern business processes: how to use a process-driven architecture to achieve flexible, efficient processes. SAPinsider **17**(1) (2016). Also available online at http://sapinsider.wispubs.com/Assets/Articles/2016/January/SPI-managing-modern-business-processes. Accessed 28 Dec 2017
2. OMG, *Business Process Model and Notation (BPMN), Version 2.0* (2017), http://www.omg.org/spec/BPMN/2.0/PDF. Accessed 27 Dec 2017
3. B. Silver, *BPMN Method and Style*, 2nd edn. (Cody-Cassidy Press, Aptos, 2011). ISBN 978-0-9823681-1-4
4. V. Stiehl, *Process-Driven Applications with BPMN*, 1st edn. (Springer, Heidelberg, 2014). ISBN 978-3-319-07217-3

Chapter 4
Analysis of Data-Flow Complexity and Architectural Implications

Daniel Lübke, Tobias Unger, and Daniel Wutke

Abstract Service orchestrations are frequently used to assemble software components along business processes. Despite much research and empirical studies into the use of control-flow structures of these specialized languages, like BPEL and BPMN2, no empirical evaluation of data-flow structures and languages, like XPath, XSLT, and XQuery, has been made yet. This paper presents a case study on the use of data transformation languages in industry projects in different companies and across different domains, thereby showing that data flow is an important and complex property of such orchestrations. The results also show that proprietary extensions are used frequently and that the design favors the use of modules, which allows for reusing and testing code. This case study is a starting point for further research into the data-flow dimension of service orchestrations and gives insights into practical problems that future standards and theories can rely on.

4.1 Introduction

The usage of analytical business processes is common in practice and has been the subject of many research projects. The logical next step, the execution of business process models, is nowadays catching up on both practical usage and a research subject.

D. Lübke (✉)
FG Software Engineering, Leibniz Universität Hannover, Hannover, Germany
e-mail: daniel.luebke@inf.uni-hannover.de

T. Unger
Opitz Consulting Deutschland GmbH, Gummersbach, Germany

D. Wutke
W&W Informatik GmbH, Ludwigsburg, Germany
e-mail: daniel.wutke@ww-informatik.de

© Springer Nature Switzerland AG 2019
D. Lübke, C. Pautasso (eds.), *Empirical Studies on the Development of Executable Business Processes*, https://doi.org/10.1007/978-3-030-17666-2_4

So far, most research has focused on the control flow of processes, e.g., the graph-based structures in BPMN [20] or the usage of activities in BPEL. For example, Hertis and Juric [7] and Lübke [9] analyzed control-flow dimensions of industrial BPEL processes.

However, for executable processes, especially those that orchestrate multiple services, the data-flow dimension is also important: data needs to be transferred between different activities in the process and needs to be converted into a format consumable by the services being orchestrated.

So far, we know no publications that deal with the implementation and the complexity of data flow in executable business processes and their relationship to the control flow.

Without knowing the data-flow dimension, existing approaches to model, test, and verify business processes cannot judge whether and to what extent they must include the data-flow dimension. Also, there are no reliable sources for practitioners working in implementation projects to estimate implementation and testing effort with regard to the data flow.

In order to fill this gap, we conducted a case study of executable business processes implemented in BPEL that is presented in this chapter. This study aims at providing metrics of data flow and comparing it to the control-flow dimension of processes collected from a number of industry projects. This is a first step to better comprehending the challenges modelers and developers face when developing executable business processes.

Research into data flow has proved difficult because all vendors of BPEL engines provide proprietary implementations and extensions. Without knowing the exact causes, this can be a sign that the technologies provided by the BPEL standard are insufficient and/or that the data-flow implementation is an important development task that vendors chose to optimize in order to better sell their products.

The case study presented in this paper was conducted based on a collection of executable BPEL processes from three companies from different domains, ranging from processes for system-internal service integration to cross-organizational business processes. The analyzed process models target one out of three different BPEL engines and are built using the respective vendor-specific modeling tool and employ the vendor-specific BPEL extension supported by the target platform.

This paper is structured according to the suggestion by Runeson et al. [16]: First, related work is discussed in Sect. 4.2 before BPEL as the modeling language of the process models used in the case study is shortly introduced in Sect. 4.3. The case study design is outlined afterward in Sect. 4.4, and its results are presented in Sect. 4.5. The latter contains subsections for detailing the metrics and their interpretation as well as possible threats to their validity. Finally, conclusions and possible future work are given in Sect. 4.6.

4.2   Related Work

4.2.1   Earlier Studies

There are not that many but still some empirical studies on the practical usage of BPEL and BPMN.

Cardoso [4] tried to empirically validate process-flow metrics for BPEL processes with a complexity metric defined by him. However, no data-flow dimensions are discussed.

zur Muehlen and Recker [20] did the first study into the practical usage of BPMN: they studied which visible BPMN elements were used by different stakeholder groups. Because the executable information, especially data input and output, is stored in non-visible attributes, the study does not contain any information about it. In addition, the analyzed process models are descriptive only.

Hertis and Juric [7] did a much larger study into metrics of BPEL processes: however, they collected process-flow-related data only, e.g., different activity counts and activity usage patterns. No data-flow metrics were described nor gathered. Also, Lübke [9] analyzed timelines of static BPEL metrics in an industry project. These metrics were process flow related, and no insights about data flow could be taken from those. Thus, data-flow dimensions of industry BPEL processes are not known.

Song et al. [18] conducted an empirical study on data-flow bugs in BPEL processes. However, the authors did not characterize the data-flow dimension itself but concentrated on three data-flow bug categories.

All in all, no empirical studies into the characterization of data-flow dimensions of executable business processes in BPEL or BPMN2 have been made to the authors' knowledge as of today.

4.2.2   Theory

One of the reasons no empirical studies about the data-flow dimension of processes have been made might be that in the history of the research into business processes. Empirical research has mainly concentrated on analytical models. Even with the rise of standardized executable languages, namely, BPEL and BPMN2, research has mostly concentrated on the already existing properties of analytical models: process-flow complexity.

As a result, not many publications about data flow are available which in turn might explain the missing empirical evidence: if no theories are created that need to be verified, empirical research has no research questions to answer.

Cardoso [5] first raised the question on how to measure data-flow metrics. The metric that would measure the code complexity of data transformations is called "interface integration complexity" by him. However, the paper is only a position paper that concludes with the question "[h]ow to calculate the interface integration complexity of BPEL4WS containers."

Parizi and Ghani [15] also raised the question of measurements for data-flow complexity. However, they only cite Cardoso's original question and offer no further theory or answers themselves.

Some related work is available from the GRID domain, in which BPEL processes have been used to orchestrate academic workflows. For example, Slomiski [17] compared different approaches and GRID-specific challenges like handling large data sets and streaming data. However, in usual business application domains, data is not that large but structured in a more complex manner: data often needs to be converted between heterogeneous data models, and conversion frequently involves conditional logic to determine the attributes that need to be copied and possibly converted.

The importance of considering data flow in addition to control flow in the context of formal verification of BPEL processes has been recognized by Moser et al. [13] and Zheng et al. [19] where the authors describe algorithms for deriving the data flow of BPEL processes and incorporating it into formal process representations, such as Petri nets or automata.

A related area to service orchestrations is the design of service choreographies, in which services are not centrally orchestrated but instead call each other. Meyer et al. [12] present an approach that relies on a global data model that is mapped to the local data model of each service. The approach visualizes mappings by the use of UML diagrams and references existing standards like OWL and XPath but does not try to assess which data transformation technique would fit the approach and how much development effort this layer requires. Nikaj et al. [14] also present an approach to derive a REST service design from BPMN choreographies. While the approach helps to identify resources and appropriate verbs, the data model is clearly marked as out of scope.

4.3   Business Process Execution Language (BPEL)

The Business Process Execution Language (BPEL) is a language for modeling executable business processes and standardized by OASIS [8]. It is focused on orchestrating web services that are described by WSDL and XML Schema.

BPEL is defined by a set of *activities* that is split into *basic activities* and *structured activities*. Basic activities perform a function, e.g., calling a service (invoke), doing data transformations (assign), or waiting for an inbound message (receive). Structured activities contain other activities and define the control flow between them, e.g., executing one activity after another (sequence) or looping (forEach, repeatUntil, while). The structured activity flow allows graph-based modeling and parallel activity execution. All other activities are block based and may only be nested hierarchically.

For handling XML data, BPEL mandates XPath and—via an XPath extension function—XSLT. XPath can be used for conditions (e.g., in an `if` or as a loop condition) or for copying data. Data copies are defined in `copy` elements inside an `assign` activity. A small code snippet copying data from a received message to a response message, for example, is implemented as follows (namespace prefixes have been omitted for clarity):

```
1  <process>
2   ...
3    <variable messageType="sayHello" name="sayHelloRequest" />
4    <variable messageType="sayHelloResponse" name="sayHelloResponse" />
5    <variable messageType="name" name="string" />
6   ...
7    <sequence>
8     <receive
9       name="ReceiveSayHello"
10      operation="sayHello"
11      variable="sayHelloRequest"
12      ... />
13    <assign name="PrepareResponse">
14      <copy>
15        <from>bpel:doXslTransform(
16          'prepareSayHelloResponse.xsl',
17            $sayHelloRequest.parameters)
18        </from>
19        <to part="parameters" variable="sayHelloResponse" />
20      </copy>
21      <copy>
22        <from>$sayHelloRequest.parameters/lastName)</from>
23            <to variable="name"/>
24          </copy>
25    </assign>
26    <reply
27      name="ReplySayHello"
28      operation="sayHello"
29      variable="sayHelloResponse"
30      ... />
31   </sequence>
32  </process>
```

A message is received by the receive activity (line 7) and copied to the variable *sayHelloRequest*. The variable *sayHelloRespnse* is prepared by an assign activity (line 13). The assign has two copy blocks. The first copy (line 14) uses XSLT via BPEL's built-in *doXslTransform* XPath function and copies the result to the response. The second copy (line 21) simply copies the result of an XPath expression to an atomic variable. The reply (line 26) sends the newly created message to the caller.

Like most WS-* standards, BPEL is designed to be extensible: new query and expression languages besides XPath can be referenced by the use of URNs, and a placeholder `extension` activity can contain vendor-specific activities.

Although BPEL has been superseded by the BPMN standard, it is still used, and many companies have large repositories of BPEL processes that contain lessons learned that apply not only to BPEL but to executable business processes and service orchestrations in general.

4.4   Case Study Design

4.4.1   Research Questions

We formulate our research goal according to the goal/question/metric (GQM) method [1]:

> The purpose of this study is to *characterize* the *implementation of data flow in BPEL processes* from the point of view of *a solution architect* in the context of *executable business process development projects*.

We refined this overall research goal into the following questions:

RQ1: Which data-flow modeling choices are preferred on specific tools?
The BPEL standard itself supports XPath and XSLT (via an XPath extension function). However, BPEL is designed with many extensibility points. One of those extensions can be the use of other languages to formulate expressions and queries on XML data. For example, many BPEL engines support XQuery (e.g., Apache ODE and its derivatives, ActiveVOS, and Oracle BPM Suite), while others allow to embed Java code or offer custom XML data mappings (both options, e.g., IBM WebSphere Process Server (WPS)). When several data-flow implementation choices are available, the question which ones are preferred (or being pushed upon) by developers arises. We hypothesize a) that the developers prefer to use the proprietary extensions provided by the tools, which in general should be more prominently offered in the development tools and should be more powerful than the standard ones because otherwise the tool vendors would have had no incentive to implement those, and b) that the most powerful options XQuery and Java are preferred over other implementation choices. We measure this by counting lines of code and expect XQuery and Java to have the largest amount of lines on ActiveVOS/Oracle and WebSphere Process Server, respectively.

RQ2: What amount of data flow is portable, i.e., standards compliant?
Because we expect the proprietary data-flow implementation choices to be preferred by the developers, our hypothesis is that no BPEL process is fully standards compliant with regard to its data-flow implementation. Because we expect XPath and XSLT to be used nevertheless in some spots (e.g., for formulating conditions and transforming XML data, where XSLT can excel in some circumstances), some portions of the data flow are expected to be standards compliant, i.e., use XPath and/or XSLT. Because we expect most XML messages to be produced by non-standards-compliant code and we expect those to make the bulk of data-flow implementation code, we hypothesize that less of 10% of

the lines of data-flow code are implemented in one of the languages offered by the BPEL standard.

RQ3: Is the data flow in executable business processes larger than the process flow? Because executable business processes possibly connect to many different systems exposing different services and business objects (BOs), we expect data transformations to be an integral and large part of a business process solution. As metrics for measuring complexity, we use the number of conditional branches (e.g., if and switch) and the number of iterations (e.g., for, while, and repeat until loops). For measuring the size, we use the number of lines of code (data flow) and the number of basic activities (process flow). For all these metrics, we hypothesize that the data-flow dimension is larger than the process-flow dimension: (1) We estimate that more lines of code are needed than there are basic activities because the XML messages usually contain more than ten elements. (2) We also expect that there are more conditions and loops. The more statements exist (regardless of the abstraction level), the more conditions and loops are required to order them. Following of (1)+(2), we expect more data-flow conditions and iterations, although we doubt any direct relationship. Originally, we planned to compare not only LOCs and counts but also the complexity of BPEL control-flow structures and the complexity of the data-flow implementations. However, while McCabe's cyclomatic complexity [11] can be easily applied to XQuery, no adaption to BPEL nor XSLT is available. Cardoso's complexity metric [3] has many weights in formulas and is not well defined for all graph-based processes (BPEL's flow activity). The weights forbid direct comparisons to McCabe's unweighted complexity metric. Therefore, we decided to use counts of iterations and conditions instead of a more sophisticated complexity metric.

RQ4: Are data-flow implementations mainly large but linear or mainly complex? From an architecture perspective, an interesting question is where complexity is located. Thus, one important question is whether the code concerned with the data flow is not only large compared to the process flow but whether it is mainly linear, thus "easy" code, or whether it contains many control-flow structures. We expect the data-flow code to be simple because we expect most of the code to simply insert values into XML templates. Only at some points we expect decisions for optional elements or loops for lists. However, we expect more conditions than loops. Therefore, we hypothesize that we have maximum one condition per four lines of data transformation code and maximum one iteration per five lines of code.

RQ5: What are possible factors for increased complexity of data flow? From an architecture point of view, it is important to know and identify drivers of data-flow complexity to better plan and estimate implementation and testing. Because we think that data flow is mainly needed to prepare messages, we hypothesize that the number of message exchange activities (receive, reply, invoke, onMessage, onEvent) correlates linearly to the lines of data-flow code. If this correlation holds, it can be used on analytical models, which contain the message exchanges, to better judge the technical implementation later on. We also hypothesize that the data-flow complexity measured by counting conditions and iterations also correlates linearly to the number of message exchange activities: the usage of conditions and iterations is probably dependent on the differences in the schemas being integrated but should behave the same within one project.

4.4.2 Case and Subject Selection

For answering the outlined research questions, we conduct a case study on processes from three different companies. All processes are BPEL processes so that the choices and metrics are comparable and influences of product choices can be isolated from the modeling language.

The processes target different BPEL engines (Informatica ActiveVOS 9.2, IBM WebSphere Process Server 7.1 and WebSphere Business Process Manager (BPM) 8.5, Oracle Business Process Management Suite 12c) and are modeled using the respective vendor-supplied modeling tool.

Informatica ActiveVOS is a BPEL engine which supports the full WS-BPEL 2.0 standard but also has proprietary extensions for modeling BPEL processes and visualizing them as BPMN. One of these extensions is the support of XQuery for expressions and queries, i.e., in all places where XPath is allowed. XQuery as a superset of XPath is more powerful and can be used to fully replace XSLT transformations.

IBM WebSphere Process Server (WPS) and its successor Business Process Manager (BPM) are workflow engines on top of a JEE application server. In addition to BPEL, IBM BPM also supports modeling and execution of processes modeled in BPMN. As this study focuses on BPEL processes, only the BPEL-specific aspects of BPM are discussed. Besides WS-BPEL 1.1 processes, WPS/BPM supports the execution of state machines and business rules. Service integration is performed via an integration solution (WebSphere ESB) that comes with the workflow engine. Regarding data flow, WPS/BPM supports standard XPath expressions as well as the vendor-specific business object maps, XML maps, and Java code embedded in the BPEL process model.

Oracle Business Process Management Suite 12c is a toolset and integration platform for development and execution of SOA-based applications. Among other components, the BPEL Process Manager supports the execution of BPEL 2.0 processes. Oracle also provides a set of vendor-specific extensions like XQuery integration in XPath, a replay activity for restarting scopes, and human tasks.

In the following, we present an overview of the processes used in the case study, following the categorization proposed in Chap. 2.

The first project that is contained in our analysis is Terravis (see Table 4.1). Terravis is a process integration platform that allows to conduct cross-organizational processes between land registries, notaries, and banks [2]. The project uses the ActiveVOS BPEL engine, which is developed by Informatica. We analyzed a

Table 4.1 Aggregated metadata for the ActiveVOS process collection (Terravis, classification according to [10])

Collection name	Terravis
Process count	86
Domain	Land register transactions
Geography	Switzerland
Time	12-2017
Boundaries	Cross-organizational 23%, intraorganizational 17%, intra-system 60%
Relationship	Calls another 17%, calls another/is being called 24%, event triggered 16%, is being called 1%
Scope	Core 34%, technical 38%, auxiliary 28%
Process model purpose	Executable
People involvement	Mostly 17%, partly 3%, none 79%
Process language	WS-BPEL 2.0, BPEL4People, plus vendor extensions
Execution engine	ActiveVOS 9.2.x
Model maturity	Productive 100%

Table 4.2 Aggregated metadata for the WPS/BPM process collection

Collection name	Banking and Insurance
Process count	75
Domain	Banking, insurance
Geography	Germany
Time	05-2017
Boundaries	Cross-organizational 4%, intraorganizational 67%, within system 29%
Relationship	Calls another 12%, is being called 64%, is being called/calls another 5%, no call 19%
Scope	Core 13%, technical 87%
Process model purpose	Executable
People involvement	None 92%, partly 8%
Process language	WS-BPEL 1.1 plus vendor extensions
Execution engine	IBM WebSphere Process Server 7.1, IBM Business Process Manager 8.5
Model maturity	Illustrative 3%, productive 73%, retried 24%

snapshot taken from the repository, which was taken in December 2017. We needed to exclude processes from this project that use XQuery 2.0 features that are not supported by our analysis tool.

The second process collection contains processes from the banking and insurance domain (see Table 4.2) with a strong focus on technical integration processes. The processes use the IBM WebSphere Process Server and IBM Business Process Manager BPEL engines and integration solutions. The analyzed snapshot was taken in May 2017.

Table 4.3 Aggregated metadata for the Oracle SOA Suite process collection

Collection name	Wholesale and Retail Trade
Process count	23
Domain	Commerce
Geography	Europe
Time	2015
Boundaries	Cross-organizational 17%, intraorganizational 83%
Relationship	Calls another 96%, is being called 4%
Scope	Technical 100%
Process model purpose	Executable
People involvement	None 96%, partly 4%
Process language	WS-BPEL 2.0 plus vendor extensions
Execution engine	Oracle SOA Suite 12.1
Model maturity	Illustrative 4%, productive 96%

Table 4.4 Proprietary extensions for data-flow definition

Informatica ActiveVOS	XQuery in assign activities, import of XQuery modules for usage in XQuery statements embedded into the assign activities
Oracle BPM Suite	XQuery in XPath
IBM WebSphere Process Server/Business Process Manager	Java, business object (BO) maps, XML maps

The Oracle process collection shown in Table 4.3 is used to integrate retailers with their suppliers.

4.4.3   Data Collection and Analysis Procedure

In the first step, the data transformations of the collected processes have been analyzed: the main goal is to identify the proprietary extensions used for defining the data flow. The extensions found are presented in Table 4.4.

The data collection for the static metrics itself was done with a custom static code analyzer named BPELStats that had been developed under the umbrella of the BPELUnit project and is now developed as a standalone project. BPELStats has been originally developed for gathering the metrics presented in [9] and is available as open source.[1]

Among other metrics, BPELStats can count BPEL activities by type and has been extended as part of this study to compute the number of occurrences, iterations,

---

[1]https://github.com/dluebke/bpelstats.

conditions, and LOCs for XPath, XSLT, XQuery, BOMaps, XMLMaps,[2] and Java code. The calculation is based on whole files: if a file is imported into the BPEL process, all functions, templates, etc. are counted toward the metrics, and no check is made whether a certain piece is actually called by the process or not. All of our extensions have been contributed to the BPELStats project and are freely available and can be reviewed.

Clean checkouts of the process projects have been done first. The total sample size contains 184 executable BPEL processes. Where necessary, a full build has been triggered before the analysis when the build is necessary to copy all external dependencies (e.g., WSDLs, XML Schemas, reused XSLT and XQuery files) to their correct positions enabling BPELStats to also follow and resolve imports of those files from the BPEL processes.

4.4.4 Validity Procedure

In order to ensure the correctness of the measurements, the BPELStats tool was tested with both unit tests and manual tests. The whole gathering routines were automated by using shell scripts in order to eliminate human error. These shell scripts were also tested by all researchers in this study in order to show that the results are correctly computed.

For allowing other researchers to replicate this study, the used scripts have been made available.[3] This also allows other researchers to check their correctness.

We tried to cover as many different BPEL toolsets as possible to strengthen external validity. With three completely different BPEL engines used in three large industrial projects at different organizations, we are confident to be able to distinguish influences imposed by the tooling and the project from those that are inherent to the problem of service orchestrations and executable business processes.

4.5 Results

Within this section, we present the plain results of our case study, which mainly include the metrics being gathered as part of our measurements. The interpretation of these measurements is presented in the following section.

---

[2]As XMLMaps are compiled to XSL transformations during build time, their metrics are calculated using the XSLT sublanguage parser and hence show up as XSLT metrics in the results with their occurrences being counted separately.

[3]The files are accessible at http://www.daniel-luebke.de/files/bpm-dataflowcomplexity.tgz.

4.5.1 Metrics

For answering our research questions, we collected the metrics required to answer them.

The first analysis computed the occurrences of data flow in the process collection and the lines of code of data-flow code. An occurrence is a place at which data-flow code is embedded into the process. If the process has five assign activities, there are at least five occurrences of data-flow mappings, depending on the number and type of copy statements. Each data-flow occurrence contains at least one line of code but can contain multiple ones. This means that the number of occurrences is equal to or less than the number of lines of code.

We aggregated the metrics as shown in Table 4.5 according to the different languages that we found in the process set. The language which has the most occurrences in our process set is XPath. However, XQuery has more lines of code. Java is the third most often used language followed by XSLT.

We aggregated this data further and clustered the languages into portable (standards compliant, i.e., XPath, XSLT) and non-portable (not mandated by the BPEL standard, i.e., XQuery, Java, BOMaps, and XMLMaps). The results are shown in Table 4.6: nearly half of the occurrences (46%) of data-flow code are portable, but only 8.96% of lines of code are written in standard-mandated languages.

In the next step, we analyzed the relationship between the process flow and the data flow. Figure 4.1 depicts the relationship between the number of basic activities and the lines of data-flow code. The plots indicate a linear relationship between basic activities and data flow. Therefore, we computed Spearson's linear correlation coefficient between these two dimensions, which is $c = 0.8162$ (Terravis), $c = 0.9035$ (Wholesale and Retail Trade), $c = 0.6962$ (Banking and Insurance), and

Table 4.5 Data-flow occurrences and LOCs by engine and implementation choice

Metric	ActiveVOS	Oracle BPM	IBM WPS/BPM
XPath occurrences	2419	2380	738
XPath LOCs	2865	2380	738
XSLT occurrences	4	0	0
XSLT LOCs	4437	0	0
XQuery occurrences	4173	108	0
XQuery LOCs	21, 888	10, 010	0
Java occurrences	0	0	2193
Java LOCs	0	0	13, 298
BOMap occurrences	0	0	32
BOMap LOCs	0	0	3676
XMLMap occurrences	0	0	0
XMLMap LOCs	0	0	0
Total occurrences	6596	2488	2963
Total LOCs	29, 190	12, 390	17, 712

Table 4.6 Percentages of used data-flow technologies	Portability	Percentage (S)LOCs	Percentage occurrences
	Portable	8.96%	46%
	Not portable	91%	54%

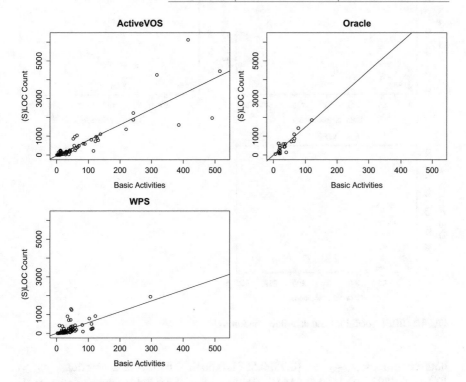

Fig. 4.1 Data-flow (S)LOC count and number of basic activities

$c = 0.848$ combined for the whole data set. Except for the Banking and Insurance data set, the relationship between the basic activities and the data-flow lines of code is linear. As such, we added regression lines to Fig. 4.1.

In order to judge whether the process-flow or data-flow dimension is larger, we computed a two-sided, paired Wilcoxon test: for the Terravis data set $p = 1.101 \times 10^{-10}$, for the Wholesale and Retail Trade data set $p = 2.886 \times 10^{-5}$, and for the Banking and Insurance data set $p = 5.947 \times 10^{-14}$. If all data sets are combined, the Wilcoxon test results in $p = 1.946 \times 10^{-31}$. All computed p-values are much smaller than 0.01, which is a commonly accepted threshold for highly significant results.

In the next step, we drilled down into the nature of the control flow and data flow and computed the number of iterations and conditions within each language. We plotted the conditions of each dimension against each other in Fig. 4.2 and the iterations against each other in Fig. 4.3. For each project alone and all combined, we again computed Spearman's linear correlation coefficient for

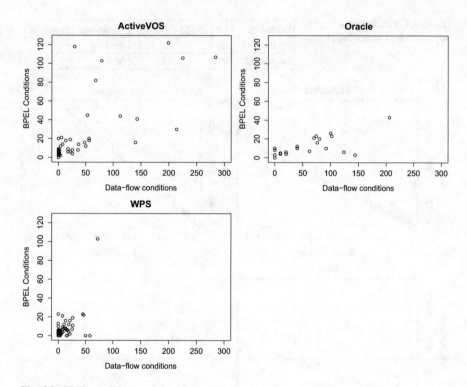

Fig. 4.2 BPEL conditions and data-flow conditions

both conditions ($c_{cond} = \{0.75, 0.5671, 0.6053, 0.6538\}$) and iterations ($c_{it} = \{0.591, 0.9503, -0.1554, 0.6444\}$). Because $|c| < 0.75|$ holds for correlation coefficients with two exceptions (conditions for Terravis and iterations for Wholesale and Retail Trade), our data cannot support any linear correlation, especially because there are also correlation coefficients with different signs (c_{it} is negative for WPS).

We also conducted a two-tailed, paired Wilcoxon test for differences between the process-flow and data-flow dimension on this data: for conditions of the three projects and all projects combined

$p_{cond} = (0.5215, 0.0001651, 0.6319, 0.07883)$

and for iterations

$p_{it} = (4.997 \times 10^{-7}, 0.0009128, 0.6768, 1.59 \times 10^{-8})$ While for all p-values concerning the conditions $p > 0.05$ holds, nearly all p-values—except for the WPS project—hold $p < 0.01$.

These differences concerning the different projects and BPEL engines led to another drill-down into the data. As shown in Fig. 4.4, we plotted the distribution of conditions and iterations in relation to the lines of data-flow code. We split this data by projects and additionally combined the processes using XQuery from the Terravis process set and the Wholesale and Retail Trade process set. The plot suggests that the number of conditions and iterations in the data flow is significantly different

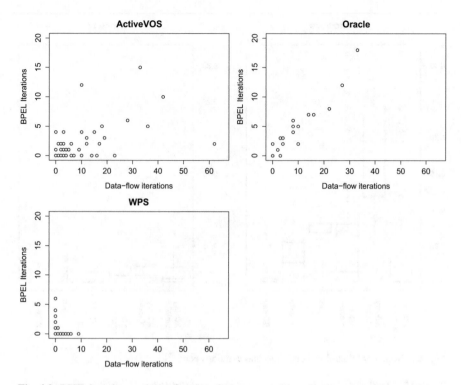

Fig. 4.3 BPEL iterations and data-flow iterations

between the data sets, also when the data sets use the same language, which is the case in Terravis and Wholesale and Retail Trade for XQuery.

The median values of conditions per lines of data-flow code are below 0.15. Except for the Wholesale and Retail Trade data set, they are even below 0.10. All values for the iterations are below 0.075, and the median values are all below 0.025. The data indicates that there are more conditions per lines of code than iterations.

For answering the last research question, we computed the number of message exchange activities in the processes and computed the correlation coefficient to the lines of data-flow code. The results are summarized in Table 4.7: For two of the three data sets, we get a correlation coefficient c with $c > 0.75$, which hints at a linear relationship. The exception is the WPS data set, which mainly uses Java. The mean of the message activities per lines of data-flow code is between 0.026 and 0.054 in the data sets.

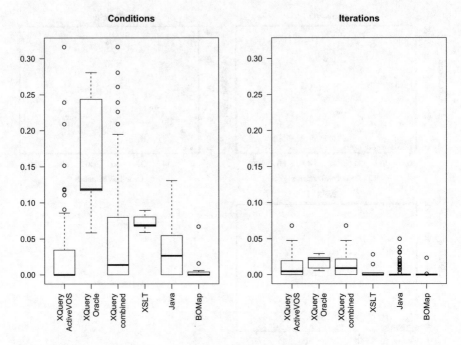

Fig. 4.4 Number of data-flow conditions and iterations per LOC

Table 4.7 Message exchanges per process collection and (S)LOC

Metric	ActiveVOS	Oracle BPM	IBM WPS
Message activities	2238	316	750
(S)LOC	41,100	12,390	17,712
Message activities/(S)LOC	0.054	0.026	0.042
Correlation coefficient	0.792	0.907	0.693

4.5.2   Interpretation

4.5.2.1   RQ1: Which Data-Flow Modeling Choices Are Preferred on Specific Tools?

The results presented in Table 4.5 confirm hypothesis (a) as well as hypothesis (b). However, the result is most succinct for the IBM WPS collection. One reason is that Java can be used almost anywhere in IBM Process Server. Furthermore, IBM's tooling supports the Java extensions very well. ActiveVOS and Oracle BPM do not support Java in conditions.

In the case of Oracle, the interpretation is not that easy. Although XQuery is a popular option for data mapping, the numbers in Table 4.5 show that also XPath is very popular. One reason is that Oracle integrates XQuery as an XPath extension function. Whenever XQuery is used, XPath is also used. This means from a

BPEL perspective you always use a BPEL standard option (XPath), because Oracle decided to extend XPath. The fact that there are much more XQuery LOCs than XPath LOCs confirms that XQuery is the preferred option for data transformation. Furthermore, Oracle provides a modeling tool for XPath.

Compared to IBM and Oracle, ActiveVOS is the most standard compliant engine. However, the disproportionately larger number of XQuery LOCs proves that the vendor extension XQuery is preferred over XPath.

Form a skill perspective, we quite often observe that BPEL processes are modeled by developers. For them, XQuery might be easier to learn than XSLT; and due to Java being a common language used for developing enterprise software, a large number of those developers are probably already familiar with Java, so they do not need to learn new languages like XPath or XSLT.

4.5.2.2   RQ2: What Amount of Data Flow Is Portable, i.e., Standards Compliant?

Table 4.6 shows that the amount of non-portable data-flow code is over 90%, i.e., porting a process would lead to a nearly complete reimplementation of the data flow. However, the occurrences of BPEL-compliant data-flow implementations and implementations using vendor extensions are nearly equal. One reason is that ActiveVOS and Oracle BPEL only support XML-based implementations in conditions. In addition, developers try to make implementation of conditions easy, i.e., XPath is sufficient by moving complicated transformation to assign activities. Ironically, the possibility to use Java in WPS also makes things easier for developers. Java provides a larger set of operators that allow to formulate conditions more easy and compact. For example, the Exclusive OR (XOR) is not supported in XPath but in Java.

Another aspect of portability is that each vendor chooses a different implementation of an extension, even if the extension itself is provided by multiple vendors. For example, the ActiveVOS XQuery extension is not compatible with Oracle's extension, and IBM Java activity is not compatible with Oracle's Java activity. Thus, portability would also not increase if comparing the process collections pairwise.

Our results also support the conclusion that there is something wrong with the standard. Maybe the standard fell victim to its extensibility because every vendor used the extensibility to differentiate its product. Maybe the vendors also only approved the standard because of its extensibility because portability was not really an issue.

For architects, this raises the question which language is the best option to model data flow. This also raises a lot of research questions: What is the best, most productive, easy-to-maintain set of data transformation languages? How to decide on a language in a concrete project setting?

4.5.2.3   RQ3: Is the Data Flow in Executable Business Processes Larger than the Process-Flow?

The highly significant p-values (all $p <= 0.01$) confirm our assumption. However, this contradicts our experience from modeling and implementing process-based systems. We spend a large part of the modeling effort on modeling the control flow. The results suggest that we should spend more effort on the data flow. Also, a lot of project guidelines we saw lack in defining rules for data flow. Therefore, guidelines should also provide rules and norms for handling the implementation of the data flow. In addition, the research domain should give data flow more attention.

4.5.2.4   RQ4: Are Data-Flow Implementations Mainly Large but Linear or Mainly Complex?

Table 4.4 shows that the measurement proves our hypothesis to some extent. However, the assumption that we expect less conditions than loops is disproved because we observed significantly different numbers (especially conditions) for each observed language. Especially, the XQuery transformations of the Wholesale and Retail Trade process collection contain more conditions than loops. This aspect needs further research. This research should also investigate whether the design of the XML Schemas, the chosen query language, or even unknown properties influence the number of loops and conditions.

4.5.2.5   RQ5: What Are Possible Factors for Increased Complexity of Data Flow?

Table 4.7 shows a strong linear correlation between message exchange activities and LOCs. One reason might be that transformations are mostly used to prepare a service invocation. In a lot of processes, we observe that an invoke activity is preceded and/or succeeded by assign activities. For example, this correlation allows to estimate effort for implementing data transformations based on the number of message exchange activities. Even if we confirmed the strong linear correlation, the slack between the projects is different. For example, the Wholesale and Retail Trade process collection shows a higher number of LOCs per message exchanges than the IBM collection. The reason for this might be similar to Sect. 4.5.2.1, i.e., the expressiveness of the data transformation language used.

4.5.3   Threats to Validity

We tried to eliminate internal threats to validity as much as possible: because we only rely on automatically and objectively measured metrics for which the metric tool and all scripts are available for public scrutiny, there should be no measurement errors.

Regarding processes built for the IBM WPS/BPM engines, we identified the following threats to internal validity due to our measurement method: WPS/BPM script elements allow the execution of arbitrary Java code, not only data transformations. The collected metrics for Java code do not differentiate between data transformation and, e.g., business logic and are calculated based on all Java code embedded in the BPEL process model. This classification would be needed to be done manually and is both time-consuming and error prone. In addition, WPS/BPM supports importing Java classes from library projects and external libraries. Both forms of imports have not been considered when calculating the Java metrics. Finally, the WPS/BPM BPEL engine comes with an integration solution (WebSphere ESB) which supports the definition and execution of so-called mediation flows. As part of the integration logic, data can be transformed in various ways, e.g., via XSL transformations or custom Java code. Data transformations defined in mediation flows have not been considered when calculating the respective data-flow metrics in the BPEL processes.

Because this case study is based on a small set of projects, there are however threats to external validity. Especially, the question of generalizability to other BPEL projects has to be raised.

This case study uses three different BPEL tool chains, and we could identify differences between the different projects. However, due to limitations in our data set, we cannot tell whether these differences arise from the tools only—which is certainly true for the different data-flow languages being offered—or whether differences are caused by other project constraints. There are no theories nor empirical evidence for possible impact factors: from our point of view, probable candidates are the difference between the service contracts of composed services and architecture choices that can distribute data transformations between different infrastructure artifacts (e.g., enterprise service bus (ESB) or process implementation) and own services (e.g., custom services implemented in a "classical" programming language like Java).

The results clearly show that more than half of the data flow is implemented with non-portable vendor extensions. To our knowledge, our data set covers all proprietary extensions except JavaScript that is, for example, offered by ActiveVOS. However, under these circumstances, we also expect that the same data-flow complexity is contained therein, even though it might be implemented differently.

Further cases will be needed to judge and strengthen the external validity and also to build and validate first theories about causalities that influence data-flow complexity. This case study will therefore serve as a first piece of the puzzle to unravel the understanding and drivers of data flow in executable business processes, but clearly further steps are required in order to exactly pinpoint influencing factors.

4.6   Conclusions and Future Work

4.6.1   *Conclusions for Researchers*

To our knowledge, this case study was the first empirical study that did not only consider the process-flow dimension but also the data-flow dimension of executable business processes—in this case modeled in BPEL.

Our study clearly shows that the data-flow dimension is larger than the process-flow dimension regarding both statements (LOCs vs. activities) and complexity (conditions and iterations). This means that theoretical concepts, e.g., for verifying process flow, fail to deliver a complete solution until they are not extended by data-flow analysis. This also means that with current techniques, verification of the process flow alone cannot replace testing of executable business processes because the tests are covering the data transformations that are otherwise left out. While "processes are not data," it is certainly true that "processes cannot be implemented without data flow."

The study also shows that BPEL processes, although they are modeled in a standardized language, are amended with many proprietary extensions. This in turn means that researchers need to have knowledge about the tools that have been used to develop the processes being researched.

Our case study resulted in a new possible estimation metric: the number of message exchanges that can be computed on the analytical process model prior to implementation of the executable model correlates very well to the lines of data-flow code. However, the average number of message exchanges per lines of data-flow code varies between 0.03 and 0.05 between the data sets.

Better formalization of data transformations would improve the possibilities to analyze the data flow from a research perspective. With this in mind, BPMN 2.0 as a standard lacks even behind BPEL with all proprietary extensions: the BPMN standardization committee opted to not standardize any technical bindings. As such, there are no data transformation languages mandated by the standard. Instead, the choice is left to the tool vendor. This means that BPMN research with the goal of gaining insights into executable BPMN in a general sense is probably impossible. A realistic goal would be to study the BPMN "dialect," which is created by the vendor implementation. With this in mind, the usage of BPEL processes as research subjects is probably easier but warrants the question of how much of the empirical results gained in BPEL processes can be generalized to BPMN executable processes.

4.6.2   *Conclusions for Practitioners*

While some BPM vendors advertise their tools with "zero code" and other buzzwords, our study clearly shows that the data-flow dimension is important and even larger and more complex than the process-flow dimension. Practitioners and especially software architects need to be aware of the implications of the "hidden logic" that is usually hidden behind nice-looking models:

- Especially, data-flow implementation seems to be highly specific to a chosen BPMS. None of the studied projects achieved portability. This means that by choosing a tool, the project will probably be dependent on this tool in the future if high migration costs are to be avoided.
- Data flow builds its own new layer of complexity. This means that effort for development and especially testing the higher number of conditions and iterations needs to be planned for. Also, architects should consider making guidelines on how to structure, format, etc. data-flow code in their projects to help developers build better and more maintainable executable processes.
- For better communication between stakeholders, it would be good to see the data flow clearer in the analytical models. Usage of data objects in BPMN is one way, which are only used in about 25% of all models [20], to better communicate which data is sent/received from where.
- We have shown that the number of message exchanges can be used to predict the lines of data-flow code. While this needs to be further improved into an estimation method, architects can leverage this knowledge.
- Although data-flow code uses conditions and iterations, it only uses few of them. This means that most of the code is fairly easy and should be easy to develop and test.
- Additionally, the overall solution architecture should address the data flow more. At which components or areas inside or outside the executable process should what type of data-flow logic be placed? In the projects analyzed as part of this research, most code was embedded directly into the BPEL processes themselves, while only a small amount was placed in surrounding areas like an enterprise service bus or supporting services. For example, Danei et al. [6] propose a multilayered approach with clear responsibilities for each layer. Empirical analysis should be used to gain further insight into benefits and drawbacks of different architectural choices.

4.6.3 Outlook and Future Work

The ultimate goal should be to identify causal relationships between projects' properties and their data-flow complexity. Most likely, this will include architectural decisions outside the modeling language itself, like the complexity and diversity of the underlying data models of the orchestrated services. Also, the use of vendor-specific functionality is very apparent. Causes for this should be subject to future research, especially with the aim to provide improvements to relevant standards. One worthwhile angle of future research would be an empirical comparison of the data-flow languages typically used with regard to development effort and understandability.

Although the case study used BPEL processes, executable processes modeled in BPMN2 also need to deal with data transformations. We expect complexity drivers for data transformations to be independent of the process modeling language. However, a further research angle would be the investigation of data flow in BPMN2 processes as well: unfortunately because BPMN2 is not standardized in the area of technical bindings, we expect research to be more difficult and the metrics harder to compare between different process engines than with BPEL.

We hope that we can pursue these possible future research topics on data flow in executable business processes together with other researchers and industry partners and hope that this case study and the published tooling help others to replicate this study and provide answers to data-flow research questions on other interesting topics!

References

1. V.R. Basili, Applying the goal/question/metric paradigm in the experience factory, in *Software Quality Assurance and Measurement: A Worldwide Perspective*, vol. 7, no.4 (Chapman and Hall, London, 1995), pp. 21–44
2. W. Berli, D. Lübke, W. Möckli, Terravis – large scale business process integration between public and private partners, in *Lecture Notes in Informatics (LNI)*, ed. by E. Plödereder, L. Grunske, E. Schneider, D. Ull. Proceedings INFORMATIK 2014, vol. P-232 (Gesellschaft für Informatik e.V., Bonn, 2014), pp. 1075–1090
3. J. Cardoso, Complexity analysis of BPEL web processes. Softw. Process Improv. Pract. J. **12**, 35–49 (2006)
4. J. Cardoso, Process control-flow complexity metric: an empirical validation, in *IEEE International Conference on Services Computing, 2006. SCC'06* (IEEE, Piscataway, 2006), pp. 167–173
5. J. Cardoso, About the data-flow complexity of web processes, in *6th International Workshop on Business Process Modeling, Development, and Support: Business Processes and Support Systems: Design for Flexibility. The 17th Conference on Advanced Information Systems Engineering (CAiSE'05)* (2015)
6. M. Danei, J. Elliott, M. Heiler, T. Kerwien, V. Stiehl, Effectively and efficiently implementing complex business processes - a case study, in *Empirical Studies on the Development of Executable Business Processes*, Chapter 3 (Springer, Cham, 2019)
7. M. Hertis, M.B. Juric, An empirical analysis of business process execution language usage. IEEE Trans. Softw. Eng. **40**(08), 738–757 (2014)
8. D. Jordan, J. Evdemon, A. Alves, A. Arkin, S. Askary, C. Barreto, B. Bloch, F. Curbera, M. Ford, Y. Goland, A. Guízar, N. Kartha, C.K. Liu, R. Khalaf, D. König, M. Marin, V. Mehta, S. Thatte, D. van der Rijn, P. Yendluri, A. Yiu, *Web Services Business Process Execution Language Version 2.0* (OASIS, Clovis, 2007)
9. D. Lübke, Using metric time lines for identifying architecture shortcomings in process execution architectures, in *2nd International Workshop on Software Architecture and Metrics (SAM), 2015 IEEE/ACM* (IEEE, Piscataway, 2015), pp. 55–58
10. D. Lübke, A. Ivanchikj, C. Pautasso, A template for categorizing empirical business process metrics, in *Business Process Management Forum - BPM Forum 2017*, ed. by J. Carmona, G. Engels, A. Kumar (Springer, Cham, 2017)
11. T.J. McCabe, A complexity measure, in *Proceedings of the 2Nd International Conference on Software Engineering, ICSE '76*, Los Alamitos (IEEE Computer Society Press, Washington, 1976), 407 pp.

12. A. Meyer, L. Pufahl, K. Batoulis, D. Fahland, M. Weske, Automating data exchange in process choreographies. Inf. Syst. **53**, 296–329 (2015)
13. S. Moser, A. Martens, K. Gorlach, W. Amme, A. Godlinski, Advanced verification of distributed ws-bpel business processes incorporating cssa-based data flow analysis, in *IEEE International Conference on Services Computing (SCC 2007)*, July 2007, pp. 98–105
14. A. Nikaj, M. Weske, J. Mendling, Semi-automatic derivation of RESTful choreographies from business process choreographies. Softw. Syst. Model. **18**(2), 1195–1208 (2019)
15. R.M. Parizi, A.A.A. Ghani, An ensemble of complexity metrics for BPEL web processes, in *Ninth ACIS International Conference on Software Engineering, Artificial Intelligence, Networking, and Parallel/Distributed Computing, 2008. SNPD '08* (2008)
16. P. Runeson, M. Höst, A. Rainer, B. Regnell, *Case Study Research in Software Engineeering – Guidelines and Examples* (Wiley, Hoboken, 2012)
17. A. Slomiski, On using BPEL extensibility to implement OGSI and WSRF grid workflows. Concurr. Comput. Pract. Exp. **18**(10), 1229–1241 (2006)
18. W. Song, C.Z. Zhang, H.-A. Jacobsen, An empirical study on data flow bugs in business processes. IEEE Trans. Cloud Comput. **PP**, 1 (2018)
19. Y. Zheng, J. Zhou, P. Krause, Analysis of BPEL data dependencies, in *33rd EUROMICRO Conference on Software Engineering and Advanced Applications (EUROMICRO 2007)* Aug 2007, pp. 351–358
20. M. zur Muehlen, J. Recker, How much language is enough? Theoretical and practical use of the business process modeling notation, in *Advanced Information Systems Engineering: 20th International Conference, CAiSE 2008 Montpellier, June 16–20, 2008 Proceedings*, ed. by Z. Bellahsène, M. Léonard (Springer, Berlin, 2008), pp. 465–479

Part III
Case Studies and Experiments

Chapter 5
Requirements Comprehension Using BPMN: An Empirical Study

Olga Lucero Vega-Márquez, Jaime Chavarriaga, Mario Linares-Vásquez, and Mario Sánchez

Abstract The Business Process Model and Notation (BPMN) has become the de facto standard for process modeling. Currently, BPMN models can be (a) analyzed or simulated using specialized tools, (b) executed using business process management systems (BPMSs), or (c) used for requirements elicitation. Although there are many studies comparing BPMN to other modeling techniques for analyzing and executing processes, there are few showing the suitability of BPMN models as a source for requirements comprehension in projects where process-aware software is built without using BPMSs. This chapter presents a study aimed at comparing the comprehension of software requirements regarding a business process using either BPMN or traditional techniques, such as use cases. In our study, we analyzed responses of 120 undergraduate and graduate students regarding the requirements comprehension achieved when using only BPMN models, only use cases, or both. The results do not show significant impact of the artifacts on the comprehension level. However, when the understanding of the requirement involves sequence of activities, using the BPMN shows better results on the comprehension time.

5.1 Introduction

The Business Process Model and Notation (BPMN) has been widely used by organizations for understanding and communicating their business processes [19, 23, 24]. Organizations also use BPMN models to automate their processes using a business process management system (BPMS) [21] or to elicit requirements [29, 33, 34].

O. L. Vega-Márquez (✉)
Universidad de los Andes, Bogotá, Colombia

Universidad de los Llanos, Villavicencio, Colombia
e-mail: ol.vegam@uniandes.edu.co; olvegam@unillanos.edu.co

J. Chavarriaga · M. Linares-Vásquez · M. Sánchez
Universidad de los Andes, Bogotá, Colombia
e-mail: ja.chavarriaga908@uniandes.edu.co; m.linaresv@uniandes.edu.co; mar-san1@uniandes.edu.co

© Springer Nature Switzerland AG 2019
D. Lübke, C. Pautasso (eds.), *Empirical Studies on the Development of Executable Business Processes*, https://doi.org/10.1007/978-3-030-17666-2_5

The benefits and critical factors of using BPMN as the foundation to implement BPMS-based solutions have been amply discussed [35], especially because some previous studies showed that BPMN is easier to comprehend by stakeholders and domain experts than other process modeling languages [3, 8, 32, 40]. However, few studies have analyzed the use of those models for software development [23] or their effectiveness for eliciting and comprehending requirements.

This chapter reports our empirical study aimed at analyzing whether BPMN models are a helpful tool for improving requirements comprehension during software development. In particular, it compares the requirements comprehension achieved by developers when using BPMN models, use cases, or both.

In this study, we used two case studies to identify the requirements comprehension achieved by the participants: (a) a credit application process and (b) a point-of-sale application. We asked participants to read a case study description and a set of artifacts describing the software requirements in the case study (BPMN model, use case specification, or both); afterward, the participants answered a questionnaire we designed to measure the comprehension level. Finally, we analyzed the responses of 120 undergraduate and graduate students from three Colombian universities. Our analysis does not show significant differences on the comprehension level that may be achieved using the different types of specification. Regarding time, the results are similar with an exception in using a BPMN model vs. using use case specifications. However, our qualitative analysis of questions showed that when software requirements were related to activity sequences, using BPMN models produced better results.

The rest of the chapter is organized as follows: Sect. 5.2 summarizes the related work. Section 5.3 describes the design of the experiment. Section 5.4 presents the results. Section 5.5 discusses the identified threats to the validity. And, finally, Sect. 5.6 draws conclusions and reports our future work.

5.2   Related Work

Several notations have been proposed to model, analyze, and support business processes. Besides the flow process charts (flowcharts) [13] proposed at the beginning of the 1900s, other types of models such as event-driven process chains (EPC) [45], YAWL [46], UML activity diagrams (UML AD) [40], ultra-light activity diagrams [6], and the BPMN standard [30] have been proposed as better ways to document and communicate business processes.

Many authors have been studying which type of modeling is the best for a specific setting. Figl [8] surveyed 279 papers studying the comprehension of processes modeled using diverse notations. These papers analyze if the medium to present the model (e.g., paper or computer), the notation, the size, or the orientation affects the comprehension level or the time required to perform some tasks on the processes. However, none of the studies referenced in [8] focus on the comprehension of the requirements regarding the implementation of the modeled processes.

Some of the above studies compared the comprehension of processes modeled using *diagrams in different notations*. For instance, Peixoto et al. [32] and Birkmeier et al. [2, 3] compared BPMN and UML AD; Gross and Doerr [16] compared EPC and UML AD; Di Cerbo et al. [6] compared the precise and ultra-light (simplified) UML AD; Gabryelczyk and Jurczuk [11] and Recker and Dreiling [36, 37] compared EPC and BPMN diagrams; Weitlaner et al. [50] studied EPC, UML AD, BPMN, and storyboard descriptions; Jošt et al. [20] studied EPC, UML AD, and BPMN; and Figl et al. [10] focused on YAWL, EPC, UML AD, and BPMN.

Some other studies include *use cases and textual descriptions* along with process models into the comparison. For instance, Ottensooser et al. [31] and Rodrigues et al. [38] compared BPMN models and use cases; and Figl and Recker [9] compared BPMN, structured text, and informal text descriptions. Ottensooser et al. compared the artifacts for domain understanding, i.e., the ability of individuals to reason and communicate the domain details where a system is rooted, including concepts, rules, constraints, inputs, outputs, etc. [12]. Rodrigues et al. and Figl and Recker were centered in the process comprehension. None of them inquired about the understanding of software requirements. Table 5.1 summarizes the works that have compared the comprehension of processes modeled with BPMN and other techniques. Note that, while some studies analyzed the data using only descriptive statistics, others used advanced techniques to determine significant differences. For instance, Sandkuhl and Wiebring [41] reported comprehension accuracy using only the average score. The highest accuracy in [41] was UML AD ($M = 11.93$), followed by EPC ($M = 11.50$), flow diagram ($M = 11.32$), and finally BPMN ($M = 11.29$). However, they did not perform further analyses on the variance of these data. In general, the papers performing other analyses did not find significant differences among BPMN and other techniques for the comprehension of processes by nontrained users.

There are few proposals to integrate business and software requirements modeling. López-Campos et al. [25] combine UML and BPMN to represent software systems; Lübke and Schneider [26] use BPMN to represent sets of use cases; Cibrán [4] and Macek and Richta [27] transform BPMN models into AD diagrams; Wautelet and Poelmans [49] propose an alignment among the elements of both modeling languages. Regretfully, these works focus on the interaction among the models but do not analyze if the use of BPMN or other process models improves the elicitation or the comprehension of the corresponding software requirements.

5.3   Empirical Study

We are interested in studying the benefits of using process models by software developers for eliciting and comprehending software requirements. To achieve this goal, we designed an experiment that measures whether the usage of BPMN models improves requirements comprehension when compared to traditional artifacts such

Table 5.1 Papers comparing BPMN with other notations

Paper	Conclusions	Models	Partic.	Analysis
BPMN vs. text or textual use cases				
Ottensooser et al. [31]	BPMN increased comprehension accuracy for users trained in process modeling. There was no significant difference for not trained users. The combination of BPMN and use cases increased comprehension accuracy	6	196	Wilcoxon rank-sum test
Rodrigues et al. [38]	BPMN increased comprehension accuracy for experienced professionals. It did not have any significant difference for nonexperienced users	1	73	Mann-Whitney test
Figl and Recker [9]	Users preferred BPMN over structured text and text	1	120	Descriptive statistics
BPMN vs. UML vs. others				
Peixoto et al. [32]	They compared BPMN and UML AD. UML was easier to answer by students in only 2 of 11 questions. They found a significant difference only in 1 question but not the others	4	35	Mann-Whitney test
Birkmeier et al. [2, 3]	They compared UML AD and BPMN. They did not find significant differences in effectiveness, efficiency, nor satisfaction by business users. UML AD had a significant difference (advantage) for the comprehension of the data handling and adequacy	1	30	ANOVA
Figl et al. [10]	They compared UML AD, BPMN, YAWL, EPC, and textual descriptions. Deficiencies (e.g., ambiguities) in the notation affect comprehension. BPMN provides a greater visual discrimination for many types of events and elements and better comprehension results	4	188	ANOVA

Weitlaner et al. [50]	They compared UML AD, BPM, EPC, and storyboards. Comprehension was the highest for storyboards and lowest for EPC	77	4	Descriptive statistics
Sandkuhl and Wiebring [41]	They compared flow diagrams, eEPC, UML AD, and BPMN. Comprehension accuracy was the highest for UML AD, followed by eEPC, flow diagrams, and BPMN. There was perception of higher performance for eEPC, followed by UML AD, BPMN, and flow diagrams	113	1	Descriptive statistics
Jošt et al. [20]	They compared BPMN, UML AD, and EPC. Different results were found for the different models. In two of the models, the comprehension accuracy was higher for UML AD than for EPC or BPMN. In the other models, they did not find significant differences	103	4	Mann-Whitney post hoc tests with Bonferroni correction

Table 5.2 GQM design template for our experiment

Overall	Purpose	Analyze and compare
Goal	Issue	Software requirements comprehension
	Object	BPMN and use cases
	Viewpoint	Developers
Goal	G_1	Compare the developer effort (i.e., time) during the comprehension task
Question	RQ_1	*Is the developer effort (in terms of time) reduced?*
Metrics	M_1	Time spent when answering the questions correctly
Goal	G_2	Compare correctness during the comprehension task
Question	RQ_2	*Is there any impact on the comprehension when using the analyzed artifacts?*
Metrics	M_2	Number of correct answers obtained by the subjects
	M_3	Number of participants with correct answers
	M_4	Average evaluation score

as use case specifications. All the artifacts used in the experiment are publicly available within our online appendix [48].

We expected this experiment to expand the research about the contribution of BPMN to the comprehension of business domain issues [31] and business processes [38] to cover the software requirements comprehension as suggested by some experiences in software development [47]. Similarly, we expected to verify in terms of time, whether users locate a requirement faster in BPMN models or in use cases [18].

The experiment was designed by following the goal/question/metric (GQM) approach [1] and the learned lessons presented by Gross et al. [17] where: (a) The research questions are stated as research goals (G). (b) Questions (Q) are defined to characterize the assessment/achievement of each goal. (c) Data metrics (M) are assigned to each question to answer it in a quantitative way.

Table 5.2 shows the overall GQM design for our experiment, based on the template proposed by Basili [1]. We defined, as the overall goal (G), *to analyze and compare the software requirements comprehension achieved when using BPMN models and use case specifications*. We subcategorized this general goal in two specific goals (Table 5.2). These goals and the corresponding metrics were used to design the experiment and analyze the results.

5.3.1 Design

We provided participants with a case study description and different modeling artifacts. The participants were expected to perform a comprehension task, i.e., read a case study, review a set of artifacts, and then answer a questionnaire with control-type questions, to identify whether the participants were able to comprehend the software requirements. In addition, we recorded the time spent by the participant to answer each question (this feature is provided by the online tool we used to create and publish the questionnaire).

Case Studies We prepared two case studies describing two different software systems that are not implemented yet. For each one, we defined (a) a case study description, (b) a BPMN model representing the process depicted in the case study, and (c) a set of use case specifications describing the software requirements. Each description was designed to be printed in less than a page and to have an average reading time of less than 10 min to reduce early dropouts of the participants. The BPMN models were created using the BPMN 2.0 notation, i.e., using elements and attributes supporting advanced events and errors. The use cases were specified using Kettenis's template [22], which resulted as the most comprehensive use case format in a recent survey [44].

Note that during the design of the experiment, we prepared six case studies and, after several discussions (among the authors), we selected the two most appropriate for the experiment. The two case studies were selected considering the number of elements in the model (i.e., selecting the cases with the same number of lanes and participants), the expected time to review all the artifacts, and the ability to answer the same questions from both the BPMN and the use cases.

The two selected case studies were a credit application system in a fictional foundation (the MSG Foundation, MSG) and a point-of-sale system in a supermarket (PS). The former is an academic case study used to teach software engineering by Schach [42], and the latter is one of the case studies used to compare use case formats in a recent paper by Tiwari and Gupta [44]. We modified the original case studies to fit the time conditions of the experiment and translated the text to Spanish. Note that the experiment was expected to be finished by the participants in about 40 min. Therefore, we tested and modified the case study descriptions to be read by the participants in a maximum time of 10 min. Tables 5.3 and 5.4 summarize the number of notational elements included in the corresponding BPMN models and use cases. It is worth noting that we created the BPMN models from scratch (for both case studies) and the use case specifications were adjusted by us to the experiment needs and translated to Spanish.[1]

Questionnaire We built a questionnaire for each case study considering the objectives defined in the GQM design questions (Table 5.2) and the abovementioned case studies and artifacts (i.e., BPMN models and use case specifications). For evaluating the comprehension time (Q1), we measured the time each participant spent in answering each comprehension question. Regarding the comprehension level (Q2), we designed 11 questions, combining free text, multiple selection, and true/false questions.

---

[1]The original use case specifications were written in English by Schach [42] and Tiwari and Gupta [44].

Table 5.3 Characteristics of the BPMN diagrams

Case study		Lanes	Gateways				Activities				Events					Total
			Parallel	Exclusive	Event	Total	Manual	User	Script	Total	Message	Activity	Attached-Msg	Attached-Err	Total	
Credit application	C1	2	1	1	1	3	1	6	6	13	5	1	1	0	7	25
Point of sale	C2	2	0	6	0	6	8	8	6	22	0	1	1	1	3	33

Table 5.4 Characteristics of the use cases

Case study		Diagrams							Specifications							
		Elements			Relations					Level				Scope		
		Actors	Use cases	Total	Include	Extend	Association	Generalization	Total	General	User	Sub-function	Total	System	Requirement	Total
Credit application	C1	3	16	19	8	0	7	2	17	1	4	0	5	1	4	5
Point of sale	C2	5	7	12	3	1	5	2	11	0	1	2	3	1	2	3

For simplicity, hereinafter we will refer to each sample with labels that describe both the case study and the artifacts. We use MSG for the MSG Foundation case study and PS for the point-of-sale case study. In addition, for the artifacts, we use B for the BPMN model, UC for the use case specification, and BU for the combination. For example, the MSG-BU label represents the sample from the participants group that received the MSG Foundation case study, a BPMN model, and a use case specification. In the same way, PS-B represents the group that received the point-of-sale case study and a BPMN model.

Pilot Test Before running the experiment with participants, we conducted a pilot test with seven volunteers that had experience in both BPMN and use case specifications. The volunteers group was composed of systems and computing engineers with at least 2 years of experience in software development and faculty members in the universities where the experiment was applied. The volunteers reviewed the artifacts and provided us with comments for improving the case study descriptions, the artifacts, and the questionnaire. With the provided feedback, we improved (a) the correctness of the artifacts, (b) the coherence between the case study descriptions, (c) the BPMN models and the use case specifications, and (d) the quality of the questions (e.g., we reduced terms' ambiguity).

5.3.2 Participants Distribution

The experiment was applied to courses in three different universities in Colombia; hereinafter, we will refer to the participants group from each course as a sample. The particular universities were Universidad de los Andes (Uniandes), Universidad Nacional de Colombia (Unal), and Universidad de los Llanos (Unillanos). We applied the experiment in ten samples. In each of them, the participants were distributed in three groups, each one receiving the same case study (just one of the two constructed) and questions, but receiving a different set of artifacts: (a) a control group provided with the BPMN model, (b) a treatment group provided with the use case specification, and (c) a second treatment group provided with both the BPMN model and the use case specification.

We got a total of 137 participants, of which 12 were discarded because they did not finish the questionnaire or wrote confusing/unrelated text in the fields where additional detail was required. Another five participants were discarded (randomly) to balance the samples in case studies and groups. The samples were balanced in the way Table 5.5 presents; we considered 60 responses for each case study, i.e., 20 responses for each set of artifacts. Thus, at the end we analyzed the responses from 120 participants.

The samples had undergraduate and graduate students from engineering programs. While the students from systems and computing engineering (SCE) were knowledgeable of both BPMN and use case specifications, the non-SCE students only had knowledge of BPMN. Note that in the non-SCE sample, we applied the experiment only with BPMN artifacts.

Table 5.5 Balanced sample characteristics

Origin			Case study: artifacts set						Total
			MSG			PS			
Poll no.	Institution	Program	B	BU	UC	B	BU	UC	Total
1	Unal	Undergrad: CS and industrial eng.	3	3	2	3	2	3	16
2	Uniandes	Graduate: spec. softw. construction	3	3	3	3	3	2	17
3	Uniandes	Graduate: M.Sc. in computing	2	4	3	3	2	1	15
4	Uniandes	Graduate: M.Sc. in computing	3	3	3	3	3	3	18
5	Uniandes	Undergrad: CS, industrial eng., and others	7	0	0	7	0	0	14
6	Unillanos	Graduate: spec. softw. eng.	0	1	4	0	2	4	11
7	Unillanos	Undergrad: CS	0	1	1	0	1	4	7
8	Unillanos	Undergrad: CS	2	2	1	1	2	1	9
9	Unillanos	Undergrad: CS	0	3	3	0	5	2	13
Totals			20	20	20	20	20	20	120
Totals per case study			60			60			120

5.3.3 Analysis Method

We started our analysis by scoring the participants' answers with a Likert scale ranging from 1 (totally incorrect) to 5 (totally correct), and the "correct answers" are considered those graded with 4 (mostly correct) and 5.

We analyzed the data in three phases: First, we conducted an *exploratory data analysis* to get an overview of the results. Then, we performed *hypothesis significance testing* to determine whether there is a significant difference in the samples corresponding to each artifact and combination. As part of our hypothesis significance testing, we first applied a Shapiro-Wilk test [43] or a Kolmogorov-Smirnov test [5] to determine the data homogeneity (normality tests) of the samples. The former is used when the sample has a size of less than 50, while the latter is used otherwise. Then, we selected the most appropriate test for each sample, according to the parametric or nonparametric nature of the data. We used ANOVA test [14] for parametric samples and Mann-Whitney test [5, p. 57] for nonparametric ones. Finally, when significant differences were found, we applied the Bonferroni correction procedure [28]; and when the significant differences were maintained, we calculated the effect size with the Cliff's d coefficient[15]. Finally, we augmented the statistical analysis with a *qualitative analysis* to identify differences at the question level.

5.4 Results and Discussion

The results are presented at two different levels: results for each case study and results when combining the data from both studies. In the latter, we collect the data without alterations, i.e., there are neither sums nor averages; this is because the questions are not related, i.e., the question x of the PS case study is not related to question x of the MSG case study. We present the results also grouped by set of used artifacts. It is worth noting that to identify the sample we are referring to, we use the same acronyms described in Sect. 5.3, e.g., MSG-BU represents the sample from the group that analyzed the MSG Foundation case study with a BPMN model and a use case specification. When presenting combined results, we use only the acronym for the set of used artifacts, e.g., the sample referred as B represents the joined data of the two case studies that used the BPMN model.

5.4.1 Exploratory Data Analysis

After grading all the answers, we processed the samples to obtain the percentage of where the participants fall in each score.

Figure 5.1a, b shows the distribution of score values for each set of artifacts in each case study. Both case studies, MSG and PS, coincide in having the highest

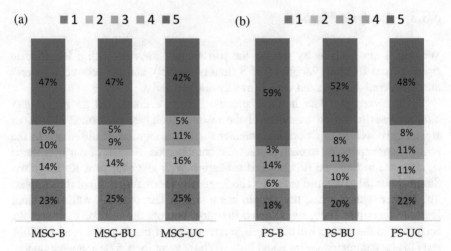

Fig. 5.1 Frequencies of each score obtained by the participants, grouped by case study and set of artifacts. (**a**) Data for MSG. (**b**) Data for PS

frequencies in the highest value in the scale, i.e., 5 is the most frequent score we assigned to the answers in both studies; then, the lowest score (1) is the second most frequent in both studies. In both cases, the frequency of 5 is close to twice the frequency of 1. Additionally, the sum of the frequencies for these values is close to the 70% of the answers in each case study. That is, more than two-thirds of the answers were totally correct or totally incorrect, where the correct answers were close to twice of the incorrect ones.

Considering each case study, in the MSG, the frequency for the score 5 is the same when the participants used BPMN and BPMN with use cases. The frequency is 47% for both sets of artifacts, but it is 42% for using only use cases. In the PS case study, the highest frequency for the score 5 was obtained using BPMN (59%), followed by using BPMN and use cases (52%). The lowest frequency was obtained using only use cases (48%). Although using BPMN and BPMN with use cases results in better frequencies for the highest score, the maximum difference is 11% (in the PS case study between B and UC), while the others frequencies have differences of 5% or lower.

Regarding the incorrect answers (i.e., the ones we scored with one (1) and denoted by the red bar in Fig. 5.1), in both study cases, those using the BPMN model have a lower frequency than those using both artifacts or only the use case specifications. That is, *in both case studies for "totally incorrect" answers, those who use the use case specifications are wrong with more frequency than those who use the BPMN model.*

Regarding the other scores (i.e., 2, 3, and 4), we note that in the MSG case study, for score 4, the artifact B shows a higher frequency than BU and UC, but the difference is only 1%. In this case study, scores 3 and 2 present more frequency in MSG-UC; but again, the difference is small, 2%. In PS case study, score 4 shows a different behavior than the one presented by MSG. In this opportunity, PS-B has a lower frequency (3%) than those of PS-BU and PS-UC (8%). However, if we consider joining scores 4 and 5 as "correct answers," we note again that there are greater frequencies for B and BU than for UC. In score 3, PS-B has greater frequency than PS-BU and PS-UC but only 4%. In score 2, the behavior is similar to score 1. The lower frequency is in PS-B and the greater in PS-UC. But again the difference is small (5%).

5.4.2 Hypothesis Significant Testing

As we defined in Sect. 5.3, our goal is *to analyze and compare the software requirements comprehension achieved when using BPMN models and use case specifications*; we subcategorized this general goal in two specific goals with their RQ and metrics (Table 5.2). In the following, we present the results for them.

5.4.2.1 RQ$_1$: *Is the Developer Effort (in Terms of Time) Reduced?*

Our first research question (RQ$_1$) aims to determine if the use of BPMN improves the comprehension time of the requirements. Thus, our analysis was focused on comparing the time spent in answering the comprehension questions correctly.

M$_1$: Time Spent When Answering the Questions Correctly Figure 5.3a, b shows the distribution of the time spent by the participants in answering questions correctly grouped by case study and the used artifacts; similarly, Fig. 5.3c shows the data when combining two samples, by used artifacts. Although the boxes present almost complete overlaps in all the cases, the data shows a lower time when the participants used only the BPMN model. For instance in Fig. 5.2c, the participants using BPMN models in both case studies had a mean time of 120.081 s (median = 88.986),

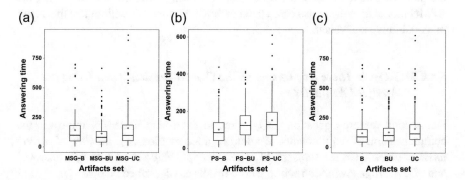

Fig. 5.2 RQ$_1$-M$_1$: Box plots comparing the time spent (in seconds) by the participants for answering correctly. (**a**) Data for the MSG study. (**b**) Data for the PS study. (**c**) Data for both (MSG and PS)

compared to 127.37 s (median = 101.058) when using both BPMN and use cases and 156.35 s (median = 115.22) when using only use cases.

In our analysis, the collected data does not exhibit a normal distribution: a Kolmogorov-Smirnov test showed that all the *p-values* are less than 0.05 (Table 5.6a). Thus, we performed further analyses using a nonparametric test, in particular the Mann-Whitney test[5] with correction for multiple comparisons. Table 5.6b shows the p-value in these comparisons.

There is a significant difference (i.e., we got a p-value less than 0.05) in the time spent answering correctly when using the BPMN model or the BPMN model and the use case specification vs. using only the use case specification (i.e., the B vs. UC and BU vs. UC samples). When multiple comparisons are applied, we noted an increment on the Type I error and applied the Bonferroni correction [5] to adjust the initial level of risk. We used $\alpha = 0.05$ with $k = 3$ comparisons, to obtain an adjusted value of $\alpha_B = \frac{0.05}{3} = 0.0167$, and analyzed the p-values again obtained in the Mann-Whitney tests (Table 5.6b) to obtain the Cliff's d when it is applicable. In Table 5.6b, we present this value and its classification according to the thresholds provided by Romano et al. [39] ($|d| < 0.147$ "negligible," $|d| < 0.33$ "small," $|d| < 0.474$ "medium," otherwise "large").

Cliff's d shows small and medium significant differences in the PS case study and in the sample resulted from analyzing both case studies in one sample. In PS case study, there is a significant difference between the time required to answer the questions correctly (a) when the participants used the BPMN vs. the BPMN and the use case specifications and (b) when they used the BPMN vs. the use case specifications. The difference between the time of BPMN and the use cases was small when we combined both case studies, but it was medium for the PS case.

Answer for RQ$_1$: Is the Developer Effort (in Terms of Time) Reduced? Only one of the pairs of sets compared has a meaningful difference in the time spent in answering questions correctly. The set of artifacts is PS-B vs. PS-UC, i.e., in the point-of-sale case study, the time spent answering correctly was less using the BPMN model than using use case specification diagrams. We will review this result in a qualitative analysis in Sect. 5.4.3.

5.4.2.2 RQ$_2$: *Is There Any Impact on the Comprehension When Using the Analyzed Artifacts?*

Our second research question (RQ$_2$) aims to determine if BPMN improves the comprehension of requirements. We defined three metrics, M_2: *number of correct answers obtained by the subjects*, M_3: *number of participants with correct answers*, and M_4: *average evaluation score*, whose results are described below.

M_2: Number of Correct Answers Obtained by the Subjects In Fig. 5.3, we can see that more answers were correct when using BPMN models (mean = 5.975, median = 6.0); this behavior is followed by the combination of BPMN model and

Table 5.6 RQ$_1$-M$_1$: Statistical treatment of sample data for time in answering correctly

(a) Kolmogorov-Smirnov test for normality evaluation

Samples	D	p-Value	Samples	D	p-Value	Samples	D	p-Value
MSG-B	0.64	2.20E−16	PS-B	0.82	2.20E−16	B	0.69	2.20E−16
MSG-BU	0.86	2.20E−16	PS-BU	0.68	2.20E−16	BU	0.91	2.20E−16
MSG-UC	0.40	3.11E−15	PS-UC	0.80	2.20E−16	UC	0.71	2.20E−16

(b) Summary of statistics for pairwise comparisons: Mann-Whitney test, Bonferroni correction, and Cliff's d

Samples compared	p-Value	Is it significant? (regarding to)		Cliff's d
		α	α$_B$	
MSG-B vs. MSG-BU	0.0983	No	–	–
MSG-BU vs. MSG-UC	0.0595	No	–	–
MSG-B vs. MSG-UC	0.7963	No	–	–
PS-B vs. PS-BU	6.09E−05	Yes	Yes	Small (0.283)
PS-BUvs. PS-UC	0.3480	No	–	–
PS-B vs. PS-UC	1.90E−06	Yes	Yes	Medium (0.343)
B vs. BU	0.1079	No	–	–
BU vs. UC	0.0488	Yes	No	–
B vs. UC	0.0005	Yes	Yes	Small (0.183)

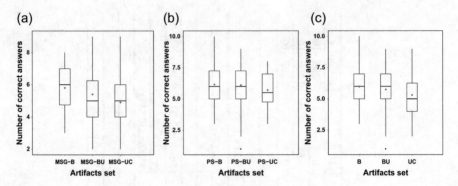

Fig. 5.3 RQ$_2$-M$_2$: Box plots comparing the number of correct answers. (**a**) Data for the MSG study. (**b**) Data for the PS study. (**c**) Data for both (MSG and PS)

use case specification (mean = 5.75, median = 6.0); the participants using only the use case specifications had the lowest number of correct answers (mean = 5.3, median = 5.0).

Table 5.7 shows the Shapiro-Wilk test that applies to small samples. The answers obtained in the point-of-sale case study using BPMN and use cases (i.e., PS-BU) have a p-value lesser than 0.05. This forced us to perform a nonparametric analysis of the data. We checked for significant differences by applying the Mann-Whitney test. Table 5.8 shows the results. There are no significant differences among the groups using different sets of artifacts.

M$_3$: Number of Participants with Correct Answers As shown in Fig. 5.4c, intuitively, there are more people with correct answers who used BPMN (mean = 10.64, median = 11.0) than those that used a combination of BPMN and use cases (mean = 10.36, median = 10.00) and those using use cases only (mean = 9.00, median = 9.46).

Table 5.7 RQ$_2$-M$_2$: Summary of statistical analysis (Shapiro-Wilk test for normality evaluation)

Sample	W	p-Value	Sample	W	p-Value	Sample	W	p-Value
MSG-B	0.910	0.065	PS-B	0.960	0.537	B	0.953	0.101
MSG-BU	0.973	0.818	PS-BU	0.888	0.025	BU	0.954	0.101
MSG-UC	0.940	0.240	PS-UC	0.921	0.102	UC	0.959	0.156

Table 5.8 RQ$_2$-M$_2$: Summary of statistical analysis (Mann-Whitney test for assessing significant differences)

Comparison	p-Value	Comparison	p-Value	Comparison	p-Value
MSG-B vs. MSG-BU	0.3711	PS-B vs. PS-BU	0.7306	B vs. BU	0.6993
MSG-BU vs. MSG-UC	0.3067	PS-BU vs. PS-UC	0.3152	BU vs. UC	0.1521
MSG-B vs. MSG-UC	0.0508	PS-B vs. PS-UC	0.4658	B vs. UC	0.0661

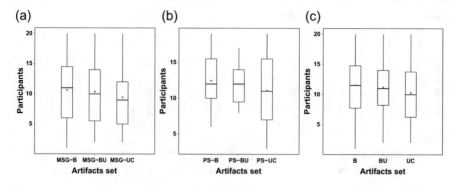

Fig. 5.4 Box plots for comparing subjects' understanding of the requirements, organized for each type of artifact: B (BPMN model), BU (BPMN model and use case specification), and UC (use case specification). (**a**) Data for the MSG study. (**b**) Data for the PS study. (**c**) Data for both (MSG and PS)

Table 5.9 RQ$_2$-M$_3$: Statistical treatment of sample data for number of subjects with correct answers

(a) Shapiro-Wilk test for normality evaluation

Samples	W	p-Value	Samples	W	p-Value	Samples	W	p-Value
MSG-B	0.971	0.894	PS-B	0.957	0.730	B	0.979	0.905
MSG-BU	0.934	0.458	PS-BU	0.947	0.606	BU	0.979	0.907
MSG-UC	0.940	0.516	PS-UC	0.957	0.739	UC	0.950	0.313

(b) ANOVA test for assessing difference

Sample	p-Value	Sample	p-Value	Sample	p-Value
MSG	0.888	PS	0.754	Both	0.701

All our data exhibits a normal distribution. Table 5.9a shows the results of the Shapiro-Wilk test. Note that all the *p*-values are greater than 0.05. Therefore, we can perform parametric analyses such as the ANOVA shown in Table 5.9b. However, there are no significant differences on the number of participants with correct answers using the different sets of artifacts.

M$_4$: Average Evaluation Score We analyzed the average score by participant, considering the Likert scale we used to grade each question. Figure 5.5 shows the distribution. Intuitively, the participants obtained upper scores when they used BPMN (mean = 10.64, median = 11.0), followed by the combination of BPMN model and use case specification (mean = 10.36, median = 10.00). The lowest scores were obtained with the use case only (mean = 9.00, median = 9.46).

Considering that the data exhibits a normal distribution, we performed an ANOVA test to determine if there are significant differences. Table 5.10a shows the results of the Shapiro-Wilk test, and Table 5.10b shows those of the ANOVA. Note that all the *p*-values greater than 0.05 show that the distribution is normal. However, the ANOVA test does not show a significant difference.

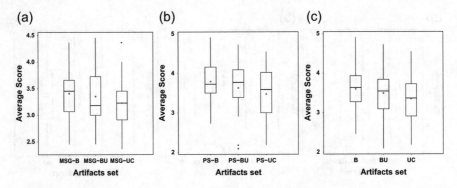

Fig. 5.5 Box plots for comparing average scores obtained, organized for each type of artifact: B (BPMN model), BU (BPMN model and use case specification), and UC (use case specification). (**a**) Data for the MSG study. (**b**) Data for the PS study. (**c**) Data for both (MSG and PS)

Table 5.10 RQ$_2$-M$_4$: Statistical treatment of sample data for number of correct answers

(a) Shapiro-Wilk test for normality evaluation

Samples	W	p-Value	Samples	W	p-Value	Samples	W	p-Value
MSG-B	0.978	0.903	PS-B	0.981	0.945	Both B	0.984	0.841
MSG-BU	0.951	0.389	PS-BU	0.922	0.107	Both BU	0.991	0.639
MSG-UC	0.958	0.509	PS-UC	0.967	0.683	Both UC	0.981	0.733

(b) ANOVA test for assessing difference

Sample	p-Value	Sample	p-Value	Sample	p-Value
MSG	0.537	PS	0.285	Both	0.171

Answer for RQ$_2$: Is There Any Impact on the Comprehension When Using the Analyzed Artifacts? Our analysis did not find significant differences using any of the artifacts, i.e., participants tend to have correct and incorrect answers independently of the type of the artifact. This will be reviewed next in our *qualitative analysis*.

5.4.3 Qualitative Analysis

Figure 5.6 shows a radar-based representation of the average scores by case study. The data is presented in Table 5.11a, b. Note that some questions show evident differences on the scores when the participants used BPMN and use cases. We performed a qualitative analysis of the questions to determine possible reasons for the differences on the scores showed by the radar graphics.

Table 5.11c, d shows, for each case study, which artifact (BPMN model, use case specification, or both) had the highest and the lowest average score and the difference between these values, for each question. Except for one in MSG (Q08),

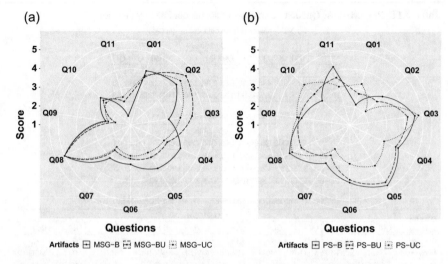

Fig. 5.6 Average score per question, organized for each type of artifact. (**a**) Data for the MSG study. (**b**) Data for the PS study

in which all participants were successful with a score of 5, our analysis of the scores obtained showed us some findings.

BPMN obtained the highest scores in most of the questions with an average score greater than 3 (the middle of the range) and a difference between the highest and lowest average scores greater than one. The only question of this group where the highest score was obtained using other artifacts was the Q03 in the MSG case study. There, the participants had to identify the users of the system. In this question, the highest score was obtained using both the BPMN and the use case specification.

Use case specifications obtained the lowest scores in most of the questions where the average score was less or equal to 3. The lowest score was obtained using other artifacts (not UC) only in one question in each case study. These questions were the Q11 for the MSG and the Q01 for the PS case studies; in both of them, the participants had to identify which users should perform some tasks in the system, and the lowest score was obtained using the BPMN artifact.

BPMN had highest scores when questions were about sequences of activities. Considering all the 22 questions, 15 were related to sequences of activities; in 13 of these, the highest score was obtained by BPMN. Of these 15 questions, 9 were in the PS study case, which could explain why a medium-sized Cliff's d occurs when comparing the response times between PS-B and PS-UC.

Using multiple artifacts solved ambiguities related to the software users, e.g., when we inquired for the users in the MSG and PS case studies, the participants using BPMN and use cases got the highest scores, but people using only the BPMN got the lowest. Checking the answers, we noted that the participants with incorrect answers confused concepts such as the lane in the BPMN model and the secondary actors in the use cases. We consider that terms such as users, actors, roles, clients,

Table 5.11 RQ$_2$-M$_4$-QA: Qualitative analysis of scores obtained by question

(a) MSG—average score obtained by question

Artifacts	Questions										
	Q01	Q02	Q03	Q04	Q05	Q06	Q07	Q08	Q09	Q10	Q11
MSG-B	4.00	4.30	3.10	4.00	3.75	3.10	3.10	5.00	2.40	3.20	1.50
MSG-BU	3.65	5.00	4.40	3.20	3.05	2.80	2.60	5.00	1.85	3.00	2.30
MSG-UC	3.75	4.60	3.75	3.00	2.75	2.65	2.40	5.00	2.25	2.80	2.55

(b) PS—average score obtained by question

Artifacts	Questions										
	Q01	Q02	Q03	Q04	Q05	Q06	Q07	Q08	Q09	Q10	Q11
PS-B	2.15	3.35	4.60	3.90	4.80	4.05	3.40	4.60	3.65	3.00	4.25
PS-BU	2.75	2.95	4.20	3.75	4.60	3.90	2.90	3.90	3.80	3.55	3.65
PS-UC	3.30	2.15	4.80	3.05	3.55	3.05	2.50	4.45	3.90	4.30	3.15

(c) MSG—artifacts set with maximum and minimum score and difference between them

Data for analysis	Questions										
	Q01	Q02	Q03	Q04	Q05	Q06	Q07	Q08	Q09	Q10	Q11
Average	3.80	4.63	3.75	3.40	3.18	2.85	2.70	5.00	2.17	3.0	2.12
Max. art. set	MSG-B	MSG-BU	MSG-BU	MSG-B	MSG-B	MSG-B	MSG-B	–	MSG-B	MSG-B	MSG-BU
Min. art. set	MSG-UC	MSG-B	MSG-B	MSG-UC	MSG-UC	MSG-UC	MSG-UC	–	MSG-UC	MSG-UC	MSG-B
Difference	0.35	0.70	1.30	1.00	1.00	0.45	0.70	–	0.55	0.40	0.80

(d) PS—artifacts set with maximum and minimum score and difference between them

Data for analysis	Questions										
	Q01	Q02	Q03	Q04	Q05	Q06	Q07	Q08	Q09	Q10	Q11
Average	2.73	2.82	4.53	3.57	4.32	3.67	2.93	4.32	3.78	3.62	3.68
Max. art. set	PS-UC	PS-B	PS-UC	PS-B	PS-B	PS-B	PS-B	PS-B	PS-UC	PS-UC	PS-B
Min. art. set	PS-B	PS-UC	PS-BU	PS-UC	PS-UC	PS-UC	PS-UC	PS-BU	PS-B	PS-B	PS-UC
Difference	1.15	1.20	0.20	0.85	1.25	1.00	0.90	0.15	0.25	1.30	1.10

(e) Background and text colors meaning

The column background color means the highest average score was obtained by participants using:			Average score > 3?
BPMN model	Use case spec.	Both	<= 3

and stakeholders are used differently by diverse authors and techniques and it is necessary to clarify these concepts if multiple types of artifacts are used in the same project.

Rare/advanced elements tend to confuse participants. In the Q09 question of the MSG case study, we got wrong responses for all artifacts. It asks about a description of the response of the system when a component fails (i.e., the behavior when the payment authorization service does not work). We expected an answer like "Whether there is a communication error or the external entity rejects the transaction, the denial is informed verbally." In regard to the BPMN model, for answering correctly, the participants required to know about two advanced elements: an exception event (without a label indicating the error) and two event links. For answering correctly using use case specifications, the participants required to know about exceptions and how they are described in the use case template; in the used template, they are specified as *extensions* in the scenarios box.

Preconceptions affect answers. Most of the wrong answers for question Q07 (*Assume that you are a buyer and you are going to a point of sale. What happens next in this system?*) were based on preconceived ideas of the participants instead of the information in the case study. We expected an answer like "The cashier will start a new sale transaction in the system"; but we obtained wrong answers such as "I pass the items, payment (. . . .), take the invoice, and withdraw the products," "Items are registered to make the purchase process," or When I go to the point of sale, a cashier serves me, receives the items I carry, and passes them through a code reader . . . ." The aforementioned answers were general descriptions of what we usually do when arriving at a point of sale, not the particular behavior described in the artifacts.

Augmented Answer for RQ$_1$: Is the Developer Effort (in Terms of Time) Reduced? We compared the characteristics of the artifacts (in Tables 5.3 and 5.4) and the types of questions in each case study, to explain why in PS the response time was less using BPMN vs. UC, compared with MSG. We found that questions showing more correct answers in less time were related to sequences, i.e., using BPMN models could improve effort in comprehension of requirements related to sequences.

Augmented Answer for RQ$_2$: Is There Any Impact on the Comprehension When Using the Analyzed Artifacts? Our qualitative analysis showed that the answers with the highest scores are usually obtained by using BPMN or BPMN and use cases and the lowest scores are obtained by using use cases only. We noted that questions related to identifying actors and users resulted in errors possibly caused by ambiguities in the terms. In addition, we noted errors caused by problems when trying to represent the same information using the diverse artifacts.

Although the statistical analysis did not show a significant difference among the compared sets of artifacts, a qualitative analysis of the radar representation suggests reasons for the better results of using BPMN instead of use cases in some situations: (a) Those that favored BPMN were questions about the description of a procedure or sequences of steps. (b) Those that favored use cases were questions where the BPMN model did not have enough detail. (c) Finally, those where some actors should be identified, participants tend to have errors independently of the type of artifact.

5.5 Threats to Validity

In this section, we identify the threats to validity following the description made by Feldt et al., to discuss *conclusion, internal, construct, and external validity* and considerations about *qualitative analysis* [7].

Conclusion validity is assured when the treatment used in the experiment is really related to the actual outcome observed, mainly from a statistical perspective. We mitigated threats of this kind by a careful statistical processing of the samples. We selected the hypothesis tests according to the normality of the samples, and for this we used the Shapiro-Wilk [43] or Kolmogorov-Smirnov [5] test for the adequate selection between parametric or nonparametric statistics. In the same way, the analyzed samples, which were collected with two different case studies, were analyzed first separately and then combined without mathematical operations (neither averages nor sums of the results); it is worth noting that the analysis of the combined samples only implied an increase in the sample size, avoiding any alteration in the results. Consequently, when we found significant differences in the distribution, we computed effect sizes to calculate their magnitude and evaluate it following the Romano et al. [39] guidelines (i.e., negligible, small, medium, large). Finally, to complement the statistical data processing and propose explanations, we realized a qualitative analysis to the samples.

To achieve *internal validity*, we must guarantee that the outcome was caused by the treatment and that we have controlled or measured other factors that could have caused the outcome. This category of validity could have been threatened by bias in the configuration of samples to which the experiment was applied. Such a bias could have happened if the sample had been formed from a group with wide or no training in one of the artifacts to be evaluated, either use case specification or BPMN modeling. This threat in the samples' conformation was mitigated by selecting the participants from different courses and universities in the following way: (a) The industrial and systems engineering undergraduate students in the Universidad Nacional de Colombia were selected from the information systems course, which ensured that the students had a minimum basic training in both artifacts. (b) The undergraduate students of the Universidad de los Llanos were taken from the fifth and ninth semesters, which ensured a sufficient training in both artifacts. (c) Undergraduate students of different engineering degrees from the Universidad de los Andes were selected from the IT in the organizations course, which provides basic training in design and analysis of business processes with BPMN. The used artifacts for this sample were only the BPMN models, to prevent applying the experiment to people who had no training in use case specifications. Finally, (d) the graduate students were selected from courses that guaranteed us training in BPMN (to avoid graduate students who had not received such training in their undergraduate programs or in their professional work).

For assuring *construct validity*, we must guarantee that the observations are only related to the treatment that we did to the sample, not caused by other circumstances or issues in the experiment. We mitigated this threat by following the learned lessons presented by Gross et al. [17]. We focused on minimizing the effects caused by comprehension issues over the artifacts and questions that could be different from the artifact content itself. This type of effects can be caused by employing a tool in the experiment, whose use can create difficulties; similarly, the notation in the models or diagrams can cause deviations in the results of understanding that obey reasons other than the understanding of the artifact content itself. Our strategies for mitigating possible threats in this validity category were as follows: (a) For minimizing comprehension difficulties in the artifacts, we used the standards notations, i.e., UML 2.5.1 specification for the use case diagram in the use case specifications and BPMN 2.0 specification for the BPMN models. (b) For the use case specification, we selected a template evaluated as the most understandable one in a recent survey [44]. (c) We delivered the artifacts in PDF and PNG formats to avoid problems regarding the handling of the tool with which the models were built (BPMN and UML). Similarly, (d) we constructed the BPMN models with the same tool used by the universities which the samples came from. Finally, (e) for avoiding difficulties in the case studies, we selected the two which satisfied the criteria of being small enough to be read in a short time and having enough elements to ask for requirements comprehension issues. For this selection, we consulted different knowledge corpora of BPMN models used in training or exhibited as successful cases in commercial tools websites and explored case studies used in research and academia in books. The selection was made by consensus among all the authors of this chapter. The use cases constructed but not selected can be consulted in the online appendix of this chapter [48]. Finally, to prevent issues in questions comprehension, we conducted a pilot test with several BPMN and use case specification experts, from academia and industry, with different levels of experience.

The *external validity* is achieved when we can generalize the results beyond the experiment scope; although we tried to mitigate this threat by configuring a considerable size and variety in the sample and using two case studies, we cannot generalize our results. Future work should be devoted to replicate the experiment with more case studies, in particular with larger models.

Regarding our *qualitative analysis*, possible threats could be in *credibility, dependability, and confirmability* [7], i.e., whether we can assure that we are confident that (a) the findings are true, (b) they are consistent and can be repeated, and (c) they are shaped by the respondents (not by the researchers). We mitigated these threats by doing the qualitative analysis guided by the results in each case study, which we presented in Table 5.11a, b for MSG and PS case studies, respectively. Next, we guided our observations by the data comparison presented in Table 5.11c, d regarding the results with each set of artifacts. Finally, we contrasted our observations with the statistical analysis.

5.6 Conclusions and Outlook

In this chapter, we reported an experiment comparing the comprehension of software requirements specified using BPMN model vs. using use case specifications. We surveyed undergraduate and graduate students using two case studies and a set of instruments especially designed to inquire on (a) the time spent in the comprehension and (b) the impact on the level of comprehension when one type of artifact is used instead of the others. A statistical analysis of a balanced sample of 120 participants showed that there is no significant difference on the level of comprehension when BPMN and use cases are used. However, a qualitative analysis of the scores per question showed us that for requirements regarding sequences of activities, BPMN exhibits better results than using BPMN with use case specifications or only use case specifications.

Regarding the time spent when using different artifacts, the results were similar, but there was a case study where people using BPMN were able to answer correctly in less time than those using use case specifications alone (the data from that case study exhibited a medium effect size in the Cliff's d indicating that conclusion). Once we analyzed qualitatively the answers provided by the participants, we found that they were mostly related to requirements that involved sequences of activities (9 of 11), which could explain why BPMN improved time response in the aforementioned case.

Conclusions for Researchers Almost all the previous studies comparing the level of comprehension did not find a significant difference among the notations used to represent the business processes [8]. Few works have shown that BPMN may increase the comprehension accuracy only when the specifications are reviewed by people trained in process modeling, not by stakeholders or final users that are not trained in the models [31, 38]. Our study shows a similar behavior for the comprehension level of software requirements. However, when analyzing the questions in our questionnaire, we found that those related to activity sequences showed better scores when using BPMN models than using the other artifacts.

Regarding the time required to comprehend the requirements, the results were similar except for one case study (our point-of-sale case study) where the participants answered the questions faster when they used BPMN instead of use case specifications. Combining our results with previous work, we recommend using BPMN model in software requirements elicitation when the following conditions are present: (a) The people are trained in BPMN models. (b) The system to be implemented shows an important presence of procedural requirements, i.e., sequence of activities, to be accomplished by the software to be implemented.

Takeaways for Practitioners A company or technical director selecting which models to use for the requirements elicitation may consider other factors instead of the typical comprehension level of BPMN and use case specifications. Factors such as the previous training and experience of the developers or the type of support provided by the development tools should also be considered. Similarly, when the type of business requires a significant number of sequences of activities, a BPMN model can contribute to a better understanding of the requirements in a shorter time. Regarding other types of business, based on previous surveys, we recommend software engineers to consider BPMN models to represent software requirements even when the application will not be implemented using a BPM execution engine. In these cases, we can confirm that (a) BPMN facilitates the communication of the business domain, between the people of the business and between them and the developers, and (b) BPMN does not harm the correctness and the time in the elicitation of requirements.

Outlook Based on the results of our experiment, we are considering three areas for further research. On the one hand, we are interested in exploring the difficulties introduced by each type of specification and the impact of the previous experience of the developers on the comprehension of BPMN and use case specifications.

We think that some types of requirements and projects may obtain more benefits using process models than the others. Thus, it is important to determine which factors affect the usefulness of these models for specifying software requirements. On the other hand, considering that BPMN models may improve the process for requirements engineering, we are interested in exploring and evaluating multiple ways to integrate the modeling of processes and software. We are planning activities and experiments to determine which combinations may result in improving the software engineering practices in a company.

Acknowledgements We would like to thank Lili Johana Rozo, Hawer Forero, Óscar Agudelo, and Carlos Andrés López from Universidad de los Llanos, Helga Duarte from Universidad Nacional de Colombia, and Andrea Herrera and Óscar González from Universidad de los Andes, for their collaboration reviewing and commenting on the case studies used in our experiments and for their help collecting data in their courses.

References

1. V.R. Basili, G. Caldiera, H.D. Rombach, *Goal Question Metric Paradigm*, vol. 1 (Wiley, New York, 1994), pp. 528–532
2. D. Birkmeier, S. Overhage, Is BPMN really first choice in joint architecture development? An empirical study on the usability of BPMN and UML activity diagrams for business users, in *6th International Conference on the Quality of Software Architectures (QoSA 2010)* (Springer, Berlin, 2010), pp. 119–134
3. D. Birkmeier, S. Kloeckner, S. Overhage, An empirical comparison of the usability of BPMN and UML activity diagrams for business users, in *18th European Conference on Information Systems (ECIS 2010)* (2010), pp. 51:1–51:12
4. M.A. Cibrán, Translating BPMN models into UML activities, in *Business Process Management Workshops (BPM 2008)*, vol. 17 (Springer, Berlin, 2008), pp. 236–247
5. G.W. Corder, D.I. Foreman, *Non Parametric Statistics for Non-Statisticians* (Wiley, New York, 2009)
6. F. Di Cerbo, G. Dodero, G. Reggio, F. Ricca, G. Scanniello, Precise vs. ultra-light activity diagrams - an experimental assessment in the context of business process modelling, in *12th International Conference on Product-Focused Software Process Improvement (PROFES 2011)* (Springer, Berlin, 2011), pp. 291–305
7. R. Feldt, A. Magazinius, Validity threats in empirical software engineering research - an initial survey, in *Proceedings of the 22nd International Conference on Software Engineering & Knowledge Engineering (SEKE'2010), Redwood City, San Francisco Bay, July 1–July 3, 2010* (2010), pp. 374–379
8. K. Figl, Comprehension of procedural visual business process models. Bus. Inf. Syst. Eng. **59**(1), 41–67 (2017)
9. K. Figl, J. Recker, Exploring cognitive style and task-specific preferences for process representations. Requir. Eng. **21**(1), 63–85 (2016)
10. K. Figl, J. Mendling, M. Strembeck, The influence of notational deficiencies on process model comprehension. J. Assoc. Inf. Syst. **14**(6), 312–338 (2013)
11. R. Gabryelczyk, A. Jurczuk, Does experience matter? Factors affecting the understandability of the business process modelling notation. Procedia Eng. **182**, 198–205 (2017). 7th International Conference on Engineering, Project, and Production Management
12. A. Gemino, Y. Wand, A framework for empirical evaluation of conceptual modeling techniques. Requir. Eng. **9**(4), 248–260 (2004). https://doi.org/10.1007/s00766-004-0204-6

13. F. Gilbreth, L. Gilbreth, *Process Charts. First Steps in Finding the One Best Way to Do Work* (The American Society of Mechanical Engineers, New York, 1921)
14. P. Goos, D. Meintrup, *Statistics with JMP: Hypothesis Tests, ANOVA and Regression* (Wiley, New York, 2016). https://books.google.com.co/books?id=GYyXCwAAQBAJ
15. R.J. Grissom, J.J. Kim, *Effect Sizes for Research: A Broad Practical Approach* (Lawrence Erlbaum Associates, Mahwah, 2005). https://books.google.com.co/books?id=4C49CGkNxLAC
16. A. Gross, J. Doerr, EPC vs. UML activity diagram - two experiments examining their usefulness for requirements engineering, in *17th IEEE International Requirements Engineering Conference (RE '09)* (2009), pp. 47–56
17. A. Gross, J. Jurkiewicz, J. Doerr, J. Nawrocki, Investigating the usefulness of notations in the context of requirements engineering - research agenda and lessons learned, in *Second IEEE International Workshop on Empirical Requirements Engineering (EmpiRE 2012)* (2012), pp. 9–16
18. C. Haisjackl, S. Zugal, Investigating differences between graphical and textual declarative process models, in *Advanced Information Systems Engineering Workshops, CAiSE 2014 International Workshops* (Springer International Publishing, Cham, 2014), pp. 194–206
19. P. Harmon, The state of business process management 2016. A BPTrends Report, 2016. https://www.bptrends.com/bptrends-surveys/
20. G. Jošt, J. Huber, M. Heričko, G. Polančič, An empirical investigation of intuitive understandability of process diagrams. Comput. Stand. Interfaces **48**, 90–111 (2016)
21. D. Karagiannis, S. Junginger, R. Strobl, Introduction to business process management systems concepts, in *Business Process Modelling* (Springer, Berlin, 1996), pp. 81–106
22. J. Kettenis, Getting started with use case modeling, White Paper, Oracle (2007)
23. M. Kocbek, G. Jošt, M. Heričko, G. Polančič, Business process model and notation: the current state of affairs. Comput. Sci. Inf. Syst. **12**(2), 509–539 (2015)
24. H. Leopold, J. Mendling, O. Günther, Learning from quality issues of BPMN models from industry. IEEE Softw. **33**(4), 26–33 (2016)
25. M.A. López-Campos, A.C. Marquez, J.F.G. Fernández, Modelling using UML and BPMN the integration of open reliability, maintenance and condition monitoring management systems: an application in an electric transformer system. Comput. Ind. **64**(5), 524–542 (2013)
26. D. Lübke, K. Schneider, Visualizing use case sets as BPMN processes, in *Requirements Engineering Visualization (REV'08)* (2008), pp. 21–25
27. O. Macek, K. Richta, The BPM to UML activity diagram transformation using XSLT, in *Annual International Workshop on DAtabases, TExts, Specifications and Objects (DATESO 2009)*, CEUR Workshop Proceedings, vol. 471 (2009), pp. 119–129
28. J.H. McDonald, *Handbook of Biological Statistics*, 3rd edn. (Sparky House Publishing, Baltimore, 2014)
29. C. Monsalve, A. April, A. Abran, On the expressiveness of business process modeling notations for software requirements elicitation, in *38th Annual Conference on IEEE Industrial Electronics Society (IECON 2012)* (IEEE, New York, 2012)
30. OMG, Business Process Model and Notation (BPMN), Version 2.0, 2011. http://www.omg.org/spec/BPMN/2.0/
31. A. Ottensooser, A. Fekete, H.A. Reijers, J. Mendling, C. Menictas, Making sense of business process descriptions: an experimental comparison of graphical and textual notations. J. Syst. Softw. **85**(3), 596–606 (2012)
32. D. Peixoto, V.A. Batista, A.P. Atayde, E.P. Borges, R. Resende, C. Isaías, P.S. Pádua, A comparison of BPMN and UML 2.0 activity diagrams, in *VII Simposio Brasileiro de Qualidade de Software*, 2008
33. M. Pichler, H. Rumetshofer, Business process-based requirements modeling and management, in *First International Workshop on Requirements Engineering Visualization (REV'06)*, 2006
34. A. Przybylek, A business-oriented approach to requirements elicitation, in *9th International Conference on Evaluation of Novel Approaches to Software Engineering (ENASE)* (IEEE, New York, 2014)

35. P. Ravesteyn, R, Batenburg, Surveying the critical success factors of BPM systems implementation. Bus. Process. Manag. J. **16**(3), 492–507 (2010)
36. J. Recker, A. Dreiling, Does it matter which process modelling language we teach or use? An experimental study on understanding process modelling languages without formal education, in *Australasian Conference on Information Systems 2007*, University of Southern Queensland (2007), pp. 356–366
37. J. Recker, A. Dreiling, The effects of content presentation format and user characteristics on novice developers' understanding of process models. Commun. Assoc. Inf. Syst. **28**(6), 65–84 (2011)
38. R.D.A. Rodrigues, M.D.O. Barros, K. Revoredo, L.G. Azevedo, H. Leopold, An experiment on process model understandability using textual work instructions and BPMN models, in *29th Brazilian Symposium on Software Engineering (SBES 2015)* (2015), pp. 41–50
39. J. Romano, J.D. Kromrey, J. Coraggio, J. Skowronek, Appropriate statistics for ordinal level data: should we really be using t-test and Cohen'sd for evaluating group differences on the NSSE and other surveys? in *Annual Meeting of the Florida Association of Institutional Research* (2006), pp. 1–3
40. N. Russell, W.M.P. van der Aalst, A.H.M. ter Hofstede, P. Wohed, On the suitability of UML 2.0 activity diagrams for business process modelling, in *3rd Asia-Pacific Conference on Conceptual Modelling - (APCCM '06)* (Australian Computer Society, Inc., Darlinghurst, 2006), pp. 95–104
41. K. Sandkuhl, J. Wiebring, Experiences from selecting a BPM notation for an enterprise, in *Business Information Systems Workshops* (Springer International Publishing, Cham, 2015), pp. 126–138
42. S. Schach, *Object-Oriented and Classical Software Engineering* (McGraw-Hill, New York, 2010)
43. S.S. Shapiro, M.B. Wilk, An analysis of variance test for normality (complete samples). Biometrika, **52**(3/4), 591–611 (1965). http://www.jstor.org/stable/2333709
44. S. Tiwari, A. Gupta, Investigating comprehension and learnability aspects of use cases for software specification problems. Inf. Softw. Technol. **91**, 22–43 (2017). https://doi.org/10.1016/j.infsof.2017.06.003
45. W.M.P. van der Aalst, Formalization and verification of event-driven process chains. Inf. Softw. Technol. **41**(10), 639–650 (1999)
46. W.M.P. van der Aalst, L. Aldred, M. Dumas, A.H.M. ter Hofstede, Design and implementation of the YAWL system, in *16th International Conference on Advanced Information Systems Engineering (CAiSE 2004)* (2004), pp. 142–159
47. O.L. Vega-Márquez, H. Duarte, J. Chavarriaga, Software development process supported by business process modeling - an experience report, in *Seventh International Symposium on Business Modeling and Software Design - Volume 1 (BMSD 2017)* (SciTePress, Setúbal, 2017), pp. 242–245
48. O.-L. Vega-Márquez, J. Chavarriaga, M. Linares-Vásquez, M. Sánchez, Requirements comprehension using BPMN models: an empirical study - ESDEBP, chapter # 3 online appendix, 2018. https://olvegam.github.io/esdebp-c3-oa/
49. Y. Wautelet, S. Poelmans. Aligning the elements of the RUP/UML business use-case model and the BPMN business process diagram, in *23rd International Working Conference Requirements Engineering: Foundation for Software Quality (REFSQ 2017)* (2017), pp. 22–30
50. D. Weitlaner, A. Guettinger, M. Kohlbacher, Intuitive comprehensibility of process models, in *S-BPM ONE - Running Processes* (Springer, Berlin, 2013), pp. 52–71

Chapter 6
Developing Process Execution Support for High-Tech Manufacturing Processes

Irene Vanderfeesten, Jonnro Erasmus, Konstantinos Traganos,
Panagiotis Bouklis, Anastasia Garbi, George Boultadakis, Remco Dijkman,
and Paul Grefen

Abstract This chapter describes the development of an information system to control the execution of high-tech manufacturing processes from the business process level, based on executable process models. The development is described from process analysis to requirements elicitation to the definition of executable business process, for three pilot cases in our recent HORSE project. The HORSE project aims to develop technologies for smart factories, making end-to-end high-tech manufacturing processes, in which robots and humans collaborate, more flexible, more efficient, and more effective to produce small batches of customized products. This is done through the use of Internet of Things (IoT), Industry 4.0, collaborative robot technology, dynamic manufacturing process management, and flexible task allocation between robots and humans. The result is a manufacturing process management system (MPMS) that orchestrates the manufacturing process across work cells and production lines and operates based on executable business process models defined in BPMN.

6.1   Introduction

The manufacturing domain is moving toward more dynamic situations [11, 20, 39]. High-tech manufacturing companies currently face compelling challenges to increase efficiency and productivity while the products they produce become more complex and more customized, order batches become smaller, and delivery times need to be shortened to stay competitive [9, 26]. This requires new ways of

I. Vanderfeesten (✉) · J. Erasmus · K. Traganos · R. Dijkman · P. Grefen
School of Industrial Engineering, Eindhoven University of Technology, Eindhoven, Netherlands
e-mail: i.t.p.vanderfeesten@tue.nl; j.erasmus@tue.nl; k.traganos@tue.nl; r.m.dijkman@tue.nl;
p.w.p.j.grefen@tue.nl

P. Bouklis · A. Garbi · G. Boultadakis
European Dynamics, Athens, Greece
e-mail: panagiotis.bouklis@eurodyn.com; anastasia.garbi@eurodyn.com; george.
boultadakis@eurodyn.com

© Springer Nature Switzerland AG 2019
D. Lübke, C. Pautasso (eds.), *Empirical Studies on the Development of Executable Business Processes*, https://doi.org/10.1007/978-3-030-17666-2_6

organizing their factories and explicit process management to deal with this required flexibility and dynamism [8].

This chapter describes the development of an information system to control the execution of high-tech manufacturing processes, based on executable process models. The system is part of the development of the EU H2020 research project HORSE [36]. The HORSE project aims to develop innovative technologies for smart factories, making end-to-end high-tech manufacturing processes, in which robots and humans collaborate, more flexible, more efficient, and more effective to produce small batches of customized products. This is done through the use of Internet of Things [25], Industry 4.0 [22], collaborative robot technology, dynamic manufacturing process management, and flexible task allocation between robots and humans.

The HORSE solution aims at bridging the IoT-oriented level of collaborative robotics and the BPM-oriented level of manufacturing processes, i.e., coupling the physical and event layers of business control with the process layer [18]. With this, it tries to answer the question whether real-time manufacturing processes can be supported and coordinated with business process management (BPM) technology. Current research in this area has focused on modeling [40] and simulation [30] of manufacturing processes and analyzing their performance without providing execution support. At best, previous efforts have demonstrated importing business process models into manufacturing execution systems to support process execution [10, 29].

As part of the overall HORSE solution, the project aims to deliver an exaptation [19] of contemporary BPM technology to the manufacturing domain and to integrate this with new technological developments on the factory floor such as collaborative robots, automated guided vehicles (AGVs), and augmented reality to support human operators. The backbone of the HORSE system is a process management system that orchestrates the manufacturing process across work cells and production lines and that operates based on executable business process models. It is termed manufacturing process management system (MPMS).

The development of the MPMS is described in this chapter, from physical structure and manufacturing process analysis to requirements elicitation to the definition and enactment of executable business processes and to a first evaluation of the system. The basis for this are the three pilot cases in the HORSE project which we treated as explorative case studies [7, 33] here. In the following sections, first, the case study approach is explained, followed by a process and requirements analysis of the case studies that leads to a general HORSE requirements framework. Next, the architecture of the system is outlined, and the executable process models are presented and reflected upon, giving detailed insights on the particular challenges we met to transform the process models developed for business analysis into executable process models. The chapter is concluded with some takeaways for researchers and practitioners and an outlook on future developments.

6.2 Approach

In order to develop the HORSE system, we used a systematic approach to analyze the current manufacturing processes, bottlenecks, potential redesigns, and requirements to the HORSE system and to develop a generic solution (see Fig. 6.1). A thorough analysis of the three pilot cases is at the core of this approach. Through interviews and observations, we first modeled their manufacturing structure and processes and then performed a systematic analysis to identify problems, bottlenecks, and challenges. The three pilot cases can therefore be seen as exploratory case studies [7, 33] that in the end led to a general requirements framework for the system to be developed. According to [7], a case study is *a technique for detailed exploratory investigations, both prospectively and retrospectively, that attempts to understand and explain phenomenon or test theories, using primarily qualitative analysis*. With these pilot cases, we intended to prospectively test whether exapted BPM theory and technology is suitable for the manufacturing domain.

Each case study is analyzed in the same systematic way:

1. **Physical hierarchy analysis**. Like an organizational chart, considering a manufacturing company from a physical hierarchy perspective is a useful starting point to identify and scope a problem. As a basis, we use the reference physical hierarchy of the widely adopted international standard IEC 62264:2013 [3]. The reference hierarchy provides a clear distinction between levels of decomposition that can be expected in a factory. A site is usually comprised of multiple production areas, which can in turn be comprised of multiple production lines. Figure 6.2 shows the reference physical hierarchy. Participants in the case

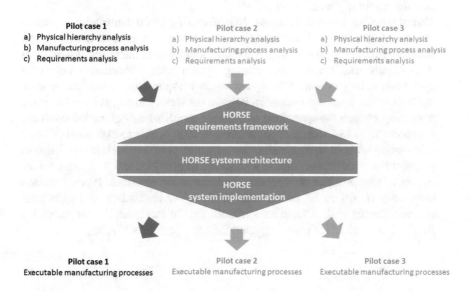

Fig. 6.1 Illustration of the case study approach

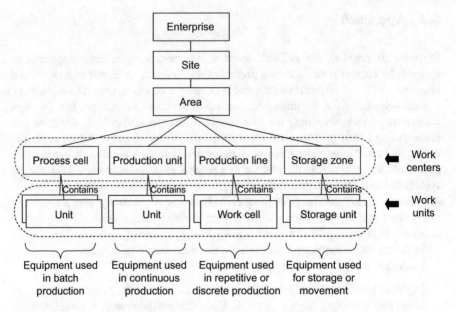

Fig. 6.2 Reference physical hierarchy for a manufacturing enterprise [21]

study analysis workshops found the top-down, hierarchical perspective easy to understand and relate to. It also benefits from an almost complete absence of notation that may be open to interpretation. Finally, the physical structure of the enterprise helps to understand the scope of the processes in the enterprise and plan the layout of process models.

2. **Manufacturing process analysis**. Manufacturing is fundamentally a process that transforms material and energy into a product. A process-oriented view therefore provides substantial information about the manufacturing system. This is especially true for a manufacturing system with a significant degree of dynamism in its processes. The dynamism is a response to the market: demand fluctuation and mass customization implore the factory to adjust its volume and frequently change its operations to produce small batches of varied products. A process model of such a manufacturing system is able to express significant information without overextending the capabilities of a model. It also helps to pinpoint the problematic point in a sequence of activities and to understand the impact of that problem on upstream or downstream activities. Process models have been shown to be useful tools to foster understanding and agreement between people with diverse backgrounds [6]. In this analysis, we adopt the BPMN 2.0 standard for modeling manufacturing processes [28, 35].

3. **System requirements analysis**. Process models can be used to effectively compare the current situation with proposed future situations. Such side-by-side comparison of the current and future scenarios is an excellent facilitator of requirements elicitation. Requirements should be stated from the perspective of the system itself, of which the process is a core aspect. Furthermore, we recommend standardized requirements specification, such as the syntax proposed by Mavin et al. [27]: «optional preconditions»«optional trigger» the «name» shall «system response». For example, the introduction of a robotic arm to an assembly activity may lead to the following requirement statement: the system shall assemble 20 products per minute. Such a requirement statement refers to the system as a whole, i.e., the future scenario where the robotic arm is an actor in the process.

Next, the elicited requirements coming from the three case studies were compared, combined, and structured in a HORSE requirements framework. The architecture of the HORSE system was designed (first from a functional perspective [14] followed by a more technical software perspective), and a prototype implementation (realization) of the HORSE system satisfying the elicited requirements was developed. Then, the pilot cases were elaborated into executable processes, and the system was deployed and evaluated on the factory floor.

The developed system builds on BPM technology (as is further explained in Sect. 6.4) and is driven by an executable business process that is a refinement of the process models resulting from the business analysis and elicitation phase. In the next sections, this approach is illustrated by a detailed elaboration of one of the pilot cases. Due to space limitations, the detailed analysis of the other two pilot cases is not included here, but an illustration can be found in the online appendix of this chapter.[1] The lessons learned on how to develop executable processes from business-level process models based on our experience with the three cases are discussed afterward.

6.3 Case Study Analysis and Requirements Elicitation

For each of the three case studies, we followed the three-step analysis approach as described in the previous section. In the next sections, these steps are detailed for the first case study, with a main focus on the process models used in this phase. Due to space limitations, the other two pilot cases are not discussed here, but additional information can be found in the online appendix (see footnote 1). The process models for all three pilot cases can be described along the lines of Lübke et al.'s [4] process classification (see Table 6.1).

---

[1] http://is.ieis.tue.nl/staff/ivanderfeesten/Papers/ESDEBP2018/.

Table 6.1 Process classification of the three case studies according to the template in Chap. 2

Process name	Case study 1	Case study 2	Case study 3
Version			
Domain	High-tech manufacturing		
Geography	Netherlands	Poland	Spain
Time	2015–2017		
Boundaries	Intraorganizational/Within department		
Relationship	Event triggered		
Scope	Business scope: core		
Process model purpose	Descriptive		
People involvement	Partly		
Process language	BPMN 2.0		
Execution engine	NA		
Model maturity	Reviewed		

6.3.1   Case Study 1

The first case study is a small high-tech factory in the south of the Netherlands. This factory produces make-to-order [12, 31, 32] sliders that allow cupboard drawers to extrude and retract. These highly customizable sliders comprise of several metal profiles and ball bearings. The metal profiles undergo various cutting, bending, and surface treatment operations, depending on the specific requirements of the customer. The final step in production is assembly of the treated profiles and ball bearings, before the sliders are placed in packaging for delivery. The company faces a huge challenge for the future: to stay competitive, they have to make production more agile and flexible to deal with an increasingly high level of customization of their products, smaller batches, and a decrease in accepted delivery time.

Physical Hierarchy As the first step in the case study analysis, the physical decomposition of the factory is described according to the physical hierarchy of IEC 62264:2013 [21]: the factory has three production areas (PAs) and a single storage zone that acts as a buffer between the production areas. Figure 6.3 shows a depiction of this decomposition. The case study covers all three production areas and the storage zone. However, in the interest of brevity, only two processes will be discussed in detail here: *tool assembly* in production area 1 (PA1) and *loading* in production area 2 (PA2).

Process Analysis As the second step in the case study analysis, the end-to-end manufacturing process is modeled in BPMN 2.0. Such an end-to-end process model is particularly useful to understand the upstream or downstream impact of a problem. The three production areas are modeled as separate pools in Fig. 6.4. This is due to a significant difference of throughput. PA1 and PA3 have much higher capacity than PA2. Therefore, the output parts from PA1 are stored in a temporary buffer before they are processed at PA2. The storage zone is not explicitly included in the process model, but rather implied as external preservation service. The operator places items in storage or retrieves them from storage.

The two processes discussed in this chapter are highlighted with bold borders in Fig. 6.4. The first process occurs in PA1 and is concerned with the preparation of tools for cold forming. These tool assemblies consist of a base plate and at least ten tooling parts. Hundreds of tooling parts are available, resulting in thousands of potential tool configurations. Figure 6.5 shows a model of the current process to assemble tooling blocks. It should be noted that this process corresponds to the PL1-1 tool assembly production line and its two work units in Fig. 6.3: WU1.1.1 single tool assembly and WU1.1.2 tool set assembly. Therefore, the single process model includes work done in two distinct work stations. This process is currently entirely manual and depends largely on the experience and skills of operators. In the future situation, the assembly activity is supported with an augmented reality system and a robot fetching the tooling parts that need to be assembled from the warehouse (Fig. 6.6).

The second process occurs in PA2—the surface treatment of the parts. Profiles coming from PA1 are loaded on (and after treatment unloaded from) racks that go into a chemical bath. This is an entirely manual activity done by human operators. It demands concentration and places physical strain on the operators. This process will undergo the most significant changes as part of the HORSE project solution and is discussed here in detail. More specifically, the *loading* process will be discussed and is highlighted with a bold outline in Fig. 6.4. Figure 6.7 shows the next level of detail of the *loading* process in PA2.

Figure 6.7 depicts a largely manual process (as indicated by many manual and user tasks), at odds with the general trajectory of automation seen in the manufacturing industry. The lack of automation is due to the product customization. The product dimensions may be different for each production order, which also affects the way profiles are loaded for surface treatment. Robotic solutions have difficulty with such highly customizable situations.

Instead of attempting to replace the human with a robot, the process as a whole should be considered. The operator has two main tasks in this process: picking a handful of profiles and then hanging each profile individually. Splitting the responsibility of those two tasks makes the potential (robotic) solution simpler and more manageable. One robot can pick the profiles (*Place parts on conveyor belt*), while the other selects the right gripper for the profile (*Change gripper*) and hangs each profile on the rack (*Grab and hang single profile*). Figure 6.8 shows how the proposed solution will change the process.

Requirements Analysis The end-to-end manufacturing process model (see Fig. 6.4) is a valuable tool to identify broader requirements. In this first case study, it can be seen that the end-to-end process is divided into three individual pools (as also indicated by the physical hierarchy in Fig. 6.3). This is to allow asynchronism between parts of the process, realized by buffered storage between the separate production areas. However, it is still necessary for a production order to make its way through all three production orders. Thus, a production order should

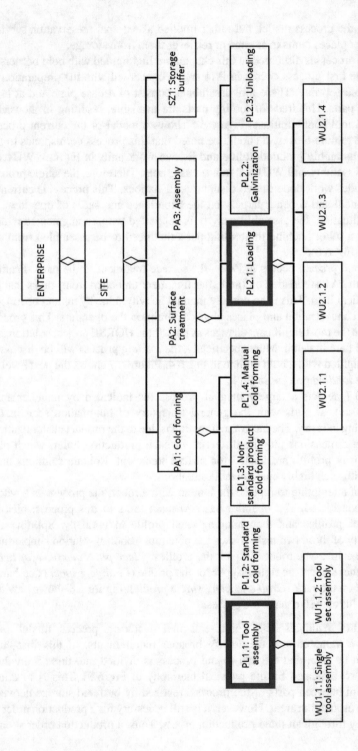

Fig. 6.3 Physical hierarchy of the manufacturing company of case study 1. The highlighted processes will be discussed in detail in the remainder of this chapter

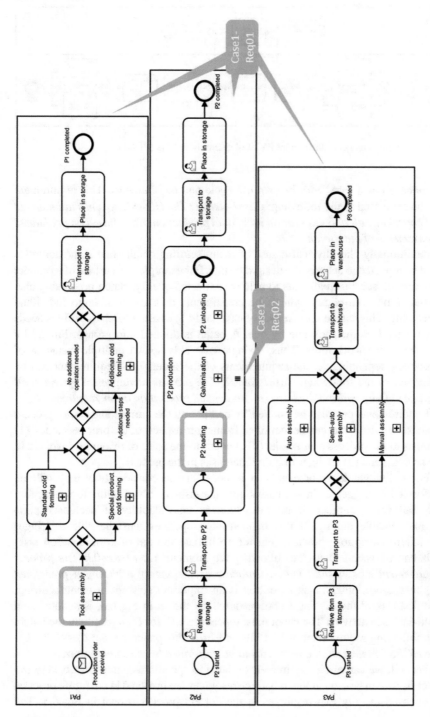

Fig. 6.4 Process model of the end-to-end production process for case study 1

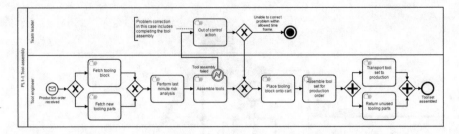

Fig. 6.5 Process model of the current PA1 tool assembly process (PL1-1)

be managed as a case, with its own life cycle and requirements. This requirement can be expressed as the following: *Case1-Req01: The HORSE system shall manage and coordinate all activities for an individual production order, based on predefined requirements of that order.*

Additionally, the physical nature of manufacturing entails that some activities must be repeated to achieve the desired results. For example, the surface of a product may require several treatments to achieve expected quality. Batch processing also entails some multiplicity, where the constituents of a batch undergo individual processing. This can be seen in PA2 of case study 1, where a batch of profiles needs to be loaded on the rack one by one. A batch is divided into groups, limited by the size of the work units. Thus, a single case may spawn multiple instances of a product, depending on the requirements of the order. This requirement can be expressed as the following: *Case1-Req02: The process management system shall manage activity multiplicity based on predefined production order requirements.*

Requirements can also be elicited by comparing the current and future process models. Requirements can be identified from three aspects of the process model: (1) changes to the process as a whole, (2) changes to the roles of resources involved in the process, and (3) changes to individual tasks in the process.

For individual tasks or events, it is necessary to consider how they will be performed or triggered. In our case study, the tasks involved in the tool assembly may fail for a number of reasons, such as unavailability of necessary parts or unacceptable quality. If this happens, the operator must be able to trigger the failure exception shown in Fig. 6.6 to initiate the out-of-normal action task. This can be specified as the following requirement: *Case1-Req03: The process management system shall manage process exceptions by initiating a predefined response.* Additionally, task repetition is an important concept in manufacturing. The first task of the Placing Robot resource, as shown in Fig. 6.8, is denoted as a multi-instance activity. The robot must repeat the task for each profile in the batch. The following requirement can be inferred from this phenomenon: *Case1-Req05: The HORSE system shall queue tasks to be performed by the same resource.*

Second, we can elicit requirements related to specific resources involved in the process. As can be seen in Fig. 6.6, three resources are involved in the future process, as opposed to only two resources in the current process shown in Fig. 6.5. The

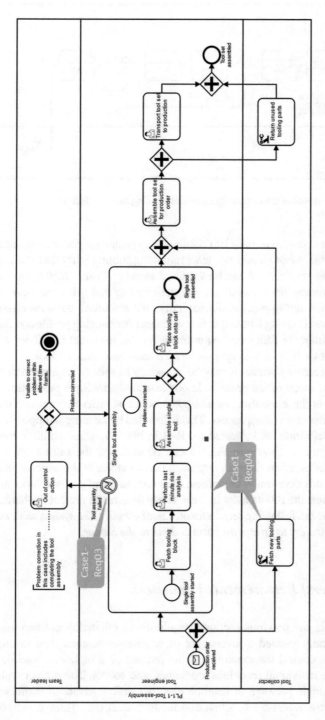

Fig. 6.6 Process model of the future PA1 tool assembly process (PL1-1). Please note that we used a BPMN extension to model robotic tasks from a business-level perspective, as defined by Aspridou [1]

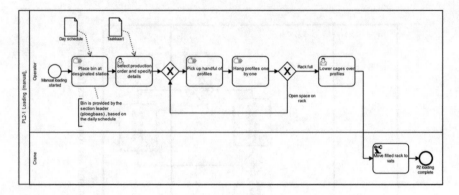

Fig. 6.7 Process model of the current PA2 (manual) loading process (PL2-1)

activities of these resources must be coordinated to ensure proper process execution. For example, the robot should not start removing tooling parts that the engineer still needs. This requirement can be specified as such: *Case1-Req04: The process management system shall coordinate the activities of multiple actors involved in the same manufacturing process.* As for individual resources, the third resource in Fig. 6.8 is named Loading Robot and is responsible for hanging profiles on the rack. Thus, we can infer the following requirement for this resource: *Case1-Req06: The Loading Robot shall be able to lift parts with a maximum mass of 5 kg.*

For the process as a whole, it may be necessary to specify requirements related to the nature or scope of the process. In our case study, multiple production orders may be active at the same time, or a single production order may require multiple executions of the same (sub)process. This is handled by creating multiple instances of a process definition, as indicated for PA2 in Fig. 6.4. Thus, multiple instances of the entire process shown in Fig. 6.8 can be active at the same time. Finally, activity automation often delivers improved performance, at the expense of safety to humans. In this case study, the human operator must still perform tasks near the two robots. Thus, the robots must include safety features to protect the human. We therefore define the following requirement: *Case1-Req07: The system shall actively monitor its proximity to ensure no harm is done to the human.*

6.3.2 General Requirements Framework

As described in the previous sections, requirements elicitation at three unrelated factories naturally yielded a diverse set of requirements, connected through the overall wish to control the execution of the process on a higher abstraction level, overseeing the individual machines, operators, and robots. The project endeavors to develop a single package of technologies that makes advanced manufacturing technology more accessible to small and medium factories. Thus, it is necessary

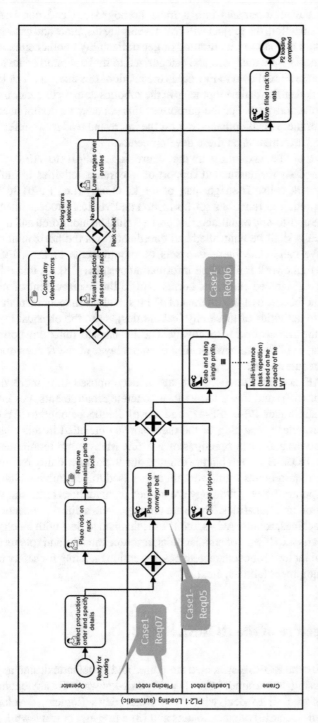

Fig. 6.8 Process model of the future PA2 (automatic) loading process (PL2-1). Please note that we used a BPMN extension to model robotic tasks from a business-level perspective, as defined by Aspridou [1]

to amalgamate the requirements into a more homogeneous and consistent set. Without homogenization, the project will risk developing disparate and case-specific subsystems that do not support integration or generalizability to other situations.

The requirements were analyzed and categorized to find common concepts. The requirements framework shown in Fig. 6.9 is the result of this analysis. The left part of this framework deals with developments in the robotics domain to better integrate human and robotic activities. For the purpose of this chapter, we do not need to go into the details of these developments; but for the interested reader, we refer to [36] for more detailed information on these developments.

The left part of the taxonomy in the figure (i.e., AF-01 to AF-04) shows the required functions for automated support of integrated activities in individual manufacturing work cells. The right part of the taxonomy (i.e., PF-01 to PF-03) shows the main required functions for horizontal and vertical process integration, meaning that the end-to-end manufacturing process shall be monitored and managed and that work cells shall be controlled and coordinated via the horizontal process management. We can relate these two sets of requirements to the AFIS four-layer reference framework for flexible information systems [18]. In this reference framework, the AF-labeled functions correspond to the management of physical entities (things in the sense of the Internet of Things) and the management of digital events (related to activities of these physical entities), so to the physical layer and event layer of the framework, respectively. The PF-labeled functions correspond to the process layer of the framework. The business layer of the framework is not covered by the requirements.

The main AF and PF functions are again decomposed into more detailed system functions (SFs) and into a large set of concrete requirements. For instance, Case1-Req01 falls under PF-01/SF-11, and Case1-Req05 belongs to AF-02/SF-07. Table 6.2 provides a mapping of the requirements included in this chapter to the system functions and main functions of Fig. 6.9. Many more requirements are specified for the HORSE system but are omitted due to confidentiality restrictions.

The HORSE requirements framework then was used to determine which extensions to contemporary BPM technology are needed to cover horizontal and vertical process integration functionalities. These are among others a direct connection with IoT devices (machines, robots, AGVs, etc.), a mechanism to deal with batching and unbatching of parts into bigger or smaller units, resource models, and role resolution mechanisms that include robot characteristics, exception handling for safety reasons and technical equipment failures, etc. [38].

6.4   Architecture of the HORSE System

In order to realize the HORSE system, a structured and systematic design approach was followed using two frameworks: (1) the well-known software engineering 4+1 framework of [24] to deal with the various views (logical, development, process, physical, scenario) of stakeholders and (2) a five-aspect framework for the

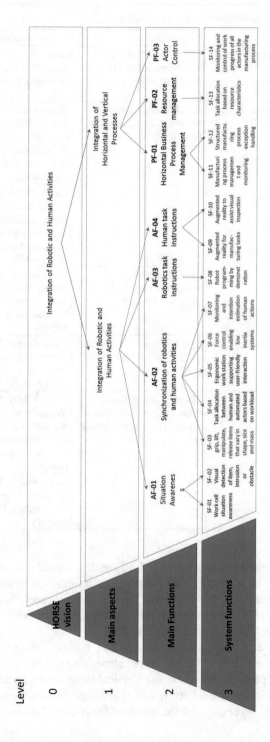

Fig. 6.9 HORSE requirements framework. Please see online appendix for a larger version

Table 6.2 Mapping of requirements to system functions

Main functions	System functions	System requirements
AF-02 Synchronization of robotic and human activities	SF-07 Monitoring and intention estimation of human actions	Case1-Req07: The system shall actively monitor its proximity to ensure no harm is done to the human
PF-01 Horizontal business process management	SF-11 Manufacturing process management and monitoring	Case1-Req01: The HORSE system shall manage and coordinate all activities for an individual production order, based on predefined requirements of that order
		Case1-Req02: The process management system shall manage activity multiplicity based on predefined production order requirements
	SF-12 Structured manufacturing process exception handling	Case1-Req03: The process management system shall manage process exceptions by initiating a predefined response
PF-02 Resource management	SF-13 Task allocation based on resource characteristics	Case1-Req06: The Loading Robot shall be able to lift parts with a maximum mass of 5 kg
PF-03 Actor control	SF-14 Monitoring and control of progress of all actors in the manufacturing process	Case1-Req04: The process management system shall coordinate the activities of multiple actors involved in the same manufacturing process
		Case1-Req05: The HORSE system shall queue tasks to be performed by the same resource

design of business information systems [15, 37] to deal with the set of enterprise information aspects of a description of a complex information system: process, data, organization, software, and platform. The full design process is documented in [14, 17]. Here, we will only summarize the logical software architecture and the realization of that architecture in a concrete system.

Based on the system requirements elicited, first, a *logical architecture* of the HORSE system was developed [14, 24], before elaborating on specific technologies in the software and platform aspects of the physical views of the architecture. The system architecture has a layered style, with a division between global and local functions. The global layer includes the functions for process management that are

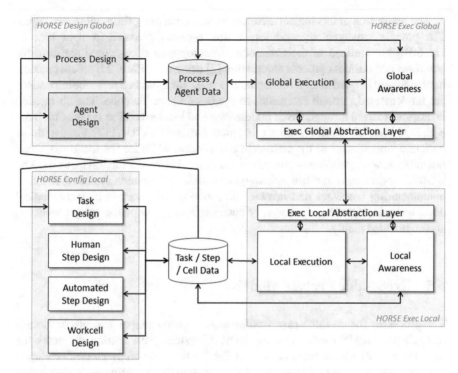

Fig. 6.10 The logical view of the HORSE system architecture; highlighted in light blue on the top left of this picture are the MPMS modules

applicable to multiple work units of the factory (work unit refers to the lowest level of the physical hierarchy shown in Fig. 6.3). The local layer provides functionality used within a single work unit. Figure 6.10 shows the *software aspect* [14, 37] of the logical architecture, at aggregation level 2. The vertical integration between global process management and local work cell execution is handled via the abstraction layers.

The architecture distinguishes between design-time and run-time functionality. Design-time functionality is used to define activities, agents, and physical constraints of the manufacturing system through (executable) process models, extended with manufacturing specific elements [1, 23]. Run-time functionality makes use of the design-time definitions to enact the processes and assign tasks to agents, within the bounds of the physical constraints. Thus, design-time functionality is used to develop the process models, and run-time functionality then enacts those process models and invokes the local layer of the HORSE system to execute activities on the factory floor.

The realization of this logical architecture was done using different technologies. The process management modules of this system (indicated in light blue in Fig. 6.10) are realized in the Camunda technology, an open-source platform for workflow and business process automation [2] using the BPMN 2.0 process modeling language [28]. Advanced functionalities (e.g., for advanced resource allocation) are implemented through extensions to the basic Camunda code. The abstraction layers are realized through OSGi middleware and local execution systems built on, e.g., ROS FlexBE, KUKA Sunrise robot platform, and OPC UA [17]. For the global part, one embodiment of the architecture is chosen; while for the local part, some flexibility in the embodiment is required to suit local infrastructures at factories. The HORSE system therefore is a lightweight, modular information system that enacts manufacturing processes and invokes the functions of a variety of technological developments, including situationally aware robotics, automated guided vehicles, and augmented reality.

6.5 Executable Process Models

The processes for all three case studies were implemented as executable models through the MPMS modules of the HORSE system. This section discusses the (development of the) executable models for the first case study and reflects upon the lessons learned and what was needed to develop these executable models based on the models used for business analysis and requirements elicitation. Due to space constraints, we only show resulting executable models for the first case study. The executable models for the other two case studies can be found in the online appendix (see footnote 1). The lessons learned, presented in Sect. 6.5.2 in the form of an extended method to develop executable processes, however, are based on our experiences with all three case studies.

6.5.1 Executable Processes for Case Study 1

As described in Sect. 6.3.1, the scope for the first case study was narrowed down to two subprocesses: the future PA1 tool assembly process and the future PA2 loading process. With the right additions and changes, which are discussed in more detail in the next section, the business process models of Figs. 6.6 and 6.8 were transformed into executable process models (see Figs. 6.11 and 6.12, respectively). An explanation of the main transformations is given in the discussion below. The executable processes can again be classified according to the process classification of Chap. 2 as indicated in Table 6.3.

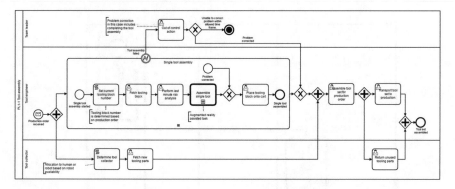

Fig. 6.11 Executable process model of the PL1-1 tool assembly process in PA1 (cf. Fig. 6.6)

The Tool Assembly Process In the future tool assembly process (cf. Fig. 6.6 vs. Fig. 6.11), several *script tasks* were added to automatically select the right agent—human or robot—for the execution of the task *Fetch new tooling parts* and to automatically retrieve additional information on the exact tooling block to be assembled for this production order.

Furthermore, the *Assemble single tool* task which was modeled as a user task in the business model was implemented in the executable model with a reusable *call activity* that represents a standardized way of communication to a device on the local level of the HORSE architecture, such as the augmented reality system that guides the human operator through the tool assembly steps. The internals of this call activity are specified by Fig. 6.13. The messages with task instructions or task events are standardized and sent to/from the local-level device through the abstraction layers.

The Loading Process In the future loading process (cf. Fig. 6.8 vs. Fig. 6.12), an exception was defined handling a failure of the robotic task *Place parts on conveyor belt*. In case something goes wrong in this task and the Placing Robot cannot properly finish it, an *out-of-control action* should happen. This was not specified at the business-level process model as it was considered a technical issue.

Furthermore, internal variables were specified for the correct handling of the multi-instance tasks *Place parts on conveyor belt* and *Grab and hang single profile*. These variables are filled in a form that is presented to the user when initiating the process instance. Ideally, this information can be automatically derived from the production order information.

Moreover, as in the tool assembly process, tasks that involve direct communication with local-level devices such as the Loading Robot, Placing Robot, and Crane were again replaced by the standardized call activity (Fig. 6.13).

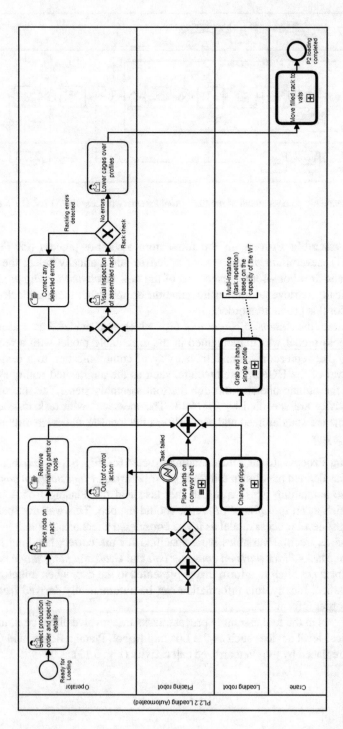

Fig. 6.12 Executable process model of the PL2-1 loading process in PA2 (cf. Fig. 6.8)

Table 6.3 Process classification of case study 1 executable process models according to Lübke et al.'s [4]

Process name	Case study 1 PL 1-1	Case study 1 PL 2-1
Version	1.0	1.0
Domain	High-tech manufacturing	High-tech manufacturing
Geography	Netherlands	Netherlands
Time	2018	2018
Boundaries	Intraorganizational	Intraorganizational
Relationship	Is being called	Is being called
Scope	Business scope, core; technical scope	Business scope, core; technical scope
Process model purpose	Execution	Execution
People involvement	Partly	Partly
Process language	BPMN 2.0	BPMN 2.0
Execution engine	Camunda	Camunda
Model maturity	Prototypical	Prototypical

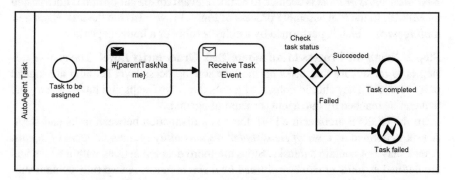

Fig. 6.13 The reusable subprocess to assign tasks and instructions to automated agents, e.g., the Crane, Loading Robot, and Placing Robot in the executable process model of the loading process in PA2 (cf. Fig. 6.12)

6.5.2   Method to Develop Executable Process Models

In order to develop the executable models for the pilot cases, again a systematic approach was followed. Dumas et al. [6] describe a five-step method to convert the business analysis process model—fit for communication and analysis purposes—into an executable model, suitable to feed into a business process execution engine: (1) Identify the automation boundaries. (2) Review manual tasks. (3) Complete the process model. (4) Bring the process model to an adequate granularity level. (5) Specify execution properties. We adopted the general guidelines of the above method and adapted and extended them where necessary, as we explain later in this section. In order to arrive at the detailed executable processes, we followed the following steps:

Step 1: Identify the Type of Tasks (Automated, User, Manual Tasks) This step is a combination of the first two steps of the method described in [6]. The aim is to assess which parts of the process can be coordinated by the MPMS and which cannot. The characterization of the type of each task (manual, user, automated, robotic) is an initial and important step that has to be done for all tasks.

In manufacturing processes, there are a lot of manual tasks, for instance, *Hang profiles* (in PA2 of the first case study), that do not add any value to a process management system. These are not executed by a process engine but can still be present in a process model. The manufacturing tasks that are interesting from an MPMS point of view are the ones performed by humans with the aid of a software application, robots, and/or automated vehicles. These are implemented as BPMN user tasks (for humans) or with the "send"-"receive" pattern (for robots) and the ones that should be configured in order to be ready for real execution. For example, in the loading process of Fig. 6.12, the task *Place rods on rack* is modeled and executed as a user task since the agent to perform it is a human operator with the assistance of a tasklist handler. On the other hand, the manual task *Remove remaining parts or tools* is deemed to be not relevant for execution and is not assisted by MPMS. In the tool assembly process of Fig. 6.11, we also see the task *Fetch new tooling parts* which is performed by a either a robot or a human operator.

Step 2: Bring the Process to Adequate Task Granularity Level The goal of this step is to make sure that tasks on the lowest subprocess level actually are logical units of work. They should consist of a coherent set of steps and have a clear goal that can be reached by one agent (or team of agents).

In the HORSE architecture [14], there is a distinction between tasks and steps. A task is defined as a *set of steps under responsibility of a single team of agents*. A task may not contain subtasks. Steps are more detailed actions within a task and are defined as *units of work performed by a single agent*. A step may contain sub-steps. A task then consists of a number of steps. Tasks, as a more high-level aspect, are handled by MPMS, while steps are handled by the local level of the HORSE architecture. An illustrative example is the robot task *Grab, lift, and hang single profile* of Fig. 6.12. This is a high-level action for which an MPMS cares for the assignment of the task to the robot and the confirmation of task completion (or failure). The internal robotic steps needed to perform the task (like "Close gripper," "Move the robot X cm," etc.) are details handled by modules of the local level, often specified in a robot execution script or taught by demonstration to the robot. Tasks should be demarcated correctly. If, on the one hand, they are too fine grained, the MPMS will continuously interrupt the agent performing the task to tell what the next task is that should be performed. For example, if "Grab profile," "Lift profile," and "Hang profile" are separate tasks, the agent must confirm each of the tasks separately and will receive separate work orders from the MPMS for each of them. If, on the other hand, tasks are too coarse grained, the agent may need to involve other agents, while it should be the MPMS that tells each agent what to do. For example, if "Hang profile" and "Paint profile" should be done by different (teams of) agents, they should be separate tasks. Otherwise, the agent who hung the profile should inform the agent who has to paint the profile. This guideline applies first of all to the business-level model, but needs to be reviewed when the executable model is created such that in case of misalignment with designed robotic tasks (in the task design module on the local configuration level), a task needs to be split or aggregated.

In our approach, we see this step as a logical sequence of the first step, in which the type of tasks (and the tasks themselves) has been identified. For this reason, we adapted the sequence of steps of the method described in [6].

Step 3: Redesign Pools and Swim Lanes for Interacting Processes In this step, the goal is to decide whether (and how) message flows between different pools in the model should be automated and to stratify communication between a main process and the (possibly multiple) related instances of its subprocesses.

Pools are used here to represent resource classes or whole processes, while swim lanes are used to partition a pool into subclasses or single resources. They are useful for a business-oriented model but have no execution semantics. When the pools are used to represent different processes, most likely they are connected to each other at some point. However, when executing such processes, it may be difficult to synchronize their instances. For example, a main production process may run in a sequential multi-instance scenario, and at some point, it calls another supplementary process that in turn has to call back the main process. The callback from the supplementary process may happen at a time in which the calling instance of the main process has been terminated (and the next instance of the multi-instance pattern has initiated). This may lead to wrong information updates or no synchronization at all. Therefore, it is preferred to model two (or more) processes in the same pool/lane in order to be executed properly and as intended to be. This was the case in case study 3, in which an alert is sent to the supervisor in case of a defected product—see the online appendix (see footnote 1). In the business process model, the supervision role is modeled as a separate pool; but in the executable process model, we had to incorporate it in the main pool, which was implemented as a multi-instance case.

This step is an addition to the approach presented in [6], since we consider it important.

Step 4: Complete the Process Model (e.g., with Exceptions) The models resulting from the elicitation phase often lack certain detailed information. The goal of this step is to enhance and complete the model with the necessary information. This step is the same as the third step of the method described in [6]. Based on our experience with the case studies, we complete Dumas et al.'s list to the following:

- Data objects. Input and output information for all tasks and decisions should be specified through (global) variables, attributes, and forms (on start events or user tasks).
- Exceptions. Alternative paths and (technical) exceptions should be specified such that the process can handle all possible situations. This requires specifying all (mutually exclusive) options after a decision gateway, alternative routes,

exceptions, timeouts, failures, corrective actions, etc. For instance, in Fig. 6.12 to make the PA2 loading process executable, all possible robot task failures must be covered. Otherwise, the process engine may get stuck when one of these failures occurs. These failures can be specified as BPMN exceptions. For example, in task *Place parts on conveyor belt*, a task failure can raise an exception leading to a standardized *out-of-control action* task.

- Resource assignment. The assignment of resources to tasks (via, e.g., direct assignees, groups (candidate users), or more advanced selections through expressions).
- Multi-instance activities. Make sure that multi-instance activities/subprocesses are repeated for the correct number of times and that the right type of multi-instance is specified (parallel or sequential). Multi-instance activities are used to deal with different abstraction levels of the case in the process. For instance, one order can lead to the production of 50 sliders that each need 3 profiles. Then on the main process level, the instance is the order, which invokes 50 instances of the slider production process and others.
- Reusable subprocesses. If similar functionality is needed, try to, if possible, define parameterizable reusable subprocesses that may be invoked from different places in the main process, e.g., the call activity of Fig. 6.13 realizing the technical communication to the robotic actors in the process.

Step 5: Integrate with Other Systems (Messaging Middleware, DB Server) An executable process rarely relies on its own execution engine system alone to run. It normally interacts with other information systems or database servers. In the HORSE system, the MPMS module needs to communicate with other modules and databases as specified in the HORSE architecture in Fig. 6.10. The goal of this step is to realize the technical integration with these systems.

Therefore, in an executable process model, there should be extra service tasks to invoke other systems (or any delegate code on user tasks or DB connectors, as we will see later on the "BPMS-specific properties" step). Such integration services could be, for instance, any web service or REST calls. In all three case studies, we implemented connections to a database, when information was needed to be retrieved or stored, and also connection to the local level of the HORSE architecture through the abstraction layers, when tasks had to be assigned to robots.

This step is also an addition to the approach described in [6], since integration of MPMS to the other modules of the HORSE architecture is vital for the whole system.

Step 6: Specify Execution Properties (i.e., Implementation Details That Are Not Depicted in the BPMN Model but Needed by the Execution Engine) In the business-oriented process model, many details are omitted for the sake of simplicity. Such details are as follows:

- Process variables, messages, signals, and errors. Process variables are used to store data information used throughout a process instance. It can be information on, e.g., a production order number, a part ID, etc. Messages, signals, and errors also have to be specified on a process model so that the engine can execute them.

- Task and event variables and their mappings to process variables. Tasks and events may have their internal variables that carry information. These have to be specified and mapped accordingly.
- Service details for service, send, and receive tasks and for message and signal events. Tasks, either service, send/receive, or user tasks, implement a business logic through a technical specification, such as a delegate code, a web service call, an execution listener, etc. In many cases, this requires the most effort from a developer to make a business-oriented model executable.
- Code snippets for script tasks. Similar to the service details of a task, some scripting may be required in some points of a workflow, for example, to update a process variable after a decision point.
- Participant assignment rules and user interface structure for user tasks. User tasks are the ones performed by a participant with the help of an application's user interface (or in the case of robot, tasks with the help of a script, implemented also as user tasks as we said previously). That means that the participant has first to be determined (either during design time or dynamically during runtime). Such a participant assignment rule is used on *Fetch new tooling parts* of Fig. 6.11, where the *script task* before will first invoke a dynamic agent allocation algorithm which will determine whether a robot or a human operator can perform the task. Then, the mechanism to notify the participant for the task assignment has to be implemented (BPMS normally has their own tasklist application; but extra notifications like emails, SMS, and push messages may be required). Finally, the user interface to present the right input information and capture the output result should be designed and implemented.
- Task, event, and sequence flow expressions. Various expressions may be needed on tasks (e.g., loop conditions), events, and sequence flows (any conditions, for instance).
- BPMS-specific properties. In addition to all of the above, extra settings and configurations may be needed on some BPMN elements to make them executable. Normally, a BPMS provides patterns for such configurations, for example, connectors.

6.6   Evaluation

At the time of writing this book chapter, the first version of the HORSE system is under installation and deployment at the pilot cases. Since these deployment experiments are not finished yet, only a first and preliminary evaluation of the PA1 (tool assembly process) solution from case study 1 can be presented here. The solution is evaluated in two ways:

1. As a proof-of-concept or feasibility test. The executable process models are defined in the MPMS modules, deployed on the factory floor, and enacted through the HORSE system enabling interaction with the augmented reality system and real process participants.
2. As an acceptance test. The process participants are interrogated regarding their perceived usefulness and ease of use.

Nineteen operators were asked to work with the system and complete the tool assembly process for one case (i.e., one tool block was assembled). Afterward, they were surveyed and interviewed to gauge their experience with the new process. The technology acceptance model (TAM) [5] is used as both survey and outline for the semi-structured interviews. The model includes twelve questions divided into two sections for perceived usefulness (PU) and perceived ease of use (PEOU). Importantly, the questions aim to determine whether the user prefers to use the new technology, compared to the previous way of working (which for the tool assembly process was completely manual as specified in Fig. 6.5). All twelve questions are measured on a Likert scale ranging from 1 (extremely likely) to 7 (extremely unlikely).

The 19 surveys and interviews generated significant data to be used for evaluation. Table 6.4 shows the 12 TAM statements posed to the interviewees and the average ratings as reported by the interviewees. As an overview, the system was rated favorably, with only two statements garnering a rating slightly unfavorably (i.e., numbers 8 and 10).

The most common complaints by participants were that the system forced them to work a certain way. Manufacturing processes that involve human participants tend to offer some flexibility to the participants on the precise order of tasks, or the resolution of mistakes and errors, especially if they are fully manual. With

Table 6.4 Average score per TAM statement

nr	Statement	Average rating (1–7)
1	Using the system in my job would enable me to accomplish tasks more quickly	2.32
2	Using the system would improve my job performance	2.26
3	Using the system in my job would increase my productivity	2.37
4	Using the system would enhance my effectiveness on the job	2.21
5	Using the system would make it easier to do my job	1.79
6	I would find the system useful in my job	2.16
7	Learning to operate the system would be easy for me	1.42
8	I would find it easy to get the system to do what I want it to do	3.53
9	My interaction with the system would be clear and understandable	1.84
10	I would find the system to be flexible to interact with	3.58
11	It would be easy for me to become skilful at using the system	1.68
12	I would find the system easy to use	1.79

an executable process enacted by an MPMS, this is no longer possible. This complaint is reflected in the average scores of the flexibility statements 8 and 10 in Table 6.1. The operators felt restricted and constrained by the system, minimizing their opportunity to pursue process improvement. However, a strict process enforced by the system would prevent many of the mistakes currently made by the human operators.

On the positive side, the participants were highly enthusiastic of the usefulness of the system. This optimism isn't necessarily related to the increased automation in the processes, leading to less burden on the operator, but rather related to the procedural nature of an MPMS-coordinated process. They acknowledged the value of having a system that encourages disciplined process execution. This is even more important for inexperienced operators, who can be trained faster to participate in complex processes. Apart from increased discipline, some participants also appreciated the lessened mental burden. The HORSE system presents the relevant information to perform a task, thus making it easier for an operator to follow instructions and perform the work.

6.7 Conclusions and Outlook

In this chapter, our experiences with developing executable processes for the high-tech manufacturing domain are discussed. We systematically derived requirements for a manufacturing process management system (MPMS) through a thorough analysis of three case studies. After the design and realization of the MPMS, we illustrated the development of the executable processes through the first case study, followed by a discussion of our lessons learned in the form of an extended stepwise method to transform a business process model into an executable model. We have already conducted some trials for the first pilot case—showing positive results. All in all, we conclude that our proof of concept shows that it is possible to support and coordinate high-tech manufacturing processes at real time with business process management technology, but that there are quite some technical and conceptual challenges to tackle and that standardization would be important for an industry strength solution.

6.7.1 Conclusions for Researchers

The research aspect behind this case study experience report is the exaptation of contemporary BPM technology (originating from the service industry) to the high-tech manufacturing domain. With these case studies and the general technology developments following that, we showed that manufacturing processes can be supported by BPM technology through, e.g., the HORSE MPMS system. This adoption of technology in a completely new and challenging domain, however, does not go without extensions. The main challenges we met here are the physical constraints in a manufacturing process (e.g., the intermediate storage and the multi-instance solutions for the different levels of granularity in the process) and the interfacing with robotic technology (for which no standard functionality or communication protocols were available yet). All in all, we conclude that the MPMS can bring many advantages to a manufacturing company but that there are still many research developments and innovations needed to make the MPMS an industry strength solution.

6.7.2   Takeaways for Practitioners

On the practical side, the three case studies have shown the possible advantages that explicit process management can bring to the manufacturing domain in order to better deal with the increasing dynamism [39]. Advantages are mainly found in a better overview of the production status and the flexible and automatic control of the process execution. The business process models turned out to be very useful for company stakeholders to get an integrated end-to-end view on their production processes, which they were often lacking. From a more technical perspective, we learned that transforming business-oriented process models into executable processes is not easy and time consuming. It requires additional specifications on various levels. We adopted a method available, but found it was not complete and, based on our experience with the three case studies, added and extended it. Our adjusted method is the most concrete contribution for practitioners as they can take it along to give structure to their efforts when creating executable manufacturing processes. Obviously, the current version of the method may be further evaluated and detailed to be of even more practical value.

6.7.3   Outlook

In this chapter, we presented a first version of the HORSE framework, mainly focused on the MPMS functionality. In the near future, this system will be further refined (e.g., including more specific manufacturing characteristics, more advanced exception handling, more advanced dynamic role resolution). Furthermore, in the next year, the HORSE framework will be extensively tested in real situations in the three pilot cases that already served as case studies here and in another seven new case studies. This will allow us to extensively evaluate the usefulness and value of the system and of our method and to further refine these. On the longer term, we envision the MPMS system could also be the basis for realizing a strong coupling of the management of manufacturing processes to the end-to-end corporate processes (i.e., from sales process to after-sales service) as discussed in [13] and even for flexible manufacturing network processes, such as described in [16, 34].

Acknowledgements The HORSE project has received funding from the European Union's Horizon 2020 research and innovation program under grant agreement no. 680734.

References

1. M. Aspridou, Extending BPMN for modeling manufacturing processes, Master thesis, Business Information Systems, TU/e, 2017. https://tinyurl.com/ya6c8czh
2. Camunda: http://www.camunda.org
3. D. Chen, Enterprise-control system integration - an international standard. Int. J. Prod. Res. **43**(20), 4335–4357 (2005)
4. L. Daniel, I. Ana, P. Cesare, A template for categorizing empirical business process metrics. BPM Forum, Barcelona (Springer, 2017), pp. 36–52
5. F.D. Davis, Perceived usefulness, perceived ease of use, and user acceptance of information technology. MIS Q. **13**(3), 319–340 (1989)
6. M. Dumas, M. La Rosa, J. Mendling, H. Reijers, *Fundamentals of Business Process Management* (Springer, Berlin, 2013)
7. S. Easterbrook et al., Selecting empirical methods for software engineering research, in *Guide to Advanced Empirical Software Engineering* (Springer, London, 2008), pp. 285–311
8. A. Estruch, J.A. Heredia Álvaro, Event-driven manufacturing process management approach, in *Business Process Management: 10th International Conference Proceedings*, ed. by A. Barros, A. Gal, E. Kindler, vol. 7481 (Springer, Berlin/Heidelberg, 2012), pp. 120–133
9. E. Filos, Four years of factories of the future in Europe: achievements and outlook. Int. J. Comput. Integr. Manuf. **30**, 18 (2015). https://www.tandfonline.com/doi/abs/10.1080/0951192X.2015.1044759
10. T. Gerber, A. Theorin, C. Johnsson, Towards a seamless integration between process modeling descriptions at business and production levels: work in progress. J. Intell. Manuf. **25**(5), 1089–1099 (2014)
11. D. Gerwin, An agenda for research on the flexibility of manufacturing processes. Int. J. Oper. Prod. Manag. **7**(1), 38–49 (1987)
12. P. Giesberts, L. Van den Tang, Dynamics of the customer order decoupling point: impact on information systems for production control. Prod. Plan. Control **3**(3), 300–313 (1992)
13. P. Grefen et al., Dynamic business network process management in instant virtual enterprises. Comput. Ind. **60**(2), 86–103 (Elsevier, 2009)
14. P. Grefen, I. Vanderfeesten, G. Boultadakis, Architecture design of the HORSE hybrid manufacturing process control system. Beta WP Series 518, TU/e (2016)
15. P. Grefen, R. Eshuis, N. Mehandjiev, G. Kouvas, G. Weichhart, *Business Information System Architecture*, Fall 2016 Edition. (Eindhoven University of Technology, Eindhoven, 2016)
16. P. Grefen, S. Rinderle-Ma, S. Dustdar, W. Fdhila, J. Mendling, S. Schulte, Charting process-based collaboration support in agile business networks. IEEE Internet Comput. **22**, 48–57 (IEEE Computer Society, 2018)
17. P. Grefen, I. Vanderfeesten, G. Boultadakis, Developing a cyber-physical system for hybrid manufacturing in an Internet-of-things context, in *Protocols and Applications for the Industrial Internet of Things* (IGI Global, 2018)
18. P. Grefen, R. Eshuis, O. Turetken, I. Vanderfeesten, A Reference Framework for Advanced Flexible Information Systems, in *Advanced Information Systems Engineering Workshops Proceedings*. LNBIP, vol. 316 (Springer, Cham, 2018), pp. 253–264
19. S. Gregor, A.R. Hevner, Positioning and presenting design science research for maximum impact. MIS Q. **37**(2), 337–356 (2013)
20. E. Hofmann, M. Rüsch, Industry 4.0 and the current status as well as future prospects on logistics. Comput. Ind. **89**, 23–34 (2017)

21. IEC, *Enterprise-Control System Integration - Part 1: Models and Terminology*, 2nd edn., vol. 1, 5 vols. (Int. Electrotechnical Commission, Geneva, 2013)
22. Industrie 4.0: Smart Manufacturing for the Future. Germany Trade and Invest (2014)
23. X. Jie-A-Looi, A method to enable ability-based resource allocation for runtime process management in manufacturing, Master thesis, TU/e, 2017. https://tinyurl.com/y75e7q8g
24. P. Kruchten, Architectural blueprints - the "4+1" view model of software architecture. IEEE Softw. **12**(6), 42–50 (1995)
25. S. Li, L. Da Xu, S. Zhao, The Internet of Things: a survey. Inf. Syst. Front. **17**(2), 243–259 (Springer, 2015)
26. D. Lucke, C. Constantinescu, E. Westkämper, Smart Factory - A Step towards the Next Generation of Manufacturing, in *Manufacturing Systems and Technologies for the New Frontier: The 41st CIRP Conference on Manufacturing Systems* May 26–28, 2008, Tokyo, ed. by M. Mitsuishi, K. Ueda, F. Kimura (Springer, London, 2008), pp. 115–118
27. A. Mavin et al., Easy approach to requirements syntax (EARS), in *2009 17th IEEE International Requirements Engineering Conference*, pp. 317–322 (2009)
28. Object Management Group. Business Process Model and Notation 2.0 specification. http://www.bpmn.org/
29. L. Prades, F. Romero, A. Estruch, A. García-Dominguez, J. Serrano, Defining a methodology to design and implement business process models in BPMN according to the standard ANSI/ISA-95 in a manufacturing enterprise. Proc. Eng. Suppl. C **63**, 115–122 (2013)
30. J.B.B. Rogers, F.W. Dewhurst, K.D. Barber, R.L.D.H. Burns, Business process modelling and simulation for manufacturing management: a practical way forward. Bus. Process. Manag. J. **9**(4), 527–542 (2003)
31. J. Romme, S. Hoekstra (eds.), *Integral Logistic Structures. Developing Customer-Oriented Goods Flow* (Industrial Press, New York, 1992)
32. M. Rudberg, W. Joakim, Mass customization in terms of the customer order decoupling point. Prod. Plan. Control **15**(4), 445–458 (2004)
33. P. Runeson, M. Host, A. Rainer, B. Regnell, *Case Study Research in Software Engineering* (Wiley, Hoboken, 2012)
34. S. Schulte, D. Schuller, R. Steinmetz, S. Abels, Plug-and-play virtual factories. Internet Comput. **16**(5), 78–82 (IEEE, 2012)
35. B. Silver, *BPMN Method and Style, with BPMN Implementer's Guide: A Structured Approach for Business Process Modeling and Implementation Using BPMN 2.0* (Cody-Cassidy Press, Aptos, 2011)
36. The HORSE project: http://www.horse-project.eu
37. J. Truijens, A. Oosterhaven et al., *Informatie-Infrastructuur: een Instrument voor het Management* (Kluwer Bedrijfs-wetenschappen, 1990) (in Dutch)
38. I. Vanderfeesten, P. Grefen, Business process management technology for discrete manufacturing. Beta WP Series 486, TU/e (2015). http://onderzoeksschool-beta.nl/wp-content/uploads/wp_486-.pdf
39. Worldwide Manufacturing Predictions for 2015 (IDC Manuf. Press Rel., 2014)
40. S. Zor, F. Leymann, D. Schumm, A proposal of BPMN extensions for the manufacturing domain, in *Proceedings of 44th CIRP International Conference on Manufacturing Systems* (2011)

Chapter 7
Developing a Platform for Supporting Clinical Pathways

Kathrin Kirchner and Nico Herzberg

Abstract Hospitals are facing high pressure to be profitable with decreasing funds in a stressed healthcare sector. This situation calls for methods to enable process management and intelligent methods in their daily work. However, traditional process intelligence systems work with logs of execution data that is generated by workflow engines controlling the execution of a process. But the nature of the treatment processes requires the doctors to work with a high freedom of action, rendering workflow engines unusable in this context. In this chapter, we describe a process intelligence approach to develop a platform for clinical pathways for hospitals without using workflow engines. Our approach is explained using a case in liver transplantation, but is generalizable on other clinical pathways as well.

7.1 Introduction

During complex patient treatments, a lot of investigations have to be conducted by an interdisciplinary medical team. In order to ensure repetition and transparency as well as patient safety in the treatment process, process documentation and quality check are necessary. This is tackled by a clinical pathway. A clinical pathway is a structured, multidisciplinary care plan that defines the steps of patient care for a certain disease in a specific hospital [33]. It is usually built upon a clinical guideline that provides a generic recommendation for a particular disease [9].

Compared to processes in industry, clinical pathways are more flexible as a treatment process varies for each individual patient. Additional therapies might be necessary, and the sequence of treatment steps might change due to interpreting patient-specific data. Furthermore, treatment processes can vary for the same disease

K. Kirchner
Technical University of Denmark, Kgs. Lyngby, Denmark
e-mail: kakir@dtu.dk

N. Herzberg (✉)
SAP SE, Dresden, Germany
e-mail: nico.herzberg@sap.com

© Springer Nature Switzerland AG 2019   143
D. Lübke, C. Pautasso (eds.), *Empirical Studies on the Development of Executable Business Processes*, https://doi.org/10.1007/978-3-030-17666-2_7

Table 7.1 Characterization of the process using the metadata template from Chap. 2

Process name	Liver transplantation pathway
Version	Prototypical version
Domain	Healthcare (liver transplantation)
Geography	Germany
Time	2011–2014
Boundaries	Intraorganizational
Relationship	Event triggered
Scope	Business scope: core
Process model purpose	Documentation, support of treatment process and monitoring
People involvement	No automation
Process language	BPMN2
Execution engine	Own developed solution
Model maturity	Prototypical

for every hospital, although they generally follow a clinical guideline. A standard process-aware information system that follows a standardized treatment process and gives no freedom to medical personnel is therefore not suitable.

Thus, we investigate the following research question: How can a flexible clinical pathway be successfully supported by an IT platform?

As an example case, we selected a rather complex pathway that includes several subprocesses with quite a number of tasks carried out in different departments of the hospital. This case study was conducted in the University Hospital of Jena (UKJ), Germany, during the PIGE (Process Intelligence in Healthcare) research project. Because the hospital is one of the German organ transplantation centers, we focus on the process of liver transplantation (Table 7.1). This process usually runs over a long period (several years), and patients have to enter the hospital several times.

The chapter is structured as follows: Sect. 7.2 describes the modeling step of our case in more detail followed by the explanation of the setup and running of the system. Theory around that topic is discussed in Sect. 7.3. In Sect. 7.4, we give an overview on our approach to establish a process intelligence system in a hospital. The technical evaluation and the user feedback are shown in Sect. 7.5. We conclude our work in Sect. 7.6.

7.2 Case Description and Pathway Modeling

As a case study, liver transplantation as a clinical pathway was selected. This pathway is rather complex: It starts from a first anamnesis of the patient and continues with the evaluation procedure for transplantation, operation, and post-operational treatment till the death of the patient. The treatment process therefore lasts several years. Medical doctors and nurses from different hospital departments are involved, and data about the treatment is saved in several clinical information systems, databases, and other data sources like spreadsheets. The treatment process steps are described in a text document in the hospital. A first step was therefore the description of the liver transplantation treatment in a formal BPMN model.

For modeling this clinical pathway, an interdisciplinary team had to be created that consisted of domain experts who were involved in carrying out the liver transplantation process, as well as of at least one process analyst. The domain experts were medical personnel, but also people from the administration, controlling, and IT departments. They were involved to cover different aspects of the clinical pathway. In order to enhance the comprehension and quality of the pathway model, an appropriate training of medical personnel was necessary. The domain experts needed to understand the basic concepts of process modeling, e.g., the basic elements of the modeling language BPMN 2.0. This was achieved in a warm-up exercise by modeling an ordinary daily process that everybody is familiar with, e.g., the process of getting ready for work in the morning [16].

The treatment process was imaged as a clinical pathway and modeled by the mentioned interdisciplinary team using best practices from a liver transplantation clinical guideline [5], existing instructions regarding patients' treatment, and the knowledge and experience of the domain experts to adjust the guidelines to the hospital's individual circumstances. Tangible Business Process Modeling (t.BPM, [7]) was used to support the collaborative modeling sessions. Based on BPMN, it uses tangible media in the form of plastic tiles symbolizing tasks, events, gateways, and documents that can be written on with a pen. The tiles can be arranged on a table where they can be connected with lines in between. t.BPM enables domain experts to participate in the modeling process. They discuss the process with the process analyst, write on the t.BPM tiles, and arrange or rearrange them on the table (Fig. 7.1). Questions of the process analyst clarify the process, and it can thus be imaged in a correct way. For the modeling, a top-down approach is used. First, the main process is designed which can later be refined in several subprocesses [17].

The resulting t.BPM models needed to be reviewed by the process analyst, adjusted as appropriate, and transferred into an electronically available BPMN model. The similarity between t.BPM and BPMN makes this an easy step. Thus,

Fig. 7.1 Modeling the clinical pathway in t.BPM

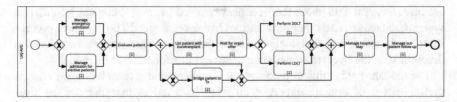

Fig. 7.2 Simplified BPMN model of liver transplantation process (level 1)

transformation into BPMN creates a formal process model. This model may then be verified and refined using the more advanced modeling options of BPMN 2.0. It should then be discussed with the domain experts to see whether the treatment process is really performed in this way and there are no missing steps. Corrections can be made directly in the BPMN model. Figure 7.2 provides a simplified BPMN model on the highest abstraction level for the liver transplantation process.

According to Fig. 7.2, the liver transplantation process can be described in a simplified way as follows: A person with a liver disease can either become a patient in an emergency case or by referral from her/his primary care physician. First, the patient is evaluated for liver transplantation, which comprises several investigations. If the patient needs a liver transplantation, she/he is registered at Eurotransplant, an organization that facilitates patient-oriented allocation and exchange of deceased organs. For patients with hepatocellular carcinoma, a bridging therapy might be necessary to diminish tumor progression while waiting for an organ. Two forms of liver transplantation are possible: deceased donor liver transplantation (DDLT) or living donor liver transplantation (LDLT) where a near relative can donate a part of her/his liver. After operation, the patient has to stay several days in hospital. Afterward, she/he has to come for follow-up investigations to the hospital regularly. The process only ends with the death of the patient.

Once designed, the business process is configured to enable the enactment by selecting the right IT systems, implement a technical solution for certain process steps, or create work instructions for rather manual executed process steps for instance. Completing this modeling phase, the process could be set live and enacted during daily operations. Within enactment, monitoring the process continually is of necessity to react on certain circumstances quickly and also enable proactive measures to avoid foreseeable circumstances.

7.3 Related Work

Raetzell and Bauer [27] as well as Köth et al. [21] described a top-down approach for defining clinical pathways. Before the pathway can be modeled, it has to be discussed which roles are involved. One member from each role should take part in the process modeling activity, creating the to-be process. Before the rollout in the hospital, the pathway should be tested and refined in several trial periods. Process mining has been applied in healthcare as well. Mans et al. mined process models for a hospital based on accounting information [23, 24]. However, there are some domain-specific challenges, i.e., the procedures in healthcare are quite complex, as the number of different activities is very high [23]. A methodology describing a mining-based information gathering process was presented by Rebuge and Ferreira [28].

While executing business processes, i.e., clinical processes, several events, in concrete real-world happenings, occur. Those occurrences are valuable for gaining insights about the processes themselves and their execution. Information about events is essential for business process intelligence applications such as process monitoring (the monitoring of running process instances) and analysis (the analysis of completed process instances) [8, 26]. Business process intelligence is the combination of techniques and methods from business intelligence and business process management aiming at analyzing and improving processes and their management. Business intelligence summarizes all technologies and methods to well-arranged information to support decision making [34]. Depending on the degree of automation of the process execution, the number of observations and representations of these events reaches from complete, e.g., for processes executed by a process engine, over more frequently in semiautomated process execution environments to rather sparse in nonautomated process execution environments, e.g., in healthcare treatment processes.

Kunz et al. proposed an approach for managing complex event processes with BPMN [22]. The authors connect the Event Processing Language (EPL) with the BPMN element directly, e.g., for getting information about attached intermediate events. For the core EPL elements, i.e., SELECT, FROM, and WHERE, a graphical representation in BPMN syntax is given. Appel et al. introduced so-called event stream processing units (SPUs) as an abstraction layer for encapsulating event stream processing in business processes [2]. The concept of SPUs is implemented and shown with a logistics scenario. They extend BPMN to allow SPU modeling [3]. In contrast to this work, the concept presented in our chapter does not introduce new graphical BPMN elements and looks for a possibility to connect events in a more fine-grained manner to the business process model nodes—independent of the model notation. Similarly, Kossak and Geist proposed a communication concept based on events while focusing on the event nodes of BPMN [20].

In contrast to the theoretical works mentioned above, the described approach in this chapter is implemented as a software system. The system is used in analyzing treatments of real patient data in a hospital's day-to-day business. During the PIGE research project from 2011 to 2014, no similar approach nor software was available.

7.4 Application of the Methodology

Establishing a process intelligence system in a hospital where no process engine is in place to control the processes is a huge challenge. In this environment, only some activities of the process models can be made observable and transparent to the process intelligence system. These are the activities where medical staff interacts with the IT infrastructure during the process or even postexecution, e.g., documenting certain treatment steps in an electronic record. In this setting, a monitoring and analysis capability is embedded to make sure the interactions happen according to the models, detect areas of deviations, and enable process improvements.

The presented approach is based on the life cycle of managed business processes [35] starting with the design, followed by configuration, execution, and evaluation. The cyclic approach, depicted in Fig. 7.3, is divided into four phases:

- Phase 1: (Re-)Design and definition of process event monitoring points (PEMPs) of interest (cf. Sect. 7.4.1)
- Phase 2: Configuring the monitoring system to establish the connection between the PEMPs defined in phase 1 and the data located in several sources of the organization's IT system landscape (cf. Sect. 7.4.2)
- Phase 3: Gathering data based on the configuration, defined in phase 2, and monitoring of the process execution with respect to information about performance, e.g., progress, time, and cost (cf. Sect. 7.4.3)
- Phase 4: Evaluating the data gathered in phase 3 regarding conformance between recorded data and designed process model, the correctness of the data, and whether the monitoring system provides the information needed (cf. Sect. 7.5.1)

Fig. 7.3 Life cycle for running a process intelligence solution

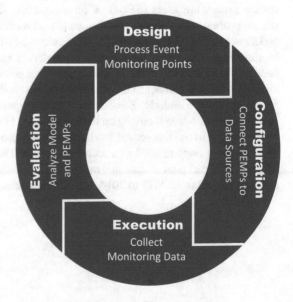

A *process event monitoring point* (PEMP) describes the position within a process model when a particular event is expected. It describes the state transition of a particular process step, e.g., a surgery process step switches from enabled to active. Such state transitions are defined in the corresponding life cycle model of a particular node, i.e., node life cycle model. For instance, for an activity in BPMN— a certain process step—the node life cycle model could be described by the states available, enabled, activated, terminated, and completed [35]. The corresponding state transitions are enable (from state active to state enabled), begin (from state enabled to state activated), terminate (from state activated to state terminated), and complete (from state activated to state completed). Formally, a PEMP is a tuple of the process model it belongs to, the corresponding node, and its state transition [12].

The design phase of the PEMPs could be in parallel with the design of the process model itself. For simplicity reasons, the following sections focus on the design, configuration, execution, and analysis of PEMPs. The modeling of the process models is described in Sect. 7.2.

In the following, it is described how a process intelligence system in the healthcare domain is set up and running. The following steps build up on a BPMN process model. The design of such a model is described in Sect. 7.2.

For this section, a simplified clinical process of the evaluation of a patient with liver disease modeled in BPMN is used as a running example (cf. Fig. 7.4). The process starts with the activity of handling a patient for admission. Afterward, the patient is examined, and a risk assessment is taken. Based on this, it is decided whether a surgery, i.e., a liver transplantation, is possible or not. If the transplantation is possible, the particular procedure is explained to the patient, and the patient is listed at Eurotransplant. Thereafter, the evaluation of the patient is completed, and the patient can be released from hospital.

7.4.1 Design Process Event Monitoring Points

Based on the process models, PEMPs have to be defined by the domain experts that can describe when a certain task started or ended, for instance, [10]. Data for these PEMPs can be later retrieved from the IT infrastructure and help to analyze and monitor the process. For that, events need to be recognized at a point of interest in the process model.

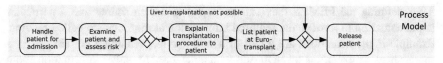

Fig. 7.4 Simplified clinical process of an evaluation of a patient with liver disease modeled in BPMN

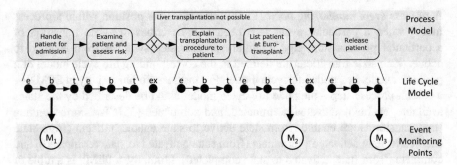

Fig. 7.5 Design and definition of PEMPs

In order to create a fine-granular positing of PEMPs, the PEMPs are not connected to the nodes itself but to their node life cycle models. Therefore, a node life cycle to each node of the process model is assigned to allow a more fine-grained positioning of the points at which an event is expected to happen. For the running example, the activity life cycle—the node life cycle for BPMN activities—adopted from [35] is simplified by combining the states *completed* and *terminated* to one state reached by one state transition called *(t)erminated*. The state transitions *(b)egin* and *(e)nable* remain unchanged (cf. Fig. 7.5). For gateways, the *(ex)cution* is of interest for our example. Nonetheless, the node life cycle could be arbitrary complex so that monitoring on different levels of detail is possible.

Based on the process model with its node life cycle models, the PEMPs of interest are defined. In the particular example, these are the following:

- M_1 describing the beginning of admitting the patient
- M_2 describing the completion of listing the patient at Eurotransplant
- M_3 describing the completion of releasing the patient

Therewith, the modeling resp. design phase ends. In the next step, it is configured which data source is delivering the information for a particular PEMP. Further, it is defined how the correlation of the event information and the concrete process instance works.

7.4.2   Connect PEMPs to Data Sources

After defining the PEMPs, they can be bound to a data source and a particular implementation to retrieve the required information at runtime—so-called binding. Example implementations are a call of a web service, reading a certain cell in a spreadsheet, or executing an SQL query on a database to gather information about process enactment.

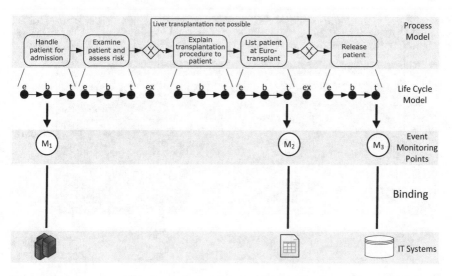

Fig. 7.6 Configuration of PEMPs. The binding is shown in more detail in Fig. 7.7

In the running example, the information about the occurrence of an event is retrieved as follows (cf. Fig. 7.6):

- Information for M_1 comes out of a service-enabled IT system by getting push notifications.
- Information for M_2 is stored in an Excel sheet. Therefore, a pull service needs to be in place to retrieve the particular data and provide it for the process intelligence application.
- Information for M_3 is stored in a database. Therefore, a pull service needs to be in place to retrieve the particular data and provide it for the process intelligence application.

The information from the data sources needs to be correlated to the particular process instance during runtime. The procedure on how to do that is part of the implementation. In hospital environments, this is possible by utilizing unique treatment case IDs and patient IDs that are used consistently across all IT systems. At the moment, this phase requires a high degree of manual effort. But also (semi-) automatic approaches could be used [11].

One PEMP is not restricted to just one data source. In practice, maybe several data sources need to be taken into account for a particular PEMP. For example, two events from different data sources must be present to meet a PEMP (AND) or just one of them (OR). Handling this correlation is part of the implementation as well.

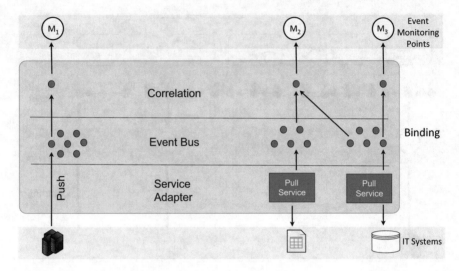

Fig. 7.7 Collecting data for process intelligence

7.4.3 Collect Monitoring Data

The configured PEMPs are used to gather process execution data and discover the occurrence of events during runtime by executing the respective implementation resp. bindings (cf. Fig. 7.7). In the running example, this is the processing of the push notifications of IT systems and the data from the pull services of Excel and the database. Having this event information in place allows the correlation of the event information to the particular process instance and to the PEMP. Further, this allows the combination of several events for a particular PEMP, as shown for M_2 where information from Excel and from the database is required. The technical implementation of such a system is described in [12] and [4]. The extracted and correlated events can be used to visualize the enactment performance in a monitoring user interface or to calculate measurements and KPIs to allow an in-depth analysis.

7.4.4 Monitor and Analyze Processes

Utilizing the event data allows monitoring of the business processes and answering questions like: Which steps were already passed by a certain instance? What are the next process steps? In the following, answering these questions for the running example is shown. We assume that an IT system pushed some information about the admission of a particular patient, i.e., with patient number 123456. Further, an entry in the Excel sheet for administrating the Eurotransplant listing was in place for that

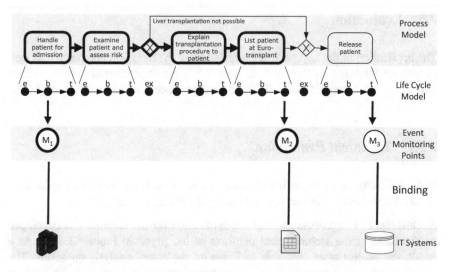

Fig. 7.8 Using data for process intelligence. Bold surrounded nodes are executed already for the particular process instance

patient too. However, the hospital's database did not contain a complete data record about patient 123456's release.

Based on that, the following could be concluded. The conclusions could be visualized as shown in Fig. 7.8:

- The admission of the patient 123456 was completed as M_1 was met.
- The patient 123456 was listed at Eurotransplant as M_2 was met.
- The patient 123456 went through examination and risk assessment as well as through the explanation of the transplantation as M_2 was already met.
- The patient 123456 was able to receive a new liver as M_2 was met. If the transplantation would not be possible, M_2 would not be met.
- The patient is still in the hospital as M_3 is not yet met.

These conclusions are made under the assumption that the patient was handled according to the process definition. Of course, there could be deviations from the model in reality. The quality of the monitoring is dependent on the quality, the quantity, and the position of the PEMPs. An approach for selecting PEMPs for optimal prediction quality is described in [30]. Further, there are approaches in identifying the most probable state of a process instance with sparse execution information [29].

An analysis of process execution data allows answering questions like: How long did an instance need from the start to the end of the process in average? How long did an instance described by certain properties need for a certain process fragment? Further, it could be analyzed with such a system whether the process executions conform to the process model [16].

7.5   Evaluation

The application of the approach is evaluated from the technical perspective as well as with an interview of the users. In Sect. 7.5.1, the implemented system with its components is described in detail. The user experience is elaborated in Sect. 7.5.2.

7.5.1   Technical Evaluation

In the following, the process intelligence system at the University Hospital of Jena (UKJ) is described. This was built up during the PIGE research project.

Architecture The process intelligence application for the hospital was developed on the basis of the technological platform of the Signavio Process Editor. As a result, the project team was able to focus on the actual analysis questions. The questions of user management or client-server communication could be built on existing technology. The system uses its own database for storing and processing the execution data, whose data schema is optimized with regard to the accepted requests. Evaluations have shown that queries can be answered faster if a main memory database is used. Through various importers, the execution data can be imported into this database and enriched. Then, users can send requests (via the browser as a client) to the system, which are processed and answered by the request layer (in the server).

Data Storage The execution data is kept in two related star schemas in the analysis database. Figure 7.9 shows the data schema in a simplified form. At the center of the stars are, on the one hand, model instances (ModelInstance cases), which depict the specific course of a patient during his treatment. On the other hand, concrete activity instances (TaskInstance), i.e., steps during the treatment of a particular patient, are at the center of a second star. In both star schemas, above all, measured

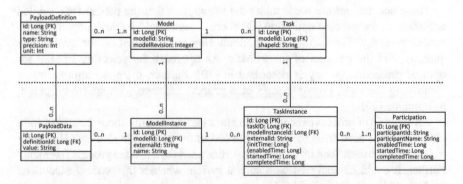

Fig. 7.9 Database schema for storing process intelligence information

timestamps (e.g., the start of a particular procedure) and data accumulated during the treatment (e.g., laboratory values) are detected. In addition, for treatment cases and for individual treatment steps, there is a relationship to the process model as well as to the process steps in the model. Through this, the data can use the process model and the process logic acquired in it during a request to the system.

Data Import During the project, various import mechanisms emerged that had data from different systems loaded (pull) or received (push). The basic difference between the two methods is which system initiates the reading of the data. At first, we worked in the area of pull procedures: data from the Business Warehouse of the UKJ was loaded via Excel and CSV. Similarly, data could be loaded from other clinical systems and SQL databases.

Various evaluations and discussions have shown that the approach to load analytic data works well on the technology, but generates organizational overhead. Therefore, an alternative push method for reading in analysis data that can be used by the applying organization was developed. This is an application programming interface (API) that can be accessed via HTTP requests. Using the API, the user can automatically load process execution data into the analysis system: treatment cases (technical: process instances including all linked data such as time stamps or case-related data) can either be recreated, updated, or deleted from the database.

The general read-in process does not differ in the two variants (pull and push): first of all, all data to be imported is transferred to a format corresponding to the database and stored there. Subsequently, the data is examined for incompleteness and logical errors (e.g., if a patient has been operated without being previously evaluated, there is an error either in the database or in the process). Finally, service-level agreements (SLAs) that are stored in the system can be checked. In the case of the PIGE project, for example, the maximum waiting time of a patient depends on his clinical evaluation data that has to be regularly taken. If the clinical values of the patient get worse, the patient will have a higher rank on the waiting list for a new organ. In the event of a violation of this time for taking his/her data, the patient's ranking may be changed on the waiting list, so it is important that the clinical process monitoring system alerts in advance (e.g., 1 week earlier) to such injuries. The stored SLAs can be expressed using a formal syntax and imported or changed to the system via the API described above.

Analysis and Visualization In order to make the system as easy to use as possible, a concept was finally chosen that is geared to the specific questions of the users. There is one "tab" in the application for each question, which shows the relevant data according to this question. In this way, the consideration of current cases and the analysis of past cases can be separated. Thus, to look at current cases, a table is available that displays all cases including some core data per case. Tables have the advantage of providing both a quick overview and the ability to sort or filter data. If a case is selected, further details and the current course of treatment can be displayed directly on the process model. Figure 7.10 shows how this is implemented in the PIGE prototype. The display of SLA violations allows all cases that are about to violate a deadline to be displayed and then prioritized within the case table.

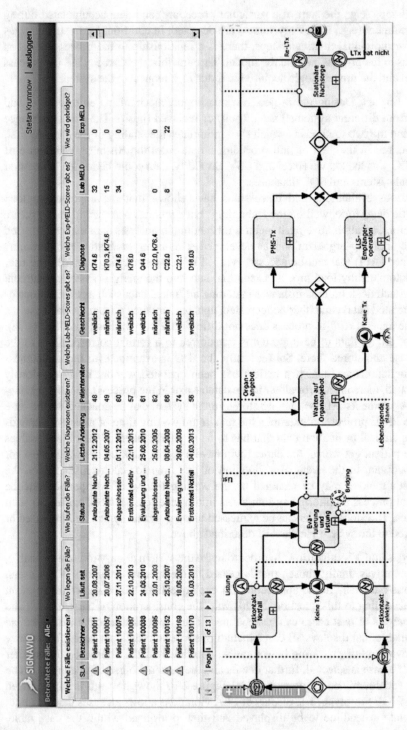

Fig. 7.10 View for monitoring current cases

In Fig. 7.10, the violations of SLAs are indicated by gray and yellow exclamation marks. These can also be used to filter and sort the data.

In addition to the tab for monitoring current cases, there are a number of analysis questions that examine either current or past cases. Examples for this are the following:

- Where is my current case currently?
- How long do the different phases of treatment last?
- How often do patients have to go through a specific step?
- What was the specific value (e.g., the ranking of a patient on the waiting list or one of his laboratory values) at a certain process step?

Figure 7.11 shows an example of such an analysis of processes. Specifically, it is visualized in which treatment phase (at which process step) are currently how many treatment cases. The process model in the lower part of the figure provides further information about the treatment phases. It allows to set filters that limit the number

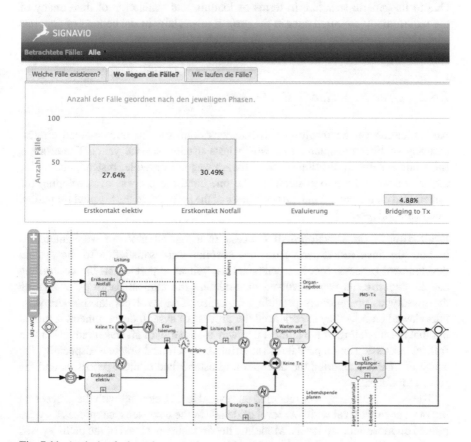

Fig. 7.11 Analysis of where the currently considered cases are

of treatment cases considered. In doing so, the filters work independently of the specifically investigated question—so they can be used in any view, regardless of whether it examines the severity of a disease or the probability of performing a particular path. The filters may be defined over periods of time (e.g., for all cases started after January 1, 2013) or on the basis of treatment data (e.g., the sex of the patient or the nature of the disease). The filters can thus be used to compare different groups of treatment cases with respect to the same question (e.g., how the turnaround time of an activity in 2012 differs from that in 2013). The results in all tabs of the questions are evaluated by a generic request concept in the backend against the imported database. Since the request layer works generically on the basis of query parameters, it is possible to freely configure the interface according to specific questions. Thus, new tabs and filters can be loaded into the application via an API for the analysis of a particular process. Any charts that the application creates can be exported as PNG graphics.

The processing of free text information was transformed in the course of the project by a transfer into structured information and its handling during the analysis. Due to its generic structure in terms of loading and evaluation of data, many of the requirements captured later in the project (especially in the context of concrete analysis questions) could easily be integrated into the system.

7.5.2 User Experience Evaluation

An evaluation of the resulting software was done for the implemented clinical pathway of liver transplantation, which lasts usually several years. Therefore, a full study for the application of the software was not possible. Instead, qualitative interviews were done to evaluate on the one hand the process of developing the system and on the other hand the usefulness of the software in the hospital for patient treatment and research.

Evaluation of the Development Process In a first attempt, we were interested in how the involved experts from the hospital were satisfied with the system development process. Medical personnel as well as experts from the controlling and IT departments were involved in modeling the clinical pathway, evaluating the prototypes or generally providing expertise. The involved stakeholders were interviewed on how they experienced the process of system development. It turned out that the modeling of the clinical pathway together with all stakeholders led to a fruitful discussion and a partial restructuring of the clinical practice. Especially, the usage of t.BPM supported the discussion of established clinical processes and the search for alternatives.

The clinical pathway was modeled on several levels, starting with the process on the most abstract level with low level of detail. In the next steps, subprocesses were refined on more detailed levels. Modeling the first, abstract level of the pathway was a challenge, because every medical doctor or nurse is only involved in some steps of the whole process. Therefore, an overview of the whole pathway had to be discussed and modeled first. Once the overall process was modeled, it was easier to go into the details of each step [16].

After modeling the overall process using t.BPM, the process was then imaged in software using BPMN 2.0. Because the medical personnel were already familiar with the main BPMN symbols and were strongly involved in modeling clinical pathways, they were able to better understand the BPMN models and give a feedback to the process analyst.

Evaluation of the Software Additionally, the medical personnel involved in liver transplantation as well as employees from the controlling and IT departments of the hospital were asked how the developed software could be used in everyday hospital tasks. Data from liver transplantation patients from the years 2004–2013 was extracted from clinical information systems and uploaded into the prototypical software. The data was extracted alongside the defined measurement points and analyzed retrospectively (Fig. 7.11). The technology acceptance model (TAM) [6] was used as a basis for an interview guideline for medical personnel. TAM helps to investigate the intention to use the software based on the usefulness of this technology in practice and the user-friendliness.

The usefulness of the software was measured with the following statements:

- Following the treatment process for a patient is simplified.
- Finding optimization potentials within the treatment process is possible, e.g., by a better planning of investigations.
- New employees can be more easily introduced to the liver transplantation pathway.
- Problems and optimization potentials within the treatment process can be found.
- The software contributes to a higher transparency of the treatment process for both patients and medical personnel.

The user-friendliness was measured via the following:

- The software can be easily learned.
- The software is easy to be used.
- The clinical pathway can be easily understood.

Furthermore, we asked how the software is intended to be used in the clinical everyday procedures and in research. Based on TAM, 15 questions were posed. Additionally, comments or ideas for further development of the system were collected during the interviews.

The interviewees agreed that the software will be useful for clinical everyday procedures. A higher transparency of the treatment process is achieved, because all treatment steps are visualized. Because the software is connected with clinical information systems, it can be seen at every point in time where a patient is currently in the pathway. Such, more structured procedures are achieved for medical doctors as well as for patients, and a higher patient safety is reached [18].

Furthermore, the software was considered as easily usable. People that were more intensively involved in the clinical pathway of liver transplantation or were even involved into the modeling of the clinical pathway evaluated the usability and the time for learning how the software works a bit better than people who did not have experiences with liver transplantation yet.

The future use of the software for research purposes was positively evaluated. Because every treatment step is connected with clinical data for the patients, the software can be also used for explaining to new employees (medical doctors and nurses) the clinical pathway, and data alongside the pathway can be analyzed for research purposes. Additionally, nearly all interviewees agreed that the software would be good for supporting other clinical pathways in the future.

Nevertheless, some improvements would be necessary to adapt the software better to the requirements of the clinical daily routines: additional data like from the laboratory system, CT images, and physicians' letters can open new potentials in the patients' treatment. Therefore, interfaces to other clinical information systems are necessary. Furthermore, the approach to develop software support for clinical pathways can be used also for the software support of other clinical pathways.

7.6   Conclusions and Outlook

In the following, we conclude our work divided by the target audience. We give a summary for researchers and takeaways for practitioners. Last, we give some outlook on further research.

7.6.1   Conclusions for Researchers

In the field of clinical pathways, various research strands are being pursued. Some research is concerned with the creation of clinical pathways. Hu et al. [15] use ontology-based technologies to model domain-specific terms and rules for clinical paths. Clinical paths are not rigid, but can be customized for patients. Alexandrou et al. [1] are developing a system for the design and execution of self-adaptive clinical pathways. Another issue is the study of the impact of clinical pathways on everyday clinical practice. Rotter et al. [32], for example, look at 3000 research articles from eight countries to examine the impact of clinical pathways on professional practice, patients, length of hospital stay, and costs. Researchers, e.g., in [31], also address the question of an effective study design for the evaluation of clinical pathways. Most studies to date are simple before/after studies comparing patients of several years. Differences between patients can be described not only by the use of clinical pathways but also by improving clinical treatment options overtime.

Processes that are executed by humans mainly challenge monitoring and analysis capabilities. As there is no central IT instance for operating these processes, such a capability is not out of the box. However, responsible people are interested at least in some places of interest within a process to get insights about process execution, e.g., time or cost consumed or issued. Therefore, based on the process model, i.e., the clinical pathways, so-called process event monitoring points are defined that are connected with the corresponding IT systems to gather the required data. A process model could help to correlate even more data, e.g., from data objects [14].

There are various solutions to visualize the execution of processes within so-called process or workflow engines. These are usually supplied together with the engine and have a smaller scope of functions than the developed support system for clinical pathways.

7.6.2 Takeaways for Practitioners

The approach described can lead to a better documentation, understanding, and support of a clinical pathway. It can not only be applied on the liver transplantation pathway but adapted to other pathways in other hospitals as well. During evaluation, it was found that the joint revision of a clinical pathway, e.g., the liver transplant pathway, led to a discussion of the previous clinic-internal processes. Through the allocation and evaluation of data along the path, improvement potential could be determined. This has made it possible, for example, to halve the average hospital stay of a living donor before transplantation.

The used questionnaire during evaluation shows that such a platform provides a quick overview of the treatment process, the identification of procedural problems, and the better planning of examinations. Future use for new employee training and data analysis for research purposes is also targeted.

The insights gathered in this use case can also be transferred to other hospital areas, so that an overall social benefit can be derived. This enables more efficient implementation of similar projects at the hospital. The path determined at a clinic can also be used in adapted form in other clinics. This results in comparability and higher transparency of processes.

Not only in healthcare but also in other areas of the economy, there are a variety of processes that are not yet directly supported by software and for process intelligence. Here, too, the scientific findings gathered in this use case can be applied. This was done for the application of production case management, [25], for instance. Further, other modeling notations should be investigated and connected to the process intelligence approach presented.

7.6.3 Outlook

We already investigated how the approach works for another business process modeling notation, i.e., Case Management Model and Notation (CMMN) [13, 19]. It would be interesting to examine in more detail whether CMMN could provide a good support for flexible clinical pathways.

In the future, data from other clinical information systems, especially medical data and doctoral letters, should be included in the system to allow a more in-depth overview of a patient and a more advanced data analysis. Further, it should be investigated more on the level of the events to clarify which scenarios conform with the process and which do not. Furthermore, the clinical data could be analyzed using data mining algorithms. It could be, e.g., predicted whether a patient that has certain lab values or body temperature might get a certain illness or complication after operation.

References

1. D.A. Alexandrou, I.E. Skitsas, G.N. Mentzas, A holistic environment for the design and execution of self-adaptive clinical pathways. IEEE Trans. Inf. Technol. Biomed. **15**(1), 108–118 (2011)
2. S. Appel, S. Frischbier, T. Freudenreich, A. Buchmann, Event stream processing units in business processes, in *Business Process Management* (Springer, Heidelberg, 2013), pp. 187–202
3. S. Appel, P. Kleber, S. Frischbier, T. Freudenreich, A. Buchmann, Modeling and execution of event stream processing in business processes. Inf. Syst. **46**, 140–156 (2014)
4. S. Buelow, M. Backmann, N. Herzberg, Th. Hille, A. Meyer, B. Ulm, T. Yin Wong, M. Weske, Monitoring of business processes with complex event processing, in *11th International Conference on Business Process Management Workshop on "Emerging Topics in BPM"* (Springer, Cham, 2013), pp. 277–290
5. P. Burra, A. Burroughs, I. Graziadei, J. Pirenne, J.C. Valdecasas, P. Muiesan, D. Samuel, X. Forns, Easl clinical practice guidelines: liver transplantation. J. Hepatol. **64**(2), 433–485 (2016)
6. F.D. Davis, Perceived usefulness, perceived ease of use, and user acceptance of information technology. MIS Q. **13**, 319–340 (1989)
7. J. Edelman, A. Grosskopf, M. Weske, L. Leifer, Tangible business process modeling: a new approach, in *Proceedings of the 17th International Conference on Engineering Design, ICED*, vol. 9 (2009), pp. 153–168
8. D. Grigori, F. Casati, M. Castellanos, U. Dayal, M. Sayal, M. Shan, Business process intelligence. Comput. Ind. **53**(3), 321–343 (2004)
9. J.M. Grimshaw, I.T. Russell, Effect of clinical guidelines on medical practice: a systematic review of rigorous evaluations. Lancet **342**(8883), 1317–1322 (1993)
10. N. Herzberg, M. Kunze, A. Rogge-Solti, Towards process evaluation in non-automated process execution environments, in *Proceedings of the 4th Central-European Workshop on Services and their Composition, ZEUS 2012* (2012), pp. 96–102. http://www.CEUR-WS.org
11. N. Herzberg, O. Khovalko, A. Baumgrass, M. Weske, Towards automating the detection of event sources, in *Service-Oriented Computing - ICSOC 2013 Workshops*. Lecture Notes in Computer Science (Springer, Berlin/Heidelberg, 2013)

12. N. Herzberg, A. Meyer, M. Weske, An event processing platform for business process management, in *Enterprise Distributed Object Computing Conference (EDOC)* (IEEE, Vancouver, 2013), pp. 107–116
13. N. Herzberg, K. Kirchner, M. Weske, Modeling and monitoring variability in hospital treatments: a scenario using CMMN, in *Business Process Management Workshops.* Lecture Notes in Computer Science (Springer, Berlin/Heidelberg, 2014), pp. 3–15
14. N. Herzberg, A. Meyer, M. Weske, Improving business process intelligence by observing object state transitions. Data Knowl. Eng. **98**, 144–164 (2015)
15. Z. Hu, J.-S. Li, T.-S. Zhou, H.-Y. Yu, M. Suzuki, K. Araki, Ontology-based clinical pathways with semantic rules. J. Med. Syst. **36**(4), 2203–2212 (2012)
16. K. Kirchner, N. Herzberg, A. Rogge-Solti, M. Weske, Embedding conformance checking in a process intelligence system in hospital environments, in *Process Support and Knowledge Representation in Health Care* (Springer, Heidelberg, 2013), pp. 126–139
17. K. Kirchner, Ch. Malessa, H. Scheuerlein, U. Settmacher, Experience from collaborative modeling of clinical pathways, in *Modellierung im Gesundheitswesen: Tagungsband des Workshops im Rahmen der Modellierung* (2014), pp. 13–24
18. K. Kirchner, H. Scheuerlein, C. Malessa, S. Krummnow, N. Herzberg, K. Krohn, M. Specht, U. Settmacher, Was ein klinischer Pfad im Krankenhaus bringt. Evaluation klinischer Pfade am Uniklinikum Jena am Beispiel des PIGE-Projekts. Chirurgische Allgemeine Zeitung **15**(7–8), 475–478 (2014)
19. K. Kirchner, N. Herzberg, Ein CMMN-basierter Ansatz für Modellierung und Monitoring flexibler Prozesse am Beispiel von medizinischen Behandlungsabläufen, in *Geschäftsprozesse. Von der Modellierung zur Implementierung* (Springer, Berlin, 2017), pp. 127–145
20. F. Kossak, V. Geist, An enhanced communication concept for business processes, in *Enterprise Modelling and Information Systems Architectures* (Gesellschaft für Informatik, Bonn, 2015)
21. H. Köth, K. Miller, M. Lein et al., Entwicklung und Effekte eines standortübergreifenden klinischen Behandlungspfades am Beispiel: "Laparoskopische Prostatektomie". Pers. Med. **1**(3), 173–180 (2009)
22. S. Kunz, T. Fickinger, J. Prescher, K. Spengler, Managing complex event processes with business process modeling notation, in *International Workshop on Business Process Modeling Notation* (Springer, Heidelberg, 2010), pp. 78–90
23. R. Mans, M. Schonenberg, M. Song, W.M.P. Aalst, P. Bakker, Application of process mining in healthcare—a case study in a Dutch hospital, in *Biomedical Engineering Systems and Technologies: International Joint Conference, BIOSTEC'08* (2009), pp. 425–438
24. R. Mans, H. Reijers, M. van Genuchten, D. Wismeijer, Mining processes in dentistry, in *Proceedings of the 2nd ACM SIGHIT Symposium on International Health Informatics* (ACM, New York, 2012), pp. 379–388
25. A. Meyer, N. Herzberg, F. Puhlmann, M. Weske, Implementation framework for production case management: modeling and execution, in *Enterprise Distributed Object Computing Conference (EDOC)* (IEEE, Ulm, 2014), pp. 190–199
26. B. Mutschler, M. Reichert, Aktuelles Schlagwort: business process intelligence. EMISA Forum **26**(1), 27–31 (2006)
27. M. Raetzell, M. Bauer, Standard operating procedures und klinische behandlungspfade, in *OP-Management: praktisch und effizient* (Springer, Heidelberg, 2006), pp. 187–198
28. Á. Rebuge, D.R. Ferreira, Business process analysis in healthcare environments: a methodology based on process mining. Inf. Syst. **37**(2), 99–116 (2012)
29. A. Rogge-Solti, M. Weske, Enabling probabilistic process monitoring in non-automated environments, in *Enterprise, Business-Process and Information Systems Modeling.* LNBIP, vol. 113 (Springer, Berlin, 2012), pp. 226–240
30. A. Rogge-Solti, N. Herzberg, L. Pufahl, Selecting event monitoring points for optimal prediction quality, in *EMISA 2012 - Der Mensch im Zentrum der Modellierung*, Vienna, Sept 13–14, 2012. Proceedings, ed. by S. Rinderle-Ma, M. Weske. Lecture Notes in Informatics, vol. 206 (Gesellschaft für Informatik, Bonn, 2012), pp. 39–52

31. Th. Rotter, L. Kinsman, E. James, A. Machotta, E.W. Steyerberg, The quality of the evidence base for clinical pathway effectiveness: room for improvement in the design of evaluation trials. BMC Med. Res. Methodol. **12**(1), 80 (2012)
32. Th. Rotter, L. Kinsman, E. James, A. Machotta, J. Willis, P. Snow, J. Kugler, The effects of clinical pathways on professional practice, patient outcomes, length of stay, and hospital costs: Cochrane systematic review and meta-analysis. Eval. Health Prof. **35**(1), 3–27 (2012)
33. Th. Rotter, L. Kinsman, A. Machotta, F.-L. Zhao, T. van der Weijden, U. Ronellenfitsch, S.D. Scott, Clinical pathways for primary care: effects on professional practice, patient outcomes, and costs. The Cochrane Library (2013). https://doi.org//10.1002/14651858.CD010706
34. W.M.P. van der Aalst et al., Process mining manifesto, in *7th International Workshop on Business Process Intelligence (BPI 2011)*, Campus des Cézeaux, Clermont-Ferrand (Springer, Berlin, 2012), pp. 169–194
35. M. Weske, *Business Process Management: Concepts, Languages, Architectures*, 2nd edn. (Springer, Berlin, 2012)

Part IV
Quality

Chapter 8
IT-Centric Process Automation: Study About the Performance of BPMN 2.0 Engines

Vincenzo Ferme, Ana Ivanchikj, Cesare Pautasso, Marigianna Skouradaki, and Frank Leymann

Abstract Workflow management systems (WfMSs) are broadly used in enterprise to design, deploy, execute, monitor, and analyze automated business processes. Current state-of-the-art WfMSs evolved into platforms delivering complex service-oriented applications that need to satisfy enterprise-grade performance requirements. With the ever growing number of WfMSs that are available in the market, companies are called to choose which product is optimal for their requirements and business models. Factors that WfMS vendors use to differentiate their products are mainly related to functionality and integration with other systems and frameworks. They usually do not differentiate their systems in terms of performance in handling the workload they are subject to or in terms of hardware resource consumption. Recent trend saw WfMSs deployed on environments where performance in handling the workload really matters, because they are subject to handling millions of workflow instances per day, as does the efficiency in terms of resource consumption, e.g., if they are deployed in the Cloud. Benchmarking is an established practice to compare alternative products, which helps to drive the continuous improvement of technology by setting a clear target in measuring and assessing its performance. In particular for WfMSs, there is not yet a standard accepted benchmark, even if standard workflow modeling and execution languages such as BPMN 2.0 have recently appeared. In this chapter, we present the challenges of establishing the first standard benchmark for assessing and comparing the performance of WfMSs in a way that is compliant to the main requirements of a benchmark: portability, scalability, simplicity, vendor neutrality, repeatability, efficiency, representativeness, relevance, accessibility, and affordability. A possible solution is also discussed, together with a use case of micro-benchmarking of open-source production WfMSs.

V. Ferme (✉) · A. Ivanchikj · C. Pautasso
Software Institute, Faculty of Informatics, USI, Lugano, Switzerland
e-mail: vincenzo.ferme@usi.ch; ana.ivanchikj@usi.ch; cesare.pautasso@usi.ch

M. Skouradaki · F. Leymann
Institute of Architecture of Application Systems (IAAS), University of Stuttgart, Stuttgart, Germany
e-mail: marigianna.skouradaki@iaas.uni-stuttgart.de; frank.leymann@iaas.uni-stuttgart.de

© Springer Nature Switzerland AG 2019
D. Lübke, C. Pautasso (eds.), *Empirical Studies on the Development of Executable Business Processes*, https://doi.org/10.1007/978-3-030-17666-2_8

The use case demonstrates the relevance of benchmarking the performance of WfMSs by showing relevant differences in terms of performance and resource consumption among the benchmarked WfMSs.

8.1   Introduction

As more and more workflow management systems (WfMSs) comply with BPMN 2.0, it is no longer just the functional requirements they satisfy that make them stand out. In addition to modeling and execution of the core BPMN 2.0 language constructs [9], the execution time and computational resource consumption, as well as the scalability and reliability of the system, become important differentiating factors. Improving these performance characteristics could lead to a competitive advantage for both WfMSs vendors and their customers. Firstly, the cycle times of the executed (semi)-automated business processes and the computational resources to enact them, they ought to buy or rent, would decrease. Secondly, they would be able to increase the volume of their operations without trading it off with system latency and downtime. The growing customers' interest in the systems' performance motivates vendors of commercial WfMSs to run internal performance analyses [1, 12]. However, such analyses are not sufficient for comparing different WfMSs due to the lack of standardization of the performed tests and the used workloads. Such comparison is necessary not only to support customers' purchase decisions but also to drive further advancements in the process engineering field. These circumstances prompt our efforts toward the creation of the first standard benchmark for BPMN 2.0 WfMSs. It is well known that standard benchmarks can significantly contribute to the improvement of the technology. Think, for instance, of the case of the Transaction Processing Performance Council (TPC)-C benchmark which improved the performance of the database management systems (DBMSs) from 54 transactions per minute in 1992 to over 10 million transactions per minute in 2010. The representativeness of a standard benchmark is increased when it is performed by an independent, non-biased third party, such as researchers or organized groups of different vendors' representatives, for example, the Standard Performance Evaluation Corporation (SPEC) [29] or the Transaction Processing Performance Council (TPC) [31]. In addition to trustworthiness and vendor neutrality, benchmarks need to satisfy other important requirements as well. They need to be repeatable, representative, portable, scalable, relevant, efficient, accessible, affordable, and simple [11, 22, 24]. Thus, their execution needs to follow a transparent and well-defined methodology, both in terms of the provided technological solutions and of the communication with the involved parties (vendors). In the rest of this chapter, we discuss the challenges that need to be faced when benchmarking the performance of WfMSs (8.2), and we propose a methodological approach for tackling them (8.3). The described methodology is developed in the scope of the BenchFlow project,[1] which targets to design and implement the first standard benchmark to assess and compare the performance of BPMN 2.0-compliant WfMSs. Thus, the main focus of this chapter is to describe a methodology for benchmarking the performance of BPMN 2.0 WfMSs. The methodology includes a technological solution addressing the abovementioned benchmarking requirements and a solution for the implementation of a communication channel with the vendors. The chapter also includes the results of a performance micro-benchmark of three open-source WfMSs as a use case of the application of the described methodology.

8.2 Challenges and State of the Art

Benchmarking WfMSs accomplishing the discussed requirements imposes significant logistic and technical challenges [20]. Logistic challenges mostly relate to managing the communication with the WfMS vendors and finding representative and suitable process models to exercise all capabilities of the WfMSs being benchmarked in a way that is fair and representative of real-world usage scenarios. Attention must be also paid to the definition of suitable and representative performance metrics and key performance indicators (KPIs). Technical challenges refer to the benchmark execution and are impacted by the complexity of the WfMSs. More specifically, they address the automation of the benchmarking process with different systems, the repeatability of tests under the same initial conditions, and the reduction of noise from the environment. A performance benchmark relies on performance testing, which by its nature requires automation, since, depending on the test type (e.g., load testing, stress testing, spike testing, capacity testing), it usually involves instantiation and execution of many instances of tests. This is particularly challenging and costly when systems are complex and the workload used as input in the tests is very diverse. This is also the case with the WfMSs. Addressing such challenges becomes only possible through a carefully designed methodology to manage the entire benchmarking process, from the deployment of the targeted system to its testing and up till the publication of the results. Various research [4, 13] and industrial [29, 31] frameworks have been proposed for the description of benchmarking methodologies applied to diverse applications and environments. The main difference between the existing methodologies in benchmarking and our approach is that the existing solutions do not deal comprehensively with the aforementioned logistic challenges [20]. Toward this direction, the SPEC and TPC organizations propose a different approach in benchmarking software systems. In this approach, the vendors execute the benchmark on their own hardware and send back the results, and the SPEC/TPC committees validate the correctness of the results before publication. Their approach is effective when a standard benchmark is well defined, as demonstrated by the large number of

---

[1] BenchFlow website: http://benchflow.inf.usi.ch.

benchmark results the vendors have submitted for validation. However, a well-defined standard benchmark does not exist yet for WfMSs. Thus, for the time being, we believe that feedback from different vendors through validation of internally calculated results is more effective. The need to create a standard benchmark for WfMSs [23, 33] is frequently discussed in the literature. Gillmann et al. [10] focus on analyzing the differences in performance between a custom-implemented WfMS and a commercial one, by using a simple e-commerce workflow. They measure the throughput of the two benchmarked WfMSs and the impact of the achieved WfMS performance on the database utilization. In their setup, the database is installed on a different server than the one used for the WfMSs. More recently, Bianculli et al. [2] propose a more comprehensive and systematic approach in the SOABench framework. SOABench provides means for the automatic generation, execution, and analysis of testbeds for testing service-oriented middleware performance and in particular Web Services Business Process Execution Language (WS-BPEL) [15] engines. The SOABench framework is used to compare the response time of three WfMSs, namely, ActiveVOS, jBPM, and Apache ODE [2]. They perform different performance tests, using a different number of clients and different think times between subsequent requests. The results have pointed to some scalability limitations of the tested systems. The main limitations of the mentioned related work about WfMS benchmarking, and other works in the area [5, 21, 27], are (1) the small number of WfMSs usually targeted; (2) the non-representativeness of the set of business processes used during the performance tests; (3) the limited number of different kinds of performance tests executed against the WfMSs; (4) the use of generic performance metrics and KPIs, which do not focus on specific characteristics of WfMSs; and (5) the focus on architectural issues of benchmarking frameworks while ignoring the methodological issues. Thus, they do not satisfy the requirements of standard benchmarks, but can be seen more as custom benchmarks.

8.3 BPMN 2.0 WfMS Performance Benchmarking Methodology

As part of the effort of designing and implementing the first standard benchmark for BPMN 2.0 WfMSs, we have designed a methodology to handle the benchmark execution and the interactions with WfMS vendors. This methodology involves vendors in both the definition of the benchmarking workload and the validation of the benchmarking results. We design the methodology around containers, a technology originally developed to ease the automated deployment of Cloud application components. The methodology aims at offering solutions to the aforementioned technical challenges by defining a benchmarking framework which benefits from the emerging containerization technology, ensuring the performance measurements can be repeated. The methodology addresses the logistic challenges by formalizing the interactions between the benchmarking team and the vendors of the WfMSs

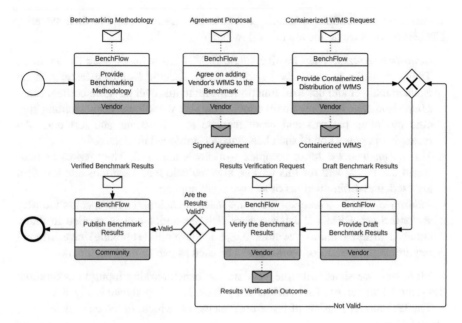

Fig. 8.1 Benchmark choreography

which are being benchmarked. Moreover, it tackles the benchmarking requirements as presented in the introduction. We argue that such formalization will foster vendor collaboration and guarantee public access to the benchmarking results. In our approach, we treat the WfMSs as a black box, as the described methodology is applicable to any WfMS released using containers.

Figure 8.1 presents the methodology using a BPMN choreography. It is comprised of six steps, starting from the sharing of the described methodology with the WfMS vendors, passing through the execution of the benchmark and the validation of the results, and up to the final release of the benchmarking results. The main stakeholders during the execution of the choreography are the benchmarking team and the WfMS vendors. In the following, we discuss each step and the exchanged artifacts.

Provide Benchmarking Methodology We share with the vendors the described benchmarking methodology. By sharing the methodology with vendors, we establish a transparent and jointly held discussion in building the real-world representative workload mixes to be used as part of the benchmark (cf. Sect. 8.3.1) and the method followed for the performance experiments (cf. Sect. 8.3.2). At this stage, we also verify with the vendors the BPMN 2.0 features their WfMSs actually support. Previous research has shown that the supported number of BPMN 2.0 features across the vendors is heterogeneous and not all the language features are always supported. For this reason, we define different kinds of benchmarks, and we discuss with the vendors to identify the ones that are applicable to their systems. The benchmarks we define are the following:

- *Nano-benchmarks:* They involve single BPMN 2.0 features, such as the timer. They are meant to study the performance of specific language features in an isolated manner and use load functions meant to discover possible bottlenecks.
- *Micro-benchmarks:* They involve more complex workflows, implementing specific modeling patterns and more realistic load functions and test data. An example of application of such benchmark is provided in Sect. 8.4.
- *Macro-benchmarks:* More complex workflows are used. They represent realworld use cases; and for this reason, also realistic load functions and test data are used, and different kinds of test types are applied.
- *Industry-driven benchmarks:* They are macro-benchmarks for specific industry sectors. Since BPMN 2.0 has a very rich semantics and is applied in many contexts, different industry sectors (e.g., finance or online booking) have different requirements in terms of workloads to be used as part of the benchmark.

Moreover, we share with the vendors the benchmarking input/process/output (IPO) model we refer to for benchmarking WfMSs, as it is shown in Fig. 8.2.

The IPO model consists of three main elements, which, in the case of WfMSs, are as follows:

1. *Input:* The workload model, that is, the process model(s) comprising the workload mix, the test data, the probabilistic data generator, and the load function. They are influenced by the test types. More details are discussed in Sect. 8.3.1.

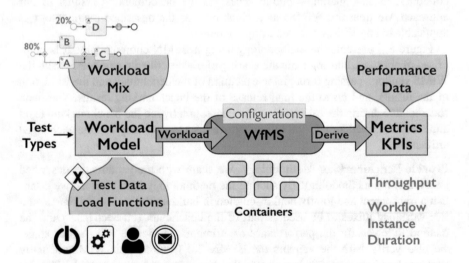

Fig. 8.2 WfMS input/process/output model

2. *Process:* The execution of the benchmark by means of an instance of the workload model, against the containers encapsulating the WfMS as well as its configuration. More details are available in Sect. 8.3.2.
3. *Output:* The performance metrics and KPIs computed based on the raw data generated during the benchmark, as described in Sect. 8.4.3.

Agree on Adding Vendors' WfMSs to the Benchmark The agreement mainly consists of discussion about the workload mixes to be used as part of the benchmark, the metrics and KPIs to be computed, the stable release version of the WfMS to be included, the availability of containerized version of the WfMS, and an agreement for publishing benchmarking results reporting vendors' product names; and to avoid an infinite loop, it is also discussed what can be considered as nonvalid results requiring a rerun of the experiments. The agreement ensures we are providing a relevant and vendor-neutral benchmark, since we transparently share all the information and methodology with all the involved vendors.

Provide Containerized Distribution of the WfMS We require a containerized distribution of the WfMS, or assistance in realizing a containerized version of the same. The containerization technology we currently support is Docker,[2] the de facto standard in this field. Docker helps us fulfill some of the benchmarking requirements. In particular, it enables the portability of the deployment process of the WfMSs across different infrastructures in the same way, thus simplifying the repeatability. Moreover, it also enhances the possibility to automate the performance experiments, thus improving the affordability and the efficiency of the benchmarking process. During the performance experiments, we use at least two containers for better isolation of the WfMS performance. One is dedicated to the WfMS and one to the DBMS it relies on. The DBMS container can refer to publicly available ones. As part of the containerized distribution, we also require the availability of a ready-to-use default configuration and the possibility to configure at least the DBMS type and connection, the logging level, and the WfMS itself.

In addition to the support of given BPMN features to be able to execute the models as part of the workload mix, a WfMS needs to provide certain APIs in order to be included in the benchmark. These APIs are required to automate the interaction with the WfMS during the performance benchmarking experiments [8]. We divide the required APIs into core and non-core ones as represented in Table 8.1. The core ones are mandatory to be supported by the WfMS that will be included in the benchmark, because they are the minimum set of APIs needed for automation of the interaction with the WfMS. The non-core APIs instead enable the possibility of executing more complex benchmarks, involving more features of BPMN 2.0 such as user tasks, web service interaction, and events. Furthermore, in order to enable the computation of performance metrics, we need to access the performance data of the WfMS, so this is a requirement toward the WfMS vendors.

---

[2]http://docker.com.

Table 8.1 WfMS APIs for benchmarking

	Functionality	Min. response data
Core APIs		
Initialization APIs	Deploy a process	Deployed process ID
	Start a process instance	Process instance ID
Non-core APIs		
User APIs	Create a user	User ID
	Create a group of users	User group ID
	Access pending tasks	Pending tasks' IDs
	Claim a task[a]	
	Complete a task	
Event APIs	Access pending events	Pending events' IDs
	Issue events	
Web service APIs	Map tasks to web service end points	

[a]Optional depending on the WfMS implementation

Provide Draft Benchmark Results Once we have the containerized version of the WfMS, we perform the benchmark using the BenchFlow framework described in Sect. 8.3.2 and provide the vendors with a draft of the benchmarking results. The benchmark results are always enriched with all the information needed to dig into the obtained results and replicate the experiments. Part of the provided data are the instance of the workload model, the complete configuration of the hardware used during the experiments as well as the configuration of the containers, and a comprehensive description of the produced metrics and KPIs.

The vendor has then the opportunity to *verify the benchmark results*, in terms of correct configuration of the WfMSs or correct input settings or measurements; and in case it is necessary, we or the vendor can repeat some of the experiments. We iterate the process until the results are validated by the vendor, based on the validation criteria stated in the signed agreement, and than we *publish the benchmark results*.

8.3.1 BPMN 2.0 Representative Workload Mixes

The Workload Model for WfMS In this section, we describe the components of a workload model, i.e., the package of components that should be issued to the WfMS for the performance tests. The workload model for benchmarking WfMSs could be compared to the one of a session-based application [32]. In both cases, the workload mix contains different types of transactions and different roles of users that execute them by following various behavior models. The concept of executing transactions, which can be compensated if an error occurs, is also present in both cases. The implementation and behavior of the workload model components are dependent on

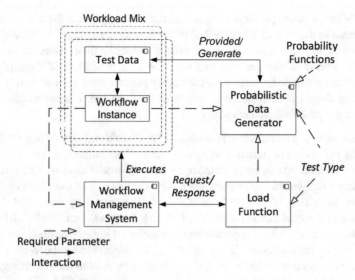

Fig. 8.3 Workload model components

the test type performed (e.g., load test, stress test, soak test [18]). The interactions among the workload model components are presented in Fig. 8.3.

- *Workflow instance* defines the executable instances of a small number of representative process models that are given as input to the targeted performance test. This set of process models is referred to as workload mix. The process models of the workload mix are representative, synthetic, process models.
- *Test data* are given as input for starting a workflow instance or are inserted/produced during the execution of the workflow instance as part of the performance test. The test data may relate to the evaluation of gateway conditions, messages for invoking web services, or persistent data required for completing a task.
- The *probabilistic data generator* generates any type of test data needed for the workflow instance execution, based on user's knowledge as an input. For example, dummy web services or dummy script tasks are generated through this component. If needed, the data are affected and generated with respect to a probability function, which defines the probability with which an exclusive or inclusive gateway will pass the control flow to each one of its outgoing branches. For example, a simple probability function may define that for every split exclusive gateway with two branches, the control will be passed to either branch with a 50% probability.
- The *load function* drives the execution of the test. Depending on the test type (e.g., load test, stress test, soak test), it defines the frequency of instantiating new workflow model instances, the number of users interacting with them, their think times, etc.

The following example summarizes the interactions between the aforementioned components in the case of a load test. Before running the system, we should deploy all the available process models on the WfMS and make them ready for execution. At the beginning of the performance test, the load function will determine how many instances should be instantiated for every process model in the workload mix. Before and during the execution of any workflow, the test data are produced with respect to the probabilistic data generator.

Definition of a Representative Workload Mix For the validity of the benchmark, especially in the case of macro- and industry sector benchmarks, it is very important that the workload mix is representative of the real-world models. Collecting and synthesizing real-world models has been identified as one of the challenges faced when benchmarking WfMS performance, to be addressed by static and dynamic analysis of real-world model collections [20, 27]. Given the fact that BPMN 2.0 is a very rich and complex language, the features included in the workload mix models need to be carefully selected. They should (1) be supported by the WfMS [9], (2) stress the performance of the WfMS, (3) be frequently used in real-world processes, and (4) be in line with the targeted performance tests and KPIs. To ensure that the workflow instance artifact of the workload mix is representative, we follow an iterative approach for its development and evaluation, referred to as process synthesizing, sketched in the top part of Fig. 8.4 and relying on Eclipse Modeling[3] and Drools[4] tools.

The overall goal of the process synthesizing methodology is to define a set of representative, synthetic, executable process models that will be then used as the workload mix input to the benchmark. These process models might reflect the general usage of a WfMS or be domain specific, as complex, domain-specific, or industry-driven test cases might require as input process models that comply with specific structural or behavioral criteria. In either case, these process models are synthesized in accordance with the process synthesizing method which uses as input a collection of BPMN 2.0 process models. The component Recurring Structures Discovery applies subgraph isomorphism testing techniques to detect a set of recurring structures in the collection. The complete definition and implementation of this methodology are described in a PhD thesis by Skouradaki [25]. The extracted recurring structures are stored and semantically annotated according to their structural characteristics and frequency of appearance [26]. Upon request, specific structures are selected by the component with respect to user-defined, benchmark-related criteria. The benchmark-related criteria can refer to size, structural metrics, metrics of external interaction, data handling and complexity [3, 17], or rate of appearance of a recurring structure [26]. Through the conduction of experiments, we define the correlation between the BPMN 2.0 language features and the performance of the WfMS, in order to consistently annotate the detected recurring structures. We

---

[3]https://www.eclipse.org/modeling/.

[4]https://www.drools.org/.

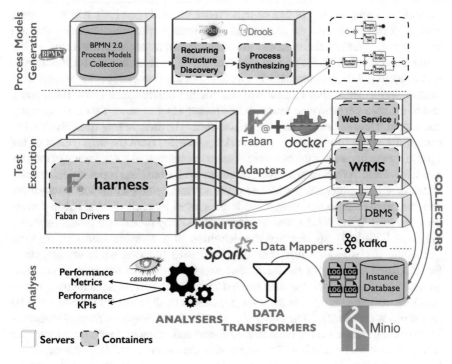

Fig. 8.4 Benchmarking framework

use that annotation to drive the meaningful selection of a workload mix with respect to the types of models whose performance test we want to target. The selected recurring structures are then combined by the process synthesizing component to synthesize representative and executable BPMN 2.0 process models that are given as input to the benchmark [28]. The executability of the synthesized BPMN 2.0 process models constitutes a challenging part, as every WfMS requires a different serialization in order to execute a model and might support a different set of BPMN 2.0 language features. What is more, the probability with which a path of the control flow graph is followed, as well as the execution duration of the process model, should be defined in such a way that the model follows a behavior which is representative for a given model collection.

8.3.2 Benchmark Execution and Results

In order to automate the execution of WfMS performance benchmarking so that reliable and repeatable results can be guaranteed, we built the BenchFlow framework. Although many [18] frameworks for executing performance tests already exist, they usually are general purpose and do not focus on a specific kind of system under test.

BenchFlow builds on top of one of these frameworks, Faban [30], that guarantees reliable performance test execution and empowers it with functionalities that are specific to the WfMSs. It also makes use of Docker for managing and automating the deployment of the WfMSs and all the BenchFlow services needed for monitoring and collecting data, as presented in Fig. 8.4. Docker introduces some overhead in system performance that can be harmful for the performance tests. However, a recent reliable performance analysis of Docker [6] has shown that, if carefully configured, Docker reaches near-zero overhead. The BenchFlow framework takes care of the entire life cycle of benchmarking WfMSs, from the deployment of the system for the purpose of the benchmark up to the automated computation of metrics and KPIs. Each WfMS uses a custom mechanism for business process deployment, instantiation, and interaction with tasks. We abstract common interaction interfaces and then map them to the actual ones implemented by each WfMS. Faban drivers issue the load to the WfMS, and we expose its API by means of a domain-specific language (DSL) [7], to simplify the definition of a reusable workload package containing the workload mix, test data, and load function while encapsulating the simulated behavior of the interacting users and external services. BenchFlow automatically collects all the data needed to compute performance metrics and to check the correct execution of the tests (e.g., errors by different WfMS components) and stores it on MinIO.[5] The client-side data (e.g., the response time of workflow instances start requests) are collected by Faban and integrated with the server-side data collected by BenchFlow. The server-side data is collected from the execution logs from all the different containers realizing the WfMS deployment, as well as from the DBMS populated by the WfMS during the test execution. In order to avoid interferences during the test execution, we collect all the data only after the WfMS completes the execution of the issued load. This is determined by first monitoring the CPU utilization of the running Docker containers and then, once the containers are idle, by checking if the number of completed workflow instances matches the number of instances started by the load driver. We exploit the logs to identify execution errors and container statistics (obtained through Docker stats API[6]) and the DBMS data to compute the performance metrics included in BenchFlow. Each WfMS has its own internal representation and structure for the logs data and the database schema. In order to define the metrics computation and the performance analysis only once for all WfMSs, we map these logs and data to a uniform representation. When transformed, the performance data are stored in a Cassandra[7] database, and the performance metrics and KPIs are computed. Cassandra is a NoSQL distributed DBMS for storing and accessing performance data in order to compute metrics on top of them. The computation, as well as the

---

[5]https://www.minio.io/.

[6]https://docs.docker.com/engine/reference/api/docker_remote_api_v1.23/#get-container-stats-based-on-resource-usage.

[7]http://cassandra.apache.org.

data transformation, is performed by relying on Apache Spark,[8] a fast, general-purpose engine for large-scale data processing. The orchestration of the performance test execution, the data collection, and the performance data analysis is delegated to Apache Kafka,[9] a publish-subscribe messaging framework. We have introduced this state-of-the-art framework to decouple the benchmark execution managed by the Faban Harness from the performance metrics computation and thus pipeline the gathering of performance data with the corresponding analytics, which can be performed offline.

8.4 WfMS Micro-Benchmarking: A Use Case

It is up to the benchmark designer to decide on the workload to be used as input to the system under test (e.g., the WfMS) and the type of metrics to be calculated and analyzed based on the obtained performance data. To showcase a sample micro-benchmark, in this section we describe the experiments we have run on three open-source WfMSs,[10] and we analyze the obtained results. For each of the workloads that are going to be described and each of the WfMSs, we executed three trials, allowing a maximum standard deviation of 5%, in order to ensure consistent behavior of the WfMS under test.

8.4.1 Workload Definition

When benchmarking a WfMS, the workload is defined by the business processes which are used in the workload mix, the frequency of workflow instance instantiation which is defined in the load function, the execution probability of the control flow paths which is defined by the probabilistic data generator, and the test data, if such is used in the selected business processes that comprise the workload mix.

8.4.1.1 Workload Mix

The set of workload mixes used in our experiments is focusing on the basic control flow and structural workflow patterns (cf. Fig. 8.5) that can be expressed by BPMN 2.0 [34]. These patterns can be seen as the most frequently used atomic operations in a WfMS. When designing the set of workload mixes, we have adhered to the

---

[8]http://spark.apache.org.

[9]http://kafka.apache.org.

[10]The publication of the results has not been explicitly confirmed by the vendors; thus, all of the participating systems under test are kept anonymized.

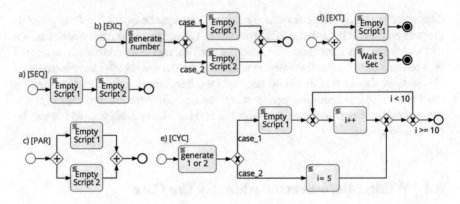

Fig. 8.5 Individual workflow patterns

following constraints: (1) The implementation of the process models needs to be as simple as possible; thus, the interactions with external participants or systems have been omitted. In this sense, all tasks have been implemented as script tasks, while human tasks and web service invocations have been excluded. This constraint aims to stress the process navigator, since the script tasks lead to the automated execution of the process model, by utilizing an embedded application logic that is co-located with the engine. (2) Script tasks need to be empty unless the implementation of the workflow pattern dictates otherwise. In this case, we are implementing the minimal amount of code and producing the minimum amount of data needed for the automated execution of the process model. (3) The execution probability of each outgoing branch of a gateway needs to be equal. (4) The models need to comply with the BPMN 2.0 standard [14] guidelines. Thus, we combine the exclusive choice workflow pattern with the simple merge [EXC] and the parallel split workflow pattern with the synchronization [PAR] workflow pattern (cf. Fig. 8.5).

More specifically, we have conducted six experiments, each comprised of three trials, using a different workload mix for each experiment. The following is a description of the set of workload mixes used in the experiments:

1. the *Sequence flow pattern* [SEQ], which consists of two sequential empty script tasks.
2. the *Exclusive choice and simple merge patterns* [EXC], which starts with a script task that randomly generates the number 1 or 2 with uniform probability. The upper or the lower branch is chosen with respect to the generated number. In both cases, an empty script task is executed.
3. the *Parallel split and synchronization patterns* [PAR], which consists of two empty script tasks that are executed in parallel.
4. the *Explicit termination pattern* [EXT], which comprises two branches that are executed in parallel. When the first branch terminates, it interrupts the execution of the remaining active branches. In our implementation, the upper branch contains an empty script task (Empty Script 1) and the lower branch a script task

with a timer of 5 s (Wait 5 s). By assigning the value of 5 s, we guarantee that the Empty Script 1 will be the fastest; thus, it will terminate first and consequently interrupt the execution of the Wait 5 s task.

5. the *Arbitrary cycle pattern* [CYC], which represents a structure with loops. In our implementation, the cyclic pattern has two entry points, at the second and the third exclusive gateways. It starts with a script task that assigns the number 1 or 2 to the variable x with uniform probability and initializes the variable $i = 0$. The first exclusive gateway evaluates the value of x and passes the control flow to the upper branch (if x equals to (1)) or to the lower branch (if x equals to (2)). The upper branch executes the Empty Script 1 and then increments the value of the variable i. This path is followed until the variable i reaches 10. Respectively, the lower branch executes the $i = 5$ script task. In order to achieve a differentiated but yet deterministic behavior of the executions, we have implemented the script $i = 5$ to assign the number 5 to the variable i. Thus, when the lower branch is followed, the cycle will be repeated fewer times compared to when the upper branch is followed.

6. a *Mix of patterns* [MIX], which is a mix of the process models defined in the previous five workload mixes expressing different workflow patterns. We have used uniform distribution to determine the contribution of each pattern to the mix.

When defining the workload mix of the experiments, we have targeted two research questions:

RQ1: How can the different WfMSs handle execution of many instances of the same workload pattern ([SEQ] or [EXC] or [EXT] or [PAR] or [CYC]), so that a comparison can be made of how the characteristics of the different workflow patterns influence the performance of the WfMSs?

RQ2: How is the performance of the WfMS affected by executing simultaneously a mix of patterns, which is closer to real-world execution, than the simultaneous execution of individual patterns?

8.4.1.2 The Load Function

The load function is defined by the load time (T_l), the ramp-up period (T_r), the number of instance producers (u), and the think time (t). We let each experiment have a *load time* of 10 min, which we find suitable for a micro-benchmark, with 30 s of *ramp-up period*. The ramp-up period defines the time it takes for all simulated instance producers to become active. Once an instance producer becomes active, it starts sending requests to the WfMS to instantiate workflow instances. In the experiments we performed, we set the limit of up to one request (t) being sent per second, provided that the response time of the system is low. This is called the *think time*, and it refers to the waiting time between a new request and the moment when the response for the previous request has been received. Since the purpose of our experiments was scalability testing, we initially set the *number of instance producers* to 1500; and if there were indications that the WfMS could not handle the load, we repeated the experiments with a lower number of instance producers. Having said that, the expected maximum number of started workflow instances (wi) can be computed using the following formula, $\sum_{j=1}^{u-1} \frac{T_r}{u} tj + \left(T_l - T_r\right)$. The actual number depends on the response time of the WfMS and the available resources on the servers where the instance producers are deployed. Based on our experience, we set a connection time-out period (T_o) of 20 s, which has proved to be sufficient to indicate if the WfMS cannot handle the issued load.

8.4.1.3   Probabilistic Data Generator

Given the simplicity of the patterns, the data that needs to be generated for the defined workload mixes is rather simple and is only necessary for the [EXC] and the [CYC] patterns. It is based on script tasks which randomly choose a number and initialize or augment a variable. For the exclusive gateway in the [EXC] pattern, a script randomly generates the number 1 or 2, to be used for the condition control at the gateway. The same is applied for the first exclusive gateway in the [CYC] pattern. To generate the data for the second exclusive gateway in the [CYC] pattern, a script augments a previously initialized variable by 1 or sets it to 5, so that the gateway condition directs the flow to the loop until the variable reaches the value of 10.

8.4.2   Environment Setup

In addition to the utilization of a well-established framework, the reproducibility of a benchmark relies heavily on the detailed description of the configuration of the benchmark environment. In these experiments, the BenchFlow framework is used for measuring the performance of three open-source WfMSs. The WfMSs under test were chosen as they satisfy the following criteria: they are broadly accepted by the industry; they have a large user community; and they are tested against conformance with the BPMN 2.0 standard [9]. Moreover, two out of three of the selected engines facilitate the reproducibility of the benchmark as they provide Docker containers with vendor-suggested configurations. Going into detail about the system configurations, we benchmark these WfMSs on top of Ubuntu 14.04.01, using Oracle Java Server 7u79. WfMS A and WfMS C were deployed on top of Apache Tomcat 7.0.62, while WfMS B was deployed on top of WildFly 8.1.0.Final. All these WfMSs utilize a MySQL Community Server 5.6.26 as a database management system (DBMS), installed in a Docker container.[11] We deployed WfMS B and WfMS C through their official Docker images, and we followed the vendor-

---

[11]MySQL Docker Hub: https://hub.docker.com/_/mysql.

suggested configurations. We configured WfMS A as suggested in the vendor's website, and we deployed it using the most popular Docker image. We updated the dependencies on the operating system and Java to be identical to the other two WfMSs, to reduce possible discrepancies introduced by using different versions. Every WfMS was given a maximum Java heap size of 32 GB, and the connection to the DBMS used the MySQL Connector/J 5.1.33 with 10 as the value for the initial thread pool size, 100 the maximum number of connections, and 10 minimum idle connections. For WfMS A, we enabled the Async executor as suggested on the vendor's website. The other configurations were as provided in the mentioned Docker images. In particular, all the WfMSs log a complete history of the workflow execution to the database (i.e., details on the execution of the workflow instances, their start and end times, as well as references to the corresponding reference process models). The containers were run by using the Docker's host network option. This option enables the containers to directly rely on the network interfaces of the physical machine hosting the Docker Engine and has been proven not to add performance overhead in the network communications [6]. The benchmark environment was distributed on three servers: one for Faban that executes the instance producers, one for the WfMS, and one for the database of the WfMS that maintains the execution information of the workflows. All the servers use Ubuntu 14.04.3 LTS (GNU/Linux 3.13.0-33-generic x86_64) as operating system and the Docker Engine version 1.8.2. The WfMS was deployed on 12 CPU Cores at 800 Mhz, 64 GB of RAM. In this way, we ensure that the machine where we deploy the instance producers (64 CPU Cores at 1400 MHz, 128 GB of RAM) can issue sufficient load to the WfMS and the database (64 CPU Cores at 2300 MHz, 128 GB of RAM) and handle the requests from the WfMS. For the interaction of the WfMS with the DBMS and of the instance producers with the WfMS, we use two different dedicated networks of 10 GB/s. Since the BenchFlow environment guarantees a repeatable benchmark, any future test that follows the suggested configuration and uses the same or a comparable hardware should reproduce results with no significant statistical difference.

8.4.3   Metrics

For each experiment trial execution, we collected the resulting raw data per workload and processed them to obtain meaningful metrics. From the collected raw data, we removed the first 1 min, to ensure that the analyzed results corresponded to a stable state of the WfMS under test. We distinguished between performance and resource consumption metrics. The raw data for the calculation of the performance metrics was gathered from the WfMS DB, while the raw data for the calculation of the resource consumption metrics was gathered from the Docker stats API.[12]

---

[12]Docker stats API: goo.gl/IlzLMn.

The statistics over the metrics are weighted due to the fact that each experiment is comprised of three trials, i.e., each workload is executed three times, due to the nondeterministic behavior of the WfMS. The weighting is based on the number of workflow instances per trial for the performance metrics and on the number of data points per trial for the resource consumption metrics. The metrics used in this use case are not exhaustive. Other metrics can be added in different use cases depending on the benchmark end users' needs.

8.4.3.1 Performance Metrics

The performance of the WfMS can be analyzed at workflow instance execution level or at an experiment level.

At *workflow instance level*, we calculated different statistics over the workflow instance duration, i.e., the time difference between the start and the completion of the workflow instance in milliseconds. They include the weighted average duration, as well as the median (the middle number in the sorted duration), the mode (the most frequent duration), and the minimum and the maximum duration across trials. To increase the precision of the weighted average duration metric, we computed also the 95% confidence interval (CI) as well as the standard deviation (Sd.). The CI sets up a range of likely values for the workflow instance duration in which we can be 95% confident [19]. Finally, we also calculated the quartiles of the duration (Q1, Q2, and Q3), which show under which value does 25%, 50%, and 75% of the data fall [19].

At *experiment level*, we calculated the average number of executed workflow instances among the trials, as well as the average throughput, i.e., the number of executed workflow instances per second [16]. We also computed the experiment duration, i.e., the average duration of the trials (in seconds).

8.4.3.2 Resource Consumption Metrics

The resource consumption metrics refer to analysis of the utilization of the CPU and RAM during the workload execution. We computed the weighted average usage of CPU (%) and RAM (MB); and due to their continuous nature, to calculate the expected value of the CPU and RAM total usage per trial, we used the trapezoidal rule on the integral overtime – $avg(itg(CPU))$, $avg(itg(RAM))$ [19]. To get further details on how efficiently the WfMS allocates the memory, we calculated the ratio between the $itg(CPU)$, $itg(RAM)$ and the product of the $max(CPU)$, $max(RAM)$ and the number of data points used to calculate that integral, respectively, for CPU and RAM. We called this metric efficiency and calculated its weighted average among the trials $wavg(e(CPU))$, $wavg(e(RAM))$. Its allowed values are between 0% and 100%, where values closer to 100% point to balanced resource use with no significant changes overtime. We also looked at the maximum CPU and RAM usage among the trials.

8.4.4   Experiment Results

In this subsection, we are going to present and discuss the experiment results.

8.4.4.1   Results Analysis

A full overview of the statistics [19] computed for every workload and for every WfMS is shown in Tables 8.2, 8.3, and 8.4, while we visualize the results of the average duration (milliseconds) (Figs. 8.6 and 8.7) and the percentages (%) of the weighted average efficiency of the CPU (Figs. 8.8 and 8.9) and RAM (Figs. 8.10 and 8.11) usage. More precisely, all tables contain data of the average measurements calculated based on the maximum load each WfMS could sustain, where the load corresponds to the number of concurrent instance producers. Under some circumstances, the WfMS could not sustain the predefined maximum load of 1500 concurrent instance producers. In these cases, we have reduced the load accordingly. The average total number of workflow model instances (#wi) each WfMS was able to complete, the average total duration (in seconds) per experiment, and the average throughput are also shown in Tables 8.2, 8.3, and 8.4 which show statistics that accompany the metrics calculated for the CPU and RAM usage, respectively.

Sequence Flow Pattern [SEQ]

The average duration of the [SEQ] workflow pattern was 0.39 ms for WfMS A, 6.39 ms for WfMS B, and 0.74 ms for WfMS C. The brief duration of this workflow pattern is accompanied by a medium average usage of the CPU which is 43.04% for WfMS A, 6.08% for WfMS B, and 36.80% for WfMS C. Respectively, the weighted average CPU efficiency is 67% for WfMS A, 28% for WfMS B, and 64% for WfMS C. In this case, we observe that a medium CPU usage is followed by a medium efficiency, which means there was a small number of fluctuations in the CPU usage. Regarding the throughput, we observe a very low mean throughput for WfMS B (63.31 wi/s), while for the rest of the WfMSs, the throughput ranges on similar values. Generally, the [SEQ] workflow pattern has the highest throughput among all the WfMSs under test. The memory utilization is 11,783.66 MB for WfMS A; WfMS B needed an average of 2923.75 MB and WfMS C 797.96 MB of RAM. In this case, the usage efficiency of the RAM is high and ranges from 80% (WfMS C) to 96% for WfMS B.

Exclusive Choice and Simple Merge Patterns [EXC]

In this workflow pattern, the first script task generates a random number, with respect to which, the exclusive gateway evaluates its condition. This condition seems to not notably impact the performance, as the values of the duration times are slightly higher than those of the [SEQ] workflow pattern. Specifically, we have an average duration time of 0.48 ms for WfMS A, 9.30 ms for WfMS B, and 0.85 ms for WfMS C. Concerning the CPU and RAM utilization and the efficiency in the resource usage, there is a similar behavior to the [SEQ] workflow pattern for all WfMSs.

Table 8.2 Performance workflow instance and experiment metrics

	Workflow instance execution duration statistics (ms)									Experiment execution statistics			
	Average and CI (=0.95)	Median	Mode	Min.	Max.	Sd.	Q1	Q2	Q3	Max load (IPs)	#Workflow instance (wi)	duration (s)	Throughput (#wi/s)
SEQ													
A	0.39 ± 0.01	0	0	0	561	1.70	0	0	1	1500	781,736	540	1447.66
B	6.39 ± 0.43	6	6	4	82	1.21	6	6	7	1500	35,516	561	63.31
C	0.74 ± 0.01	1	1	0	682	2.29	0	1	1	1500	786,664	540	1456.79
EXC													
A	0.48 ± 0.01	0	0	0	485	2.07	0	0	1	1500	775,455	540	1436.03
B	9.30 ± 0.05	9	9	6	131	2.11	9	9	10	1500	27,805	567	49.04
C	0.85 ± 0.01	1	1	0	627	2.51	0	1	1	1500	765,274	540	1417.17
EXT													
A	14.10 ± 0.06	11	10	5	858	13.45	10	11	14	1500	770,229	540	1426.35
B	2622.00 ± 237.68	5012	11	8	5047	2500	13	5012	5016	1500	1703	4498	0.38
C	0.40 ± 0.01	0	0	0	74	1.03	0	0	1	1500	784,614	539	1455.68
PAR													
A	13.29 ± 0.06	10	8	4	456	11.99	9	10	13	1500	772,013	540	1429.65
B	10.06 ± 0.06	10	10	7	145	2.22	9	10	10	1500	27,718	567	48.89
C	0.70 ± 0.01	1	1	0	691	2.10	0	1	1	1500	773,883	540	1433.12
CYC													
A	6.23 ± 0.13	2	2	0	478	18.68	1	2	3	800	347,770	540	644.02
B	39.36 ± 0.40	43	50	25	146	9.52	30	43	47	1500	8695	646	13.46
C	3.06 ± 0.04	2	2	0	353	4.43	2	2	3	600	177,770	542	327.99
MIX													
A	8.16 ± 0.07	2	0	0	663	14.65	1	2	12	1500	758,659	541	1402.33
B	540.02 ± 122.30	12	11	6	5195	1525	10	12	38	1500	2392	1343	1.78
C	1.22 ± 0.02	1	0	0	434	4.21	0	1	1	1500	575,210	542	1061.27

Table 8.3 CPU resource consumption metrics

	CPU (%)					
	wavg(CPU) and CI (=0.95)	sd(avg(CPU))	max(CPU)	avg(int(CPU)) and CI (=0.95)	sd(avg(int(CPU)))	wavg(e(CPU))
SEQ						
A	43.04 ± 0.02	0.01	64.40	51,606.55 ± 21.55	8.67	67%
B	6.08 ± 0.02	0.01	21.70	7557.53 ± 26.69	10.74	28%
C	36.80 ± 0.01	0.00	57.91	44,221.75 ± 12.06	4.86	64%
EXC						
A	57.33 ± 0.01	0.00	86.88	68,749.51 ± 12.43	5.01	66%
B	6.00 ± 0.02	0.01	21.42	7527.03 ± 21.71	8.74	28%
C	40.99 ± 16.13	6.49	63.33	49,251.41 ± 19,381.43	7802.07	52%
EXT						
A	60.03 ± 0.01	0.01	79.03	72,130.57 ± 14.82	5.97	76%
B	0.26 ± 0.02	0.01	19.90	2315.17 ± 153.00	61.59	1%
C	33.50 ± 0.01	0.00	63.33	40,245.96 ± 14.40	5.80	53%
PAR						
A	65.74 ± 0.02	0.01	90.35	79,003.30 ± 27.12	10.92	73%
B	5.87 ± 0.02	0.01	19.69	7382.02 ± 22.84	9.19	31%
C	41.81 ± 0.04	0.02	72.19	50,235.56 ± 51.86	20.88	58%
CYC						
A	83.57 ± 0.01	0.00	97.92	100,419.62 ± 6.22	2.50	86%
B	4.83 ± 0.01	0.01	24.60	6835.68 ± 18.55	7.47	20%
C	41.88 ± 0.00	0.00	89.05	50,407.19 ± 1.30	0.52	47%
MIX						
A	77.10 ± 0.04	0.02	96.00	92,812.54 ± 49.43	19.90	81%
B	0.75 ± 0.08	0.03	17.00	2108.73 ± 214.35	86.29	4%
C	48.62 ± 0.19	0.08	80.97	58,565.97 ± 24.64	9.92	60%

Table 8.4 RAM resource consumption metrics

| | RAM (MB) | | | | | |
	wavg(RAM) and CI (=0.95)	sd(avg(RAM))	max(RAM)	avg(int(RAM)) and CI (=0.95)	sd(avg(int(RAM)))	wavg(e(RAM))
SEQ						
A	11,783.66 ± 0.05	0.02	12,545.00	14,131,141.27 ± 57.51	23.15	94%
B	2923.75 ± 0.02	0.01	3058.58	3,634,312.88 ± 28.02	11.28	96%
C	797.96 ± 0.01	0.00	998.75	958,382.91 ± 15.29	6.15	80%
EXC						
A	11,762.39 ± 0.03	0.01	12,473.00	14,108,016.85 ± 32.28	12.99	94%
B	2962.97 ± 0.04	0.01	3098.60	3,718,632.92 ± 44.30	17.83	96%
C	814.40 ± 0.00	0.00	993.73	978,152.16 ± 2.56	1.03	82%
EXT						
A	11,561.36 ± 0.03	0.01	12,451.84	13,889,937.29 ± 39.52	15.91	93%
B	2746.40 ± 0.01	0.00	2820.06	24,962,073.97 ± 47.93	19.29	97%
C	786.03 ± 0.02	0.01	979.43	944,044.81 ± 22.92	9.23	80%
PAR						
A	11,746.54 ± 0.03	0.01	12,473.14	14,112,493.71 ± 42.58	17.14	94%
B	2923.44 ± 0.06	0.02	3107.76	3,674,992.09 ± 75.31	30.32	94%
C	819.11 ± 0.03	0.01	1044.90	983,762.38 ± 38.98	15.69	78%
CYC						
A	12,050.98 ± 0.02	0.01	12,483.56	14,478,419.89 ± 22.88	9.21	96%
B	2886.16 ± 0.02	0.01	3018.67	4,084,012.52 ± 28.80	11.59	96%
C	919.26 ± 0.02	0.01	959.25	1,106,035.08 ± 29.83	12.01	96%
MIX						
A	11,874.58 ± 0.04	0.01	12,493.80	14,290,147.61 ± 43.49	17.51	95%
B	2782.67 ± 0.00	0.00	2876.38	7,816,580.17 ± 11.86	4.77	97%
C	976.64 ± 1.48	0.60	1074.05	1,176,024.34 ± 2425.00	976.19	91%

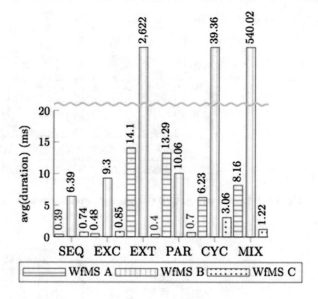

Fig. 8.6 Average duration (ms) per workflow pattern and mix

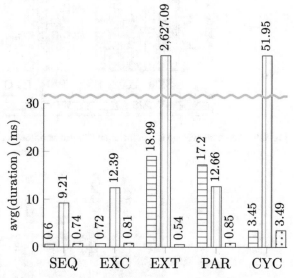

Fig. 8.7 Detailed average duration (ms) per workflow pattern in the mix

Explicit Termination Pattern [EXT]

The [EXT] workflow pattern was the longest workflow pattern in terms of duration for WfMS A resulting in an average duration of 14.1 ms, while WfMS C maintained a small average duration of 0.40 ms. Concerning the resource utilization, we observe a stable behavior for both engines, with WfMS A having 60.03% CPU average usage and WfMS C 33.5% CPU usage. Likewise, the memory utilization remains

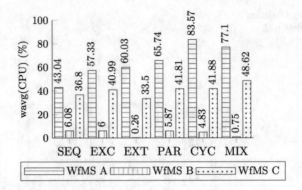

Fig. 8.8 Weighted average CPU (%) usage per workflow pattern and mix

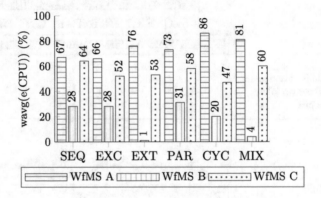

Fig. 8.9 Weighted average CPU efficiency (%) per workflow pattern and mix

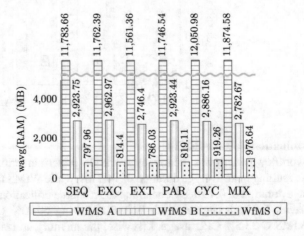

Fig. 8.10 Weighted average RAM usage (MB) per workflow pattern and mix

Fig. 8.11 Weighted average
efficiency (RAM) (%) per
workflow pattern and mix

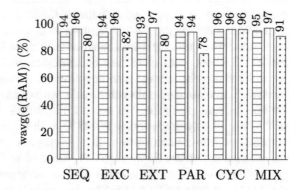

relatively stable to 11,561.36 MB for WfMS A and 786.03 MB for WfMS C. The
efficiency of the CPU usage is in a medium and rather better for WfMS A which
reaches the 76%. The RAM is used efficiently by all three WfMSs. In this workflow
pattern, WfMS B had a different behavior and has resulted in very high duration for
the execution of this pattern. After further analysis, we have noticed that during the
executions, WfMS B deviates from the guidelines of the BPMN 2.0 standard (cf.
Sect. 8.4.1.1, [EXT]) by sequential (pseudo-parallel) execution of each path, with
an average percentage of 52.23% on following the Wait 5 s script path and 47.77%
for following the Empty Script 1 path. Since the waiting script needs 5 s for its
completion, every time the Wait 5 s script is chosen, the average duration time adds
a 5 s overhead on the overall duration. Although the efficiency on the RAM usage
for this pattern seems to remain unaffected, the CPU is used very inefficiently and
presented many fluctuations. This dropped the value of $wavg(e(CPU))$ to 1%.

Parallel Split and Synchronization Patterns [PAR]
In this pattern, we observe some impact of the parallelism on the performance.
Namely, for WfMS A and WfMS B, the duration times increase to 13.29 ms and
10.06 ms, respectively. In this case, WfMS B seems faster than WfMS A. However,
we should notice that WfMS B has an overall execution of 27,718 workflow
instances in 567 s, while WfMS A executed 772,013 instances in 540 s. As far as
WfMS C is concerned, it seems to handle parallelism very fast, with a mean duration
of 0.70 ms. The resource utilization in the [PAR] workflow pattern has a relatively
stable behavior, with 65.74% usage for WfMS A, 5.87% usage for WfMS B, and
41.81% usage for WfMS C. Respectively, the RAM usage ranges 11,746.54 MB for
WfMS A, 2923.44 MB for WfMS B, and 819.11 MB for WfMS C. From this, we
may conclude that the CPU resource utilization is a little bit higher for WfMS A
compared to the [SEQ], [EXC], and [EXT] patterns. The efficiency of RAM and
CPU usage is again stable and similar to the previously discussed patterns.

Arbitrary Cycle Pattern [CYC]
Compared to the other workflow patterns, the [CYC] is more complex, both
statically, in terms of the number of language elements, and dynamically, in terms of
the logic executed by the script tasks which was expected to add certain execution
overhead. Furthermore, the presence of a loop introduces variability in the instance

execution duration, depending on whether the loop is executed five times or ten times. With a connection timeout limit set to 20 s, connection timeout errors have been noted when running a load function with more than 600 instance producers for WfMS C and with more than 800 instance producers for WfMS A. While Table 8.1 shows the average workflow instance duration with the maximum load per WfMS, to make the results comparable, we looked at the duration of all WfMSs for 600 instance producers. We noticed that WfMS A with an average duration of 2.92 ms slightly outperforms WfMS C with an average duration of 3.06 ms. WfMS B performs much worse with an average duration of 38.65 ms. Regarding the resource utilization, the average CPU usage of WfMS B (4.83%) and WfMS C (41.88%) remains in the same range with the other patterns. The same applies for the RAM for WfMS B (2886.16 MB), while slight increase to 919.26 is recorded for WfMS C. An increase in both CPU (83.57%) and RAM (12,050.98 MB) utilization compared to the other patterns is noticeable for WfMS A, but followed at the same time by greater CPU and RAM usage efficiency. These numbers are relative to the maximum number of instance producers. When analyzed with 600 instance producers, WfMS A uses on average 70.09% of CPU and 12,201.16 MB RAM. If we look at the change in metrics when the load was increased from 600 to 800 instance producers for WfMS A, we notice doubling of the average duration from 2.92 to 6.23 ms. The increase in load from 800 to 1500 instance producers for WfMS B results in hardly any increase in performance due to the increase in response time.

Mix [MIX]
The results of the [MIX] generally could lead to the conclusion that they express a cumulative value of the mean duration time derived by each workflow pattern. In this case, the throughput is comparably smaller for all the WfMSs. However, WfMS A keeps it on the same range as with its other workloads at 1402.33 wi/s. Figure 8.7 shows the separate duration times for each workflow pattern in the mix. There, we observe a small increase on the duration time of all patterns, as compared to the duration times we gathered by executing each workflow pattern individually. For the resource utilization in the [MIX] pattern, the engines have a different behavior. For example, we observe outlier values for WfMS A, which utilizes 77.1% CPU. This is its second biggest value after the [CYC] pattern. Likewise, WfMS B utilizes 0.75% CPU, which is the second lowest value of usage after the [EXT] pattern. These results on CPU utilization are also proportionally similar on the CPU efficiency. On the contrary, WfMS C has a slightly increased value of 48.62% CPU usage in comparison to the rest of the workflow patterns. Regarding the RAM usage and efficiency, we observe values close to the rest of the patterns, without remarkable fluctuations regarding the efficiency of the resource.

8.4.4.2 Results Discussion

As described in Sect. 8.4.4.1, WfMS B has very different results than the other two WfMSs. This particular behavior has also been observed by Bianculli et al. [2] for the WS-BPEL version of WfMS B. In order to explain this peculiarity, we have further investigated the documentation of WfMS B. The WfMS uses a synchronous API to execute processes. Thus, clients calling the REST API of the execution server will be blocked until the execution of the workflow instance has completed. This has an impact on the performance of WfMS B. In our experiments, all the instance producers initialize requests to the WfMS through the REST API and with a think time of 1 s. In the expected case of asynchronous communication, the instance producers would need to wait for the completion of their previous requests before initializing the next ones. However, in the case of WfMS B, the synchronous calls force the instance producers to wait for the entire workflow instance execution before the next request initialization. This fact introduces a high overhead that is reflected on the performance of WfMS B. In order to examine whether it is reasonable to repeat the experiments on WfMS B with higher load (i.e., instance producers), we have executed a scalability test for WfMS B. The assumption for this test was that under higher load, we could reach a number of executed workflow instances that can be more comparable to those executed by WfMS A and WfMS C. Thereby, we have executed the experiment for the load of 500, 1000, 1500, and 2000 instance producers. This resulted in the following response times: 7.15, 15.19, 22.58, and 30.89 s, respectively. The throughput for this experiment remained stable with a mean value of 62.23 workflow instances per second. This result indicates that it is meaningless to increase the number of instance producers and expect the WfMS throughput to grow accordingly. Another issue raised by the behavior of WfMS B is the execution of the [EXT] pattern. According to the specification of the BPMN 2 language [14], the parallel path with the empty script should end first and interrupt the execution of the Wait 5 s script, leading to the immediate termination of the execution of the workflow instance. However, in the case of WfMS B, we have observed many executions which lasted for 5 s. Thus, the Wait 5 s script was executed in its entirety. This behavior is explained by the documentation of WfMS B. WfMS B chooses to pseudo-parallel execute the parallel scripts, by dedicating a single thread to them. This decision leads to a nondeterministic serialization of the parallel paths. These two facts lead us to a better explanation of the results derived by the experiments on WfMS B. Namely, the WfMS B has higher values for the duration of the workflow execution, while it resulted in much lower rates concerning the resource utilization. This can be justified by the lack of parallelism within the same workflow instance. The other two WfMSs share some architectural similarities as WfMS C was originally a fork of WfMS A. Still, their behavior is not identical, and let us conclude to some interesting points. WfMS C has low duration values for all the workflow patterns, but for the [SEQ] and [EXC] patterns, where WfMS A is slightly better. Additionally, WfMS A seems to be affected by the parallelism, as we observed an increased duration values and resource utilization for the [EXT], [PAR], and [MIX] workflow patterns. On the contrary, WfMS C seems to be unaffected by the parallelism, by maintaining a relatively stable behavior for the aforementioned patterns. On the whole, we may conclude that WfMS C performed better and more stably in comparison to the other two WfMSs. Apropos of the resource utilization, we may generally conclude that WfMS B and WfMS C have a more stable behavior.

On the other side, WfMS A shows a direct increase when it is stressed, but had better behavior concerning the efficient usage of resources. Observing the resource utilization as a whole, the RAM is used generally in an efficient and stable manner, while the CPU is used less efficiently. Finally, concerning the impact of the BPMN 2 language constructs on the performance of the WfMSs (RQ1), we have observed that the [SEQ] workflow pattern resulted in the lowest duration times, most stable performance, and highest throughput for all the WfMSs. The condition evaluation on the [EXC] pattern seems to have a slight impact on the performance. The patterns that contain parallelism (i.e., [EXT], [PAR]) and more complex structures ([CYC]) seem to stress the WfMSs more and have an impact on the performance and resource utilization. These conclusions indicate that small, sequential workflows can be used toward discovering the maximum throughput of the WfMSs, while the parallel and more complex workflows make better candidates for stressing the WfMSs in terms of resource utilization. Concerning the behavior derived by the [MIX] execution (RQ2), it seems that the concurrent execution of different workflow patterns does not have a significant impact on the performance, while it seems to slightly affect the resource utilization and efficiency. It is suggested that further research is applied toward this direction. These observations should be considered when designing the workload of more complex, realistic cases and macro-benchmarks.

8.5   Lessons Learned and Conclusion

Our effort in building the first benchmark for BPMN 2.0 WfMS performance has led us to characterize the challenges researchers and practitioners have to deal with to accomplish this task. The main outcome of our effort is the realization that in order to define a benchmark involving real-world production systems, one needs to define and provide vendors with a clear methodology. Transparency toward the vendors is mandatory in these settings, since their involvement is necessary to build real-world and realistic benchmarks using realistic processes and data, as well as realistic configuration settings for the benchmarked systems. Moreover, it helps defining an agreement for the publication of results, since it is often the case that vendors would not allow you to publish results with their names, if they cannot reproduce and validate them. Other big challenges relate to the complexity of the BPMN 2.0 semantics and the diversity in the WfMS usage. They introduce the necessity of defining different benchmarks, based on the complexity level of the BPMN 2.0 features or based on the specific industry area. Moreover, a specific methodology is also necessary to deal with the heterogeneity and the need of defining a small subset of representative models for the purpose of performance benchmarking. The BPMN 2.0 WfMSs, in addition to implementing a semantically rich and complex language, are themselves complex in terms of configuration and deployment options. Executing performance benchmarking on such complex systems requires automation, which brings us to the need of a framework to support it and to mitigate the diversity in the interfaces available for interaction with different WfMSs, as well as a framework which scales with the amount of data to be analyzed. To develop such a framework, we relied on the state-of-the-art framework for performance testing and big data analysis, thus providing a complete solution for benchmarking WfMSs. As seen in this chapter, applying our methodology to the first simple micro-benchmark we defined on three open-source WfMSs has already identified differences in performance, thus proving the necessity and the relevance of providing further benchmarks in this context, such as macro-benchmarks with more realistic processes that go beyond the use of script tasks and simplistic data flow. We have found a bottleneck in scaling with the number of users for one of the engines included in our micro-benchmark. Moreover, we also found differences in performance and resource consumption between the other two engines for which major bottlenecks did not appear. The results of our initial micro-benchmark emphasize the importance of such an undertaking, especially nowadays. The results are important for both the end users of such systems and for the vendors and developers. The former might want to compare performance and resource consumption of different engines based on their use cases, in order to select the right solution in accordance to their requirements while achieving certain cost savings. The latter need fine-grained and detailed information on the performance and resource utilization of their systems, so that they can improve them by understanding and dealing with the potential bottlenecks. This becomes especially relevant as more and more vendors start providing Cloud-based deployment of their systems, where inefficient use of the allocated resources directly leads to money loss.

References

1. Active Endpoints Inc. Assessing ActiveVOS Performance (2011), http://www.activevos.com/content/developers/technical_notes/assessing_activevos_performance.pdf
2. D. Bianculli, W. Binder, M.L. Drago, SOABench: performance evaluation of service-oriented middleware made easy, in *2010 ACM/IEEE 32nd International Conference on Software Engineering*, vol. 2 (IEEE, Piscataway, 2010), pp. 301–302
3. J. Cardoso, Business process control-flow complexity: metric, evaluation, and validation. Int. J. Web Serv. Res. **5**(2), 49–76 (2008)
4. M.B. Chhetri, S. Chichin, Q.B.Vo, R. Kowalczyk, Smart CloudBench—a framework for evaluating cloud infrastructure performance. Inf. Syst. Front. **18**(3), 413–428 (2016)
5. F. Daniel, G. Pozzi, Y. Zhang, Workflow engine performance evaluation by a black-box approach, in *Proceedings of the International Conference on Informatics Engineering & Information Science (ICIEIS '11)*, ICIEIS '11 (Springer, Berlin, 2011), pp. 189–203
6. W. Felter, A. Ferreira, R. Rajamony, J. Rubio, An updated performance comparison of virtual machines and linux containers, in *2015 IEEE International Symposium on Performance Analysis of Systems and Software (ISPASS)* (IEEE, Piscataway, 2015), pp. 171–172
7. V. Ferme, C. Pautasso, A declarative approach for performance tests execution in continuous software development environments, in *ICPE '18*(ACM, New York, 2018), pp. 261–272
8. V. Ferme, A. Ivanchikj, C. Pautasso, M. Skouradaki, F. Leymann, A container-centric methodology for benchmarking workflow management systems, in *CLOSER (2)* (SciTePress, Setúbal, 2016), pp. 74–84

9. M. Geiger, S. Harrer, J. Lenhard, G. Wirtz, On the evolution of bpmn 2.0 support and implementation, in *2016 IEEE Symposium on Service-Oriented System Engineering (SOSE)*(IEEE, Piscataway, 2016), pp. 101–110

10. M. Gillmann, R. Mindermann, G. Weikum, Benchmarking and configuration of workflow management systems, in *Proceedings of the 7th International Conference on Cooperative Information Systems (CoopIS '00), CoopIS '00* (Springer, Berlin, 2000), pp. 186–197

11. J. Gray, *Benchmark Handbook: For Database and Transaction Processing Systems* (Morgan Kaufmann Publishers Inc., Burlington, 1992)

12. IBM, Sap netweaver business process management performance, scalability, and stability proof of concept. IBM White Paper WP102045 (2011), http://www-01.ibm.com/support/docview. wss?uid=tss1wp102045&aid=1

13. A. Iosup, R. Prodan, D. Epema, IaaS cloud benchmarking: approaches, challenges, and experience, in *Cloud Computing for Data-Intensive Applications* (Springer, New York, 2014), pp. 83–104

14. D. Jordan, J. Evdemon, *Business Process Model and Notation (BPMN) Version 2.0* (Object Management Group, Needham, 2011), http://www.omg.org/spec/BPMN/2.0/

15. D. Jordan, J. Evdemon et al., Web Services Business Process Execution Language (WS-BPEL) Version 2.0, in *OASIS Standard* (2007), pp. 1–264

16. E.D. Lazowska, J. Zahorjan, et al., *Quantitative System Performance: Computer System Analysis Using Queueing Network Models* (Prentice-Hall, Upper Saddle River, 1984)

17. J. Mendling, *Metrics for Process Models: Empirical Foundations of Verification, Error Prediction, and Guidelines for Correctness* (Springer, Berlin, 2008)

18. I. Molyneaux, *The Art of Application Performance Testing: Help for Programmers and Quality Assurance*, 1st edn. (O'Reilly, Sebastopol, 2009)

19. D.C. Montgomery, G.C. Runger, *Applied Statistics and Probability for Engineers* (Wiley, Hoboken, 2010)

20. C. Pautasso, D. Roller, F. Leymann, V. Ferme, M. Skouradaki, Towards workflow benchmarking: open research challenges. *Datenbanksysteme für Business, Technologie und Web (BTW 2015)* (Gesellschaft für Informatik, Bonn, 2015)

21. C. Röck, S. Harrer, G. Wirtz, Performance benchmarking of BPEL engines: a comparison framework, status quo evaluation and challenges, in *Proc. SEKE 2014* (2014), pp. 31–34

22. F. Rottensteiner, G. Sohn, M. Gerke, J.D. Wegner, U. Breitkopf, J. Jung, Results of the ISPRS benchmark on urban object detection and 3D building reconstruction. ISPRS J. Photogramm. Remote Sens. **93**, 256–271 (2014)

23. N. Russell, W.M.P. van der Aalst, A.H.M. ter Hofstede, All that glitters is not gold: selecting the right tool for your BPM needs. Cut. IT J. **20**(11), 31–38 (2007)

24. S.E. Sim, S. Easterbrook, R.C. Holt, Using benchmarking to advance research: a challenge to software engineering, in *Proceedings of the 25th International Conference on Software Engineering (ICSE '03)* (IEEE Computer Society, Washington, 2003), pp. 74–83

25. M. Skouradaki, Workload mix definition for benchmarking BPMN 2.0 Workflow Management Systems. PhD thesis, Institute of Architecture of Application Systems (IAAS), University of Stuttgart, 2017

26. M. Skouradaki, F. Leymann, Detecting frequently recurring structures in BPMN 2.0 process models, in *Proceedings of the 9th Symposium and Summer School On Service-Oriented Computing: SummerSOC'15* (IBM, North Castle, 2015), pp. 102–116

27. M. Skouradaki, D.H. Roller et al., On the road to benchmarking BPMN 2.0 workflow engines, in *Proceedings of the 6th ACM/SPEC International Conference on Performance Engineering, ICPE '15* (ACM, New York, 2015), pp. 301–304

28. M. Skouradaki, V. Andrikopoulos, F. Leymann, Representative BPMN 2.0 process model generation from recurring structures, in *2016 IEEE International Conference on Web Services (ICWS)* (IEEE, Piscataway, 2016), pp. 468–475

29. Standard Performance Evaluation Corporation. SPEC CPU2006 Version 1.2 (2011)

30. S. Subramanyam, Faban - helping measure performance, http://faban.org

31. Transaction Processing Council (TPC), TPC Benchmark C (Online Transaction Processing Benchmark) Version 5.11 (1997)
32. A. van Hoorn, C. Vögele, et al., Automatic extraction of probabilistic workload specifications for load testing session-based application systems, in *Proc. VALUETOOLS '14* (ICST, 2014), pp. 139–146
33. B. Wetzstein, P. Leitner, et al., Monitoring and analyzing influential factors of business process performance, in *2009 IEEE International Enterprise Distributed Object Computing Conference, EDOC '09* (IEEE, Piscataway, 2009), pp. 141–150
34. P. Wohed, W.M.P. van der Aalst, M. Dumas et al., On the suitability of BPMN for business process modelling, in *Business Process Management*. LNCS, vol. 4102 (Springer, Berlin, 2006), pp. 161–176

Chapter 9
Effectiveness of Combinatorial Test Design with Executable Business Processes

Daniel Lübke, Joel Greenyer, and David Vatlin

Abstract Executable business processes contain complex business rules, control flow, and data transformations, which makes designing good tests difficult and, in current practice, requires extensive expert knowledge. In order to reduce the time and errors in manual test design, we investigated using automatic combinatorial test design (CTD) instead. CTD is a test selection method that aims at covering all interactions of a few input parameters. For this investigation, we integrated CTD algorithms with an existing framework that combines equivalence class partitioning with automatic BPELUnit test generation. Based on several industrial cases, we evaluated the effectiveness and efficiency of test suites selected via CTD algorithms against those selected by experts and random tests. The experiments show that CTD tests are not more efficient than tests designed by experts, but that they are a sufficiently effective automatic alternative.

9.1 Introduction

Many organizations rely on *executable business processes* (XBPs) to orchestrate distributed services in order to satisfy critical business needs. Therefore, the correctness of each XBP must be thoroughly validated via tests. However, complex business rules, process flow, and data transformations make it difficult to engineer effective test suites [11].

Ideally, to catch all bugs, an XBP should be tested with all possible combinations of input parameter values, but this is intractable in practice. Equivalence class partitioning can help abstract from the single input values and partition the range for each input parameter into a few sets of values where it is assumed that the

D. Lübke (✉) · J. Greenyer · D. Vatlin
Leibniz Universität Hannover, Fachgebiet Software Engineering, Hannover, Germany
e-mail: daniel.luebke@inf.uni-hannover.de; greenyer@inf.uni-hannover.de

© Springer Nature Switzerland AG 2019
D. Lübke, C. Pautasso (eds.), *Empirical Studies on the Development of Executable Business Processes*, https://doi.org/10.1007/978-3-030-17666-2_9

XBP exhibits equivalent behavior. Sometimes, it is then possible to cover all combinations of the parameters' equivalence classes. Usually, however, this will still require too many tests; even with automated tests, a single XBP test can take up to minutes and is thus resource intensive.

In the industrial project Terravis, which develops a process integration platform between land registers, notaries, and banks throughout Switzerland [2], approximately hundred XBPs are constantly improved and extended; so tests must be designed, maintained, and executed regularly. For efficient systematic testing, the *classification tree generator* (CTG) framework [19] was developed, which combines equivalence class partitioning via classification trees [6] with automated generation of BPELUnit [11, 16] tests.

CTG aids testers in defining equivalence classes and selecting and generating tests. The test selection determines which input messages an XBP under test receives. Moreover, requirements can be formalized as constraints, so that also assertions on the output values can be generated automatically.

Selecting a good test set, however, is still a time-consuming and error-prone expert task. To address this problem, we investigated employing *combinatorial test design* (CTD) [21] to automate the selection of effective and efficient tests. CTD is a test planning approach which relies on the observation that whether a software bug is executed, which is necessary for finding it in a test, usually depends on the interaction of only a few input parameters [9, 20]. For example, if a system has three Boolean input parameters, there are eight ($|\mathbb{B} \times \mathbb{B} \times \mathbb{B}|$) tests for the system. All pairwise combinations of these parameter values, however, would already be covered by five test cases, for example, those with inputs $(0, 0, 0)$, $(0, 1, 1)$, $(1, 0, 0)$, $(1, 0, 1)$, and $(1, 1, 0)$—and these would be sufficient for finding any bug that depends on any particular value combination of any two parameters. When dealing with many input parameters, but only covering t-wise parameter interactions where t is small, the reduction of tests w.r.t. testing all possible inputs is significant.

Automatic algorithms exist for synthesizing sets of test inputs that cover all t-wise interactions of parameter values, for example, the IPOG algorithm [10, 23]. CTD can be combined with expert-based equivalence class partitioning of input parameters as mentioned above.

Applying CTD for the testing of XBPs is currently not an established nor researched practice, so we aim to answer the following research questions:

RQ1: What value of t is typically required for CTD tests of executable business processes in order to be effective?

RQ2: How does the effectiveness and efficiency of the CTD-generated tests, with different t-values, compare to (a) tests created by experts and (b) tests selected randomly?

In order to answer these questions, we implemented an automated CTD procedure and conducted experiments with the industrial XBPs provided by the Terravis project. Terravis provides many large BPEL processes and is thus a good candidate for exploring the effects of testing methodologies.

Because the CTG framework and BPELUnit [11, 16] are already in use in the Terravis project, we integrated CTG with the two most common CTD algorithms, IPOG-C [10, 23] and AETG-SAT [4, 5]. Through the use of BPELUnit, we could easily measure the test case sizes and test coverage with respect to activities and decisions in the process [14]. We used the latter as a metric for the effectiveness of a test suite, i.e., its capability of discovering bugs.

To our knowledge, applying CTD to the business process domain is new or has not been published previously. The contribution of our paper is, first, that we show CTD can be applied to XBPs and, second, we present results of experiments carried out on industrial cases; the results allow practitioners to judge when and how to apply these methods.

Structure We introduce preliminaries in Sect. 9.2 and overview of related work in Sect. 9.3. The design and results of our experiments are described in Sects. 9.4 and 9.5. Finally, we conclude in Sect. 9.6.

9.2 Preliminaries

In this section, we explain the basic features of the classification tree generator (CTG) framework and how we combined it with CTD algorithms.

Suppose the process under test is a simple online shop process modeled in BPMN as shown in Fig. 9.1. Initially, a customer places an order. The product may not be available; but if it is, the customer receives an order confirmation, and the freight company receives an order, upon which the freight company returns a packaging label. At this point, it may still turn out that the shipment is not possible, for example, because the product is out of stock (and stock-level data is inconsistent). If the shipment is possible, it is handed to the freight company, and an invoice is sent to the customer.

The order placed by the customer is a document that contains different parameters, like the ID of the ordered product, amount, payment information, customer ID, etc. Of course, it is not possible to test the process for each possible order, and so we use equivalence class partitioning of the different input parameters. For example, we assume that different payment methods (credit card, Maestro, or wire transfer) will lead to different behaviors, but the actual credit card number, for example, does not influence the process behavior. Likewise, the process will behave similarly for available products for which shipment is possible, which shows that there can also be a multidimensional partitioning with interdependencies, for example, a shipment can only be successful when the product is available.

We thus use a classification tree-based approach [6] for the selection of test inputs. A classification tree for the online shop process is shown in Fig. 9.2. It is displayed as a spreadsheet where, below the tree structure that makes the table

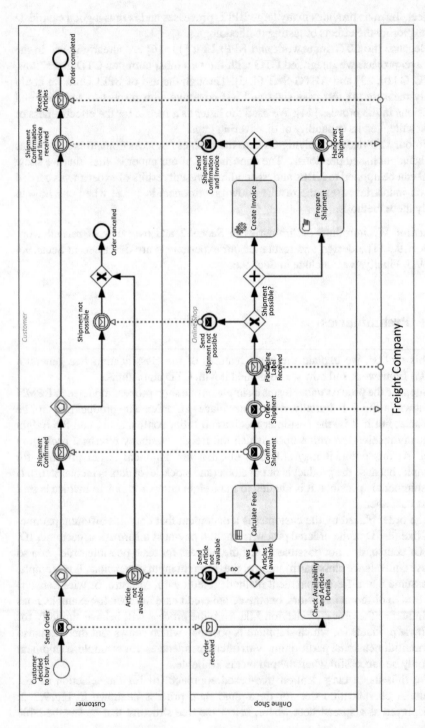

Fig. 9.1 Simple online shop process

TestCases:	Article Available? Shipment possible? Success	Problem	Not Available	Shipment Size Maxi Letter	Package	Bulk	Payment Method Credit Card	Maestro	Wire Transfer
TC1			X	X				X	
TC2			X		X				X
TC3			X			X	X		
TC4	X			X					X
TC5	X				X		X		
TC6	X					X		X	
TC7		X		X			X		
TC8		X			X			X	
TC9		X				X			X

Fig. 9.2 Classification tree for the sample online shop process used in [19]

heading, tests can be configured by selecting from the equivalence classes resulting from the classification tree-based partitioning.

For each leaf of the classification tree, a corresponding snippet of a BPEL-Unit [11, 16] test case is created. Then, given a test input selection, a test case can be generated automatically by composing the corresponding snippets. Constraints on input and output values can be added to the classification tree, so that also assertions can be generated automatically. The classification tree is not only used to configure parameters of initial input messages but also to specify the contents of intermediate messages.

In current practice, the test selection as in Fig. 9.2 is done by an expert who has detailed knowledge of the process in order to select a test set that is *effective* and *efficient*, i.e., will successfully detect bugs, and does so with few tests. For an average-size XBP, with thousands of possible tests to choose from, it can take hours to create a good test set; for big processes, with hundreds of thousands of possible tests, the expert easily loses oversight.

When testing with BPELUnit, the tester has some support in assessing the quality of a test suite: it is possible to measure how many of the activity nodes and branches in the process were covered by a test suite. However, such a measure is only available after running the test suite, and so iteratively refining the test suite based on these results is time consuming.

Ultimately, we aim to automate the test selection process. For this purpose, we integrated automatic CTD algorithms in the test case selection framework. In particular, we chose IPOG-C [23] and AETG-SAT [5] for an experimental comparison: IPOG-C is a variant of the IPOG (*In Parameter Order General*) algorithm [10] that is extended to also consider constraints on possible parameter combinations. Similarly, AETG-SAT is an extension of the AETG (*Automatic Efficient Test case Generator*) algorithm [4] that considers constraints on possible parameter combinations, by employing a SAT solver. In our case, the constraints on the possible combinations of inputs are given through the classification tree or additional manually added constraints, e.g., shipment cannot be successful for unavailable product.

IPOG and AETG take a different approach on selecting tests that yield a full *t*-wise coverage of the input parameter space. IPOG starts by building all *t*-tuples of the first *t* parameters and then incrementally extends this set horizontally, by including more and more parameters, and vertically, adding more and more tuples as needed, until all *t*-tuples of all parameters are covered. AETG, on the other hand, uses a heuristic approach for incrementally extending a set of test inputs. In each step, a number of new candidate test inputs is generated, partly randomized, in order to cover as many yet uncovered *t*-tuples as possible. Then, one of these candidates that covers most uncovered *t*-tuples is chosen to be included in the test set. This process is repeated until all *t*-tuples of all parameters are covered. Due to the random component in AETG, the algorithm may produce different results between different runs and the same inputs. IPOG, by contrast, is a deterministic algorithm.

Both algorithms, IPOG and AETG, do not guarantee that the test set is of minimal size. Also, there are no conclusive studies on which approach yields the smallest test set; and, therefore, we decided to investigate whether IPOG-C or AETG-SAT creates more efficient test suites in our approach.

9.3 Related Work

The empirical study of testing techniques is an important subject [3]. The testing of business processes, in particular, is becoming increasingly important, as more and more business and government processes are automated. However, applying CTD for XBPs has not been studied previously; we therefore overview existing work on CTD in related areas.

Kruse et al. [7] and Puoskari et al. [17] studied the effectiveness and efficiency of applying CTD to test an IT management system at IBM. In particular, they also combined a classification tree-based test selection method with CTD algorithms in a commercial tool, which is now called TESTONA (Assystem Germany GmbH). They compared the classification tree + CTD test design approach with established testing techniques at IBM for the system under study and concluded that the former could improve the effectiveness of the tests. For measuring the effectiveness of the generated test suites, Kruse et al. measured the test suites' abilities to find manually injected faults. In this paper, we instead use activity and branch coverage as a metric for the test suites' effectiveness; as future work, we also plan to use measure the detection rate of faults created via systematic and automatic mutation.

Qi et al. [18] used CTD in combination with automated dynamic exploration testing of web applications. The CTD approach can be used successfully to systematically generate interacting inputs for forms, which accelerate the dynamic exploration.

Kuhn and Reilly [8] conducted an experiment with a browser and server modules, where they ran tests with different *t*-levels of AETG against the software. Because they knew the number of existing bugs, they could check how many bugs were found with which t-level. For both test sets, all bugs were found with $t = 6$. For efficiency reasons, the authors recommended $3 <= t <= 6$ as an advice.

Kuhn et al. [9] did an empirical study for analyzing fault interactions. They queried bug databases on how many conditions influenced a defect. The authors analyzed seven systems and found that the upper bound of parameter interactions was also 6.

9.4 Experiment Design

9.4.1 Research Questions

Following the goal-question-metric (GQM) method [1], we formulate our research goal as follows:

> The purpose of this study is to *evaluate* the *effectiveness and efficiency of CTD-based testing* from the point of view of *software testers* in the context of *executable business processes*.

When aiming to apply CTD in XBP development projects, the main challenge is to find a suitable t-value and to evaluate the quality of automatically chosen tests by CTD algorithms compared to expert test designs and random tests. The latter serve as a control group in our experiments: random tests are an automated test selection method, which is easy to implement. With some confidence, it can be assumed that random tests will exercise many different cases. As such, we refine our goal into the following two research questions:

1. **What value of t is typically required for executable business processes in order to be effective?** When projects want to use CTD, they need to know which configuration of the CTD algorithms will likely yield the intended results. The higher the t-value is, the more tests are generated and, thus, the more effective the test set will be. But the tests will also run longer, which is a critical factor when tests will be included in continuous builds. However, if the chosen t-value is too low, the tests will likely not be able to detect defects. Therefore, testers need to be able to choose an optimum t-value. Therefore, we want to demonstrate in our experiments with which t-value most if not all business processes are tested with 100% test coverage measured as (a) basic activity coverage (BPEL equivalent of statement coverage) and (b) decision coverage. These coverage criteria are not a direct measure for the effectiveness of a test suite, but a generally accepted effectiveness metric.

2. **How does the effectiveness and efficiency of the CTD-generated tests, with
   different t-values, compare to (a) tests created by experts and (b) a set of
   tests of equivalent size selected randomly?** When deciding whether to use
   a CTD-based testing approach, the main question is how such an approach
   performs compared to a test selection by an expert and to an easy-to-implement
   random approach. Thus, we compare the efficiency of the test suites generated
   with IPOG-C and AETG-SAT to those of an expert selection and randomly
   chosen test suites with the same size.

9.4.2   Case Selection

For studying the effectiveness of the CTD test case selection algorithms, we required
a set of XBPs with classification trees. We had access to processes of the Terravis
project [2]. Many XBPs in this project are mature; but extensions, improvements,
and new processes are released frequently [12]. The project applies the (yet
new) CTG framework for five processes, which we included in our experiments.
In addition, we used two BPEL processes that were used as examples for the
classification tree generator by Schnelle [19] for comparison.

   We compare the different characteristics of the business processes in the classification table (see Tables 9.1 and 9.2) in a template structure as suggested by Lübke
et al. [15].

   In addition to the main part of the template, we show static BPEL metrics and
the metrics of the classification trees. Static BPEL metrics include the number of
basic activities, structured activities, and structured activities without the sequence
activities (nonlinear structured activities) in order to show the process sizes.
The metrics for the classifications are shown following the notation in [10]: the
parameters of the classifications are notated in the form of x^y, which means that
there are y parameters with x values.

9.4.3   Data Collection Procedure

Before analyzing and evaluating the results, we describe the testing process and the
tools used for data collection.

   Given an XBP to be tested, a test suite is generated as follows: First, the test
designer creates the classification tree for the CTG framework as described above,
including constraints and underlying BPELUnit fragments.

   The classification tree is then to be filled out. This can be done manually; a
specified number of tests can be automatically generated at random, or a selection
can be generated automatically using two alternative CTD algorithms, IPOG-C or
AETG-SAT.

Table 9.1 Classification according to Lübke et al. [15] of the processes in this study (1/2)

	Online shop	Credit approval	Land register notifications
Version	–	–	–
Domain	E-commerce	Banking	Mortgage transactions
Geography	None	None	Switzerland
Time	2016	2016	2017
Boundaries	–	–	Cross-organizational
Relationship	No call	No call	Is being called
Scope	Core	Core	Auxiliary
Purpose	Execution	Execution	Execution
People involvement	None	None	None
Process language	BPEL 2.0	BPEL 2.0	BPEL 2.0 plus vendor extensions
Execution engine	Apache ODE[a]		Informatica ActiveVOS 9.2
Model maturity	Illustrative	Illustrative	Productive
Basic activities	19	25	84
Structured activities	8	12	85
Nonlinear struct. a.	6	14	38
Parameters	3^3	$4^1 \cdot 2^4$	$2^7 \cdot 3^7 \cdot 6^1$
Constraints	0	3^1	$3^5 \cdot 2^1 2$
Allowed configurations	27	52	69,888

[a]For our analysis, the processes were executed on Informatica ActiveVOS 9.2

The IPOG-C algorithm can be used with the application developed by Vatlin [22], which integrates the IPOG-C implementation of the NIST- [23] Advanced Combinatorial Testing System (ACTS) with the CTG framework. The AETG-SAT algorithm can be used with the help of the generator developed by Schnelle and Lübke [19].

With a given test selection, the BPELUnit test cases can then be generated and executed.

During generation, we measured the size of the test suite; and after test case execution, we measured the coverage metrics. A BPEL process consists of basic activities and structured activities. Basic activities describe the elementary steps of the process and represent single actions. Structured activities determine the control flow and describe the sequence of activities in BPEL business processes. Structured activities describe conditional and iterative executions of activities.

For the assessment of the used procedure, tools, and their interaction, this paper will regard the activity coverage, branch coverage, number of test cases, and number of test activities.

Test coverage was measured by analyzing the process logs extracted from the BPEL engine as described by Lübke [13]. We calculated two coverage metrics as described in [14]: (Basic) Activity coverage calculates the fraction of executed basic activities within a BPEL process. (Conditional) Branch coverage calculates the fraction of branches taken in a test suite. There are further test coverage metrics

Table 9.2 Classification according to Lübke et al. [15] of the processes in this study (2/2)

	Creditor transfer	Transfer approval	Approver process	Depot check
Version	–	–	–	–
Domain	Mortgage transactions			
Geography	Switzerland			
Time	2017			
Boundaries	Cross-organizational			Within dep.
Relationship	Calls another			No call
Scope	Core	Core	Core	Auxiliary
Purpose	Execution	Execution	Execution	Execution
People involvement	None	Partly	None	None
Process language	BPEL 2.0 with vendor extensions			
Execution engine	Informatica ActiveVOS 9.2			
Model maturity	Productive	Productive	Productive	Productive
Basic activities	235	33	30	40
Structured activities	234	34	37	52
Nonlinear struct. a.	71	9	10	16
Parameters	$12^1 . 9^1 . 5^2 . 3^1 . 2^2$	$3^2 . 2^4$	$4^1 . 3^2$	$6^2 . 5^1 . 2^4$
Constraints	$8^1 . 7^2 . 5^4 . 2^{12}$	2^8	2^3	$20^1 . 13^1 . 7^1$ $. 6^1 . 5^1 . 2^3 . 1^1$
Allowed configurations	7031	27	10	128

defined for BPEL (handler coverage and link coverage), which we decided not to use because activity coverage and branch coverage should cover all relevant process elements.

9.4.4 Analysis Procedure

For our study, we captured the following metrics for every process project:

- Number of test cases, number of test activities, basic activity coverage, and branch coverage for the *expert*-selected test suites
- Number of test cases, number of test activities, basic activity coverage, and branch coverage for the *IPOG-C, t* $\in \{1, 2, 3, 4\}$-generated test suites
- Number of test cases, number of test activities, basic activity coverage, and branch coverage for the *AETG-SAT, t* $\in \{2, 3, 4\}$-generated test suites
- Number of test cases, number of test activities, basic activity coverage, and branch coverage for the randomly chosen test suites, which have the same size as their IPOG-C, $t \in \{1, 2, 3, 4\}$ counterparts

For all test strategies with randomness (all randomly chosen test suites and all AETG-SAT test suites), 20 test suites were generated, and the mean from the measures was computed in order to account for variances.

For classification trees with fewer than four parameters, we could not generate $t = 4$-level test suites (and their random counterparts). This applies to the Online Shop and Approver Process.

From these measurements, we computed the efficiency of the tests as $Eff_y(x) = Cov(x)/|y|$ with $x \in \{activity, branch\}$ being the coverage metric and $y \in \{TC, TA\}$ being the number of test cases or test activities.

In order to answer our research questions, we compared the efficiency of the different strategies. However, we excluded strategies that did not reach at least 75% of the maximum achievable coverage, because we deemed such a low coverage to be too low for practical reasons. Originally, we wanted to use a strict 75% threshold. However, we found that depending on the classification tree, not 100% coverage could be reached for all processes. As such, we defined *maximum coverage* as the maximal coverage value that could be achieved with the provided classification tree. Test case selection strategies that reach maximum coverage are the most *effective* ones.

9.5 Results

In this section, we present our measurement results and their interpretations with regard to our research questions. Last, we assess the validity of our results.

9.5.1 Measurements

The measurements gathered as described above are shown in the boxplots in Figs. 9.3 and 9.4. Figure 9.3 shows the activity coverage of the different test suites, and Fig. 9.4 shows the branch coverage.

The boxplots **aetgx** and **ipogx** show the values for both AETG-SAT$_{t=x}$ and IPOG-C$_{t=x}$ algorithms. The **random-ipogx** plots show the values of the random test suites with the same number of test cases as the test suites generated with IPOG-C$_{t=x}$.

We can see that the general coverage for both activities and branches is usually above 75% for all strategies. Only IPOG-C$_{t=1}$ and the random test suites often score near or below this threshold. AETG-SAT$_{t=3}$ and IPOG-C$_{t=3}$ however usually score the maximum coverage.

Tables 9.3, 9.4, 9.5, 9.6, 9.7, 9.8, and 9.9 show more detailed information for each XBP.

The data shows that the classifications for the processes "Approver Process" and "Depot Check" are not complete because at least one coverage metric maximizes

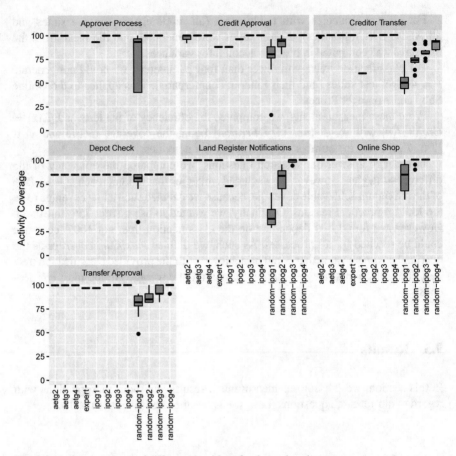

Fig. 9.3 Activity coverage of different algorithms for the analyzed processes

at below 100%. Interestingly, the "Depot Check" process has full basic activity coverage but misses 100% branch coverage. Upon investigation, it became clear that fault handlers managing exception flow were not triggered which contained basic activities. Because handlers were not included in this test coverage metric, the test gap became only apparent in the basic activity coverage metric.

9.5.2 Interpretation

RQ1 (Required t-Value) For all processes and the given classification trees that are part of our experiments, both IPOG-C and AETG-SAT generate the maximum coverage at $t = 3$. Higher t-values have offered no additional coverage benefits in our data set. From an efficiency point of view, $t = 2$ yields more effective

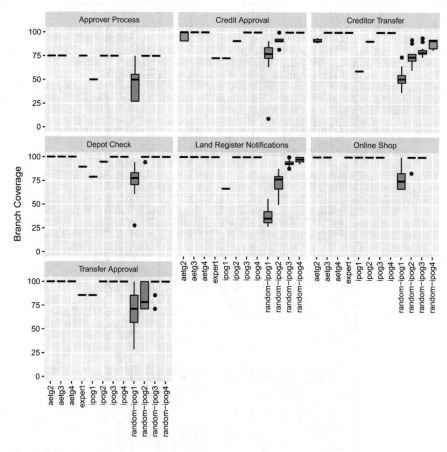

Fig. 9.4 Conditional branch coverage of different algorithms for the analyzed processes

results with often maximum coverage and in other cases only a small penalty while requiring only a fraction of test cases compared to $t = 3$. No process profited from a further increase of t to $t = 4$; the test suites become very large without any coverage benefit.

This is in contrast to other types of software (see [8, 9]), where some defects in certain kinds of applications are only triggered with $t = 6$. This is a significant difference because less test cases are required for XBPs to fully cover the software than with "traditional" software.

RQ2 (Efficiency and Effectiveness) Looking at the data, IPOG-C and AETG-SAT deliver comparable test coverage for the same t-level. Sometimes one algorithm scores better and sometimes the other. Better performance is not bound to any particular process. For one t-level for one given process, one algorithm can score better than the other while scoring worse for another t-level on the same process.

Table 9.3 Measurements for the **Online Shop** process: because this process has only three parameters, no $t = 4$-level test suites could be generated

Strategy	t-Level	Test cases	Test activities	Cov(Act)	Cov(Branch)	Eff-TC(Act)	Eff-TC(Cond)	Eff-TA(Act)	Eff-TA(Cond)
IPOG-C	1	3	15	100.0	100.0	33.33	33.33	33.33	33.33
IPOG-C	2	9	45	100.0	100.0	11.11	11.11	11.11	11.11
IPOG-C	3	27	135	100.0	100.0	3.70	3.70	3.70	3.70
IPOG-C	4	–	–	–	–	0.25	–	–	–
Random I1		3	15	84.2	75.0	28.07	25.00	28.07	25.00
Random I2		9	47	100.0	100.0	11.11	11.11	11.11	11.11
Random I3		27	135	100.0	100.0	3.70	3.70	3.70	3.70
Random I4		–	–	–	–	–	–	–	–
AETG-SAT	2	10	49	100.0	100.0	10.00	10.00	10.00	10.00
AETG-SAT	3	27	135	100.0	100.0	3.70	3.70	3.70	3.70
AETG-SAT	4	–	–	–	–	–	–	–	–
Expert		9	45	100.0	100.0	11.11	11.11	11.11	11.11

100% activity and branch coverage is reached by all strategies except the random test suites with the same size as IPOG-C$_{t=1}$. Both the expert and IPOG-C$_{t=2}$ select the most efficient test suites with 9 test cases and 45 test activities each. AETG-SAT creates slightly larger test suites for $t = 2$. IPOG-C and AETG-SAT create the same-size test suites for $t = 3$, which, however, have no improvement over $t = 2$. The expert in this case is not the most efficient one because he designed more test cases than both algorithms with $t = 1$

Table 9.4 Measurements for the **Credit Approval** process: the expert does not achieve 100% coverage for this process, although IPOG-C with $t \in \{3, 4\}$ and AETG-SAT with $t \in \{2, 3, 4\}$ achieve this goal

Strategy	t-Level	Test cases	Test activities	Cov(Act)	Cov(Branch)	Eff-TC(Act)	Eff-TC(Cond)	Eff-TA(Act)	Eff-TA(Cond)
IPOG-C	1	4	18	88.0	72.7	22.00	18.18	22.00	18.18
IPOG-C	2	8	36	96.0	90.9	12.00	11.36	12.00	11.36
IPOG-C	3	24	111	100.0	100.0	4.17	4.17	4.17	4.17
IPOG-C	4	40	180	100.0	100.0	2.50	2.50	2.50	2.50
Random I1		4	18	80.0	77.3	20.00	19.32	20.00	19.32
Random I2		8	36	94.0	90.9	11.75	11.36	11.75	11.36
Random I3		24	106	100.0	100.0	4.17	4.17	4.17	4.17
Random I4		40	170	100.0	100.0	2.50	2.50	2.50	2.50
AETG-SAT	2	10	42	100.0	100.0	10.00	10.00	10.00	10.00
AETG-SAT	3	22	99	100.0	100.0	4.55	4.55	4.55	4.55
AETG-SAT	4	41	182	100.0	100.0	2.44	2.44	2.44	2.44
Expert		4	18	88.0	72.7	22.00	18.18	22.00	18.18

Also the random equivalences for IPOG-C $t \in \{3, 4\}$ achieve the same coverage. Interestingly, the most efficient test suite is created by AETG-SAT with $t = 2$. For $t = 3$, AETG-SAT also outperforms IPOG with a smaller test suite on average, and even the randomly generated test suites are more efficient than the IPOG-C ones because they use fewer test activities with the same amount of test cases. In this case, the expert does not achieve maximum coverage nor the best efficiency value (superseded by the random equivalent for IPOG-C $t = 1$ with regard to branch coverage)

Table 9.5 Measurements for the **Land Register Notifications** process: the expert scores best with 100% coverage for both measures and the fewest test cases (25) for this coverage level

Strategy	t-Level	Test cases	Test activities	Cov(Act)	Cov(Branch)	Eff-TC(Act)	Eff-TC(Cond)	Eff-TA(Act)	Eff-TA(Cond)
IPOG-C	1	6	29	72.6	66.7	12.10	11.11	12.10	11.11
IPOG-C	2	30	140	100.0	100.0	3.33	3.33	3.33	3.33
IPOG-C	3	125	593	100.0	100.0	0.80	0.80	0.80	0.80
IPOG-C	4	401	1959	100.0	100.0	0.25	0.25	0.25	0.25
Random I1		6	33	38.1	35.4	6.35	5.89	6.35	5.89
Random I2		30	162	83.3	76.8	2.78	2.56	2.78	2.56
Random I3		125	684	100.0	93.0	0.80	0.74	0.80	0.74
Random I4		401	2217	100.0	97.7	0.25	0.24	0.25	0.24
AETG-SAT	2	32	152	100.0	100.0	3.08	3.08	3.08	3.08
AETG-SAT	3	124	600	100.0	100.0	0.81	0.81	0.81	0.81
AETG-SAT	4	410	2006	100.0	100.0	0.24	0.24	0.24	0.24
Expert		25	112	100.0	100.0	4.00	4.00	4.00	4.00

IPOG-C and AETG-SAT with $t \in \{2, 3, 4\}$ also achieve 100% coverage for both measures, which is not reached by any random test suites. Those fail with regard to branch coverage. IPOG-C and AETG-SAT require more test cases than the expert. IPOG-C creates a smaller test suite than AETG-SAT for $t \in \{2, 4\}$, while for $t = 3$ AETG-SAT is more efficient

Table 9.6 Measurements for the **Creditor Transfer** process: both IPOG-C and AETG-SAT achieve 100% activity and branch coverage for $t \in \{3, 4\}$, but both also fail to achieve this coverage with $t = 2$

Strategy	t-Level	Test cases	Test activities	Cov(Act)	Cov(Branch)	Eff-TC(Act)	Eff-TC(Cond)	Eff-TA(Act)	Eff-TA(Cond)
IPOG-C	1	14	133	59.6	59.3	4.26	4.23	4.26	4.23
IPOG-C	2	68	768	99.6	90.7	1.46	1.33	1.46	1.33
IPOG-C	3	268	3151	100.0	100.0	0.37	0.37	0.37	0.37
IPOG-C	4	934	11,024	100.0	100.0	4.35	4.35	4.35	4.35
Random I1		14	164	49.6	50.9	3.54	3.64	3.54	3.64
Random I2		68	834	73.5	74.1	1.08	1.09	1.08	1.09
Random I3		268	3244	80.3	78.7	0.30	0.29	0.30	0.29
Random I4		933	11,083	93.0	91.7	0.10	0.10	0.10	0.10
AETG-SAT	2	67	747	99.6	90.7	1.49	1.35	1.49	1.35
AETG-SAT	3	279	3234	100.0	100.0	0.36	0.36	0.36	0.36
AETG-SAT	4	968	11,434	100.0	100.0	0.10	0.10	0.10	0.10
Expert		35	741	100.0	100.0	2.86	2.86	2.86	2.86

Interestingly, the expert achieves 100% coverage with less test cases than both $t = 2$-level algorithms and thus is the most efficient one to reach maximum coverage

Table 9.7 Measurements for the **Transfer Approval** process: the expert misses the 100% coverage goal with this process and scores like IPOG-$C_t = 1$ 97% activity coverage and 85.7% branch coverage

Strategy	t-Level	Test cases	Test activities	Cov(Act)	Cov(Branch)	Eff-TC(Act)	Eff-TC(Cond)	Eff-TA(Act)	Eff-TA(Cond)
IPOG-C	1	4	26	97.0	85.7	24.24	21.43	24.24	21.43
IPOG-C	2	8	61	100.0	100.0	12.50	12.50	12.50	12.50
IPOG-C	3	15	122	100.0	100.0	6.67	6.67	6.67	6.67
IPOG-C	4	23	194	100.0	100.0	4.35	4.35	4.35	4.35
Random l1		4	31	81.8	71.4	20.45	17.86	20.45	17.86
Random l2		8	69	84.8	78.6	10.61	9.82	10.61	9.82
Random l3		15	126	90.9	100.0	6.06	6.67	6.06	6.67
Random l4		23	195	100.0	100.0	4.35	4.35	4.35	4.35
AETG-SAT	2	8	61	100.0	100.0	12.50	12.50	12.50	12.50
AETG-SAT	3	12	95	100.0	100.0	8.33	8.33	8.33	8.33
AETG-SAT	4	22	190	100.0	100.0	4.44	4.44	4.44	4.44
Expert		4	28	97.0	85.7	24.24	21.43	24.24	21.43

All random test suites miss the 100% target as well. IPOG-C and AETG-SAT with levels $t \in \{2, 3, 4\}$ all reach 100% activity coverage and branch coverage. Both IPOG-C and AETG-SAT with $t = 2$ create the most efficient test suites with 8 test cases and 61 test activities. Coverage cannot increase with higher t-levels. However, AETG-SAT creates smaller test suites than IPOG-C with these levels

Table 9.8 Measurements for the **Approver Process**: because this process has only three parameters, no 4-level test suites could be generated

Strategy	t-Level	Test cases	Test activities	Cov(Act)	Cov(Branch)	Eff-TC(Act)	Eff-TC(Cond)	Eff-TA(Act)	Eff-TA(Cond)
IPOG-C	1	4	14	93.3	50.0	23.33	12.50	23.33	12.50
IPOG-C	2	10	42	100.0	75.0	10.00	7.50	10.00	7.50
IPOG-C	3	10	42	100.0	75.0	10.00	7.50	10.00	7.50
IPOG-C	4	–	–	–	–	4.35	–	–	–
Random I1		4	15	93.3	50.0	23.33	12.50	23.33	12.50
Random I2		10	42	100.0	75.0	10.00	7.50	10.00	7.50
Random I3		10	42	100.0	75.0	10.00	7.50	10.00	7.50
Random I4		–	–	–	–	–	–	–	–
AETG-SAT	2	10	42	100.0	75.0	10.00	7.50	10.00	7.50
AETG-SAT	3	10	42	100.0	75.0	10.00	7.50	10.00	7.50
AETG-SAT	4	–	–	–	–	–	–	–	–
Expert		6	32	100.0	75.0	16.67	12.50	16.67	12.50

Except for IPOG-C$_t$ = 1 and its random counterpart, which reach 93.33% activity coverage and around 50% branch coverage, all strategies deliver 100% test coverage and 75% branch coverage. With 6 test cases and 32 test activities, the expert has selected the most efficient test suite that delivers the same coverage like the remaining strategies but with fewer test cases. IPOG-C and AETG-SAT create test suites with the same amount of test cases and test activities for this process project

Table 9.9 Measurements for the **Depot Check** process: the maximum coverage for activities is 85% meaning that the classification tree is not complete

Strategy	t-Level	Test cases	Test activities	Cov(Act)	Cov(Branch)	Eff-TC(Act)	Eff-TC(Cond)	Eff-TA(Act)	Eff-TA(Cond)
IPOG-C	1	7	45	85.0	79.0	12.14	11.28	12.14	11.28
IPOG-C	2	35	194	85.0	94.7	2.43	2.71	2.43	2.71
IPOG-C	3	81	450	85.0	100.0	1.05	1.23	1.05	1.23
IPOG-C	4	128	726	85.0	100.0	0.66	0.78	0.66	0.78
Random I1		7	38	81.2	77.8	11.61	11.11	11.61	11.11
Random I2		35	193	85.0	100.0	2.43	2.86	2.43	2.86
Random I3		81	454	85.0	100.0	1.05	1.23	1.05	1.23
Random I4		128	726	85.0	100.0	0.66	0.78	0.66	0.78
AETG-SAT	2	35	195	85.0	100.0	2.43	2.86	2.43	2.86
AETG-SAT	3	77	427	85.0	100.0	1.10	1.30	1.10	1.30
AETG-SAT	4	128	726	85.0	100.0	0.66	0.78	0.66	0.78
Expert		8	43	85.0	89.5	10.62	11.18	10.62	11.18

Both algorithms regardless of the t-value reach the maximum activity coverage. This is also true for the random test suites equivalent in size to the IPOG-C $t > 1$ suites. Only the random test suite corresponding to IPOG-C $t = 1$ does not achieve maximum activity coverage. IPOG-C $t = 2$ and the expert additionally miss the maximum branch coverage. However, the expert creates the most efficient test suite with regard to branch coverage, while the random test suite relating to IPOG-C $t = 1$ is the most efficient test suite with regard to activity coverage

Random test case selection scores worse with regard to both effectiveness and efficiency across our XBP set, so structured test selection with IPOG-C and AETG-SAT beats pure randomness. Also IPOG-C$_{t=1}$ is not very effective, but on that low level of effectiveness, it is quite efficient.

For industry XBPs, the expert is the most efficient "strategy"—especially because the expert selection usually reaches maximum possible coverage. Sometimes, however, even the expert fails to achieve the maximum coverage although this is possible with the given classification tree. Thus, while being more efficient than IPOG-C and AETG-SAT for the same test suite size, the expert is not as effective as the automatic test case selection algorithms.

Both algorithms and experts cannot perform better than the input data: the testers for three industry processes failed to provide a classification tree that is sufficient to reach 100% coverage.

During our analysis, we observed one property of the current test coverage metric definitions for BPEL that is distinctively different from the properties for other programming languages: the power of branch coverage compared to the power of activity coverage. Usually, branch coverage is stricter than activity coverage (called statement coverage for programming languages.) However, BPEL allows the modeling of several handler types that are modeled outside the main control flow and are thus not included in the branch coverage definition—test managers should be aware of this difference. We observed a lower activity coverage measure in the Depot Check process, where it was possible to reach 100% branch coverage (e.g., with AETG-SAT$_{t=2,3}$ and IPOG-C$_{t=2,3}$), but the maximum activity coverage was 85%. Our analysis revealed that this process contains further basic activities in two fault handlers. Because all branches in the normal process flow were triggered, branch coverage was 100%; but the basic activities in the handlers were not executed, thereby lowering activity coverage below 100%.

9.5.3 Evaluation of Validity

Our data set only contains processes from one project and is quite small: we covered five industrial XBPs and two synthetic ones. Also for all XBPs, only one expert selected test cases manually, and these were the first processes for which the CTG framework was applied. Therefore, the results that we obtained for the expert choices may not be representative.

However, our data set consisted of XBPs of very different sizes, with different numbers of constraints and classification tree sizes. Therefore, we think that our results are still generalizable with regard to chosen t-values and efficiency.

9.6   Conclusion and Future Work

Our work demonstrates that CTD can be successfully applied to the domain of executable business processes. We developed a novel testing technique for executable business processes that combines automatic CTD algorithms with automatic BPELUnit test generation based on classification trees. We conducted experiments with industrial processes that indicate that CTD algorithms can replace the expert in the selection of the test cases. For the processes that we considered, a t-level of 3 for both IPOG-C and AETG-SAT was always sufficient to reach the maximum coverage that was possible with a given classification tree.

IPOG-C and AETG-SAT delivered comparable efficiency for a given t-level. For some processes, IPOG-C created smaller test suites than AETG-SAT and vice versa.

However, the expert could create test suites that were more efficient, i.e., they required less test cases for a given efficiency. The expert also missed the maximum coverage in some processes. All in all, the automatic selection of test cases is more reliable but a bit less efficient.

One interesting finding is that in our experiments, coverage for XBPs maximizes at $t = 3$, while in other studies the coverage for some types of software systems maximizes with t up to 6. If further studies strengthen this finding, an evaluation of differences in the structure of the software should be done to explain this significant difference.

9.6.1   Conclusions

From the practitioners' point of view, our conclusion is as follows: The implementation of the described automated CTD technique within the Terravis project was successful, and our experiments showed that automatic selection of test cases from test classification trees with IPOG-C and AETG-SAT meets the requirements of practice.

Especially the huge number of constraints requires algorithms that consider these constraints and can calculate test cases quickly. Both IPOG-C and AETG-SAT can handle the classification trees of the studied project well. For all studied processes, $t = 3$-level covered the possible maximum activities and branches in the processes. $t = 2$-level generated less test cases and covered more activities/branches per test case but failed to reliably cover all activities and branches.

Regarding industry usage, test managers need to decide whether efficiency or maximizing coverage is more important.

While IPOG-C and AETG-SAT are comparable for generating test case selections, due to the random component within AETG, the result is nondeterministic, and coverage varies between different generation runs, which might be problematic in industry projects that cannot afford to rerun tests multiple times but want to save time.

While the expert was able to create more efficient test case selections than both IPOG-C and AETG-SAT, the expert sometimes missed test cases to create full coverage. The task of selecting test cases is especially burdensome if the classification tree becomes large, which is the case with the executable processes in our study. Therefore, we think that under most circumstances, the added efficiency by the tester does not outweigh the required effort. However, the exact characterization of this topic and the required considerations are left to future work.

An important aspect is the completeness of the classification tree that must be created manually by the testers: we observed that for some executable processes, the classification tree was incomplete, and thus neither the expert nor any algorithm could achieve 100% coverage. Industry projects require methods for detecting such problems. In this regard, an automated CTD-based approach can even help pinpoint the problem: if coverage is below 100% for an automatically generated test set for $t = 3$, this is a strong indicator that the problem is an incomplete classification tree. By contrast, a test expert who is in an hour-long process of improving the test selection to increase coverage may realize only late that the classification tree is the problem. Both approaches benefit from using coverage measurement tools in order to detect missing cases on a technical level and fix this by adding business-driven equivalence classes to the classification tree.

9.6.2 Future Work

While we are happy that we could conduct an experiment with industrial implementations, such possibilities are yet too rare. We would especially like to see (or help doing) case studies that can be replicated by others. Having an even larger executable business process set is desirable as well.

Replicated case studies will hopefully strengthen our findings but will also enable better predictions on which t-levels for the different algorithms are appropriate to reach maximum coverage. Future research should identify properties of processes or heuristics that can predict which t-level is likely sufficient for achieving maximum coverage for a given classification tree beforehand.

We have also seen that the expert selects more efficient test cases for executable business processes than the algorithms do. Further research into why this is the case and extensions or optimizations of the existing algorithms are a valuable research target in order to further enhance the efficiency of generated test suites.

Furthermore, we have seen that the current definitions of BPEL test coverage are not totally satisfactory: in order to know whether everything process flow related has been covered during testing, both basic activity coverage and branch coverage are required. Extending branch coverage by handler coverage would eliminate the problem and make the new metric more powerful than basic activity coverage. However, even with such an extended metric, the data-flow code hidden in the executable business processes is not taken into account. Due to this, we would like to proceed further by incorporating test coverage metrics that also take the data flow into account into our research. Possible effectiveness metrics could be derived by using systematically seeded faults (mutations) in the process and dataflow-dependent metrics.

References

1. V.R. Basili, Applying the goal/question/metric paradigm in the experience factory. Softw. Qual. Assur. Meas. Worldw. Perspect. **7**(4), 21–44 (1993)
2. W. Berli, D. Lübke, W. Möckli, Terravis – large scale business process integration between public and private partners, in *Lecture Notes in Informatics (LNI), Proceedings INFORMATIK 2014*, volume P-232, ed. by E. Plödereder, L. Grunske, E. Schneider, D. Ull (Gesellschaft für Informatik e.V., Bonn, 2014), pp. 1075–1090
3. L.C. Briand, A critical analysis of empirical research in software testing, in *First International Symposium on Empirical Software Engineering and Measurement (ESEM 2007)* (IEEE, Piscataway, 2007), pp. 1–8
4. D.M. Cohen, S.R. Dalal, M.L. Fredman, G.C. Patton, The aetg system: an approach to testing based on combinatorial design. IEEE Trans. Softw. Eng. **23**(7), 437–444 (1997)
5. M.B. Cohen, M.B. Dwyer, J. Shi, Constructing interaction test suites for highly-configurable systems in the presence of constraints: a greedy approach. IEEE Trans. Softw. Eng. **34**(5), 633–650 (2008)
6. M. Grochtmann, Test case design using classification trees, in *Proceedings of the International Conference on Software Testing Analysis & Review (STAR 1994), Washington* (1994), pp. 93–117
7. P. Kruse, O. Shehory, D. Citron, N. Condori-Fern'andez, T. Vos, B. Mendelson, Assessing the applicability of a combinatorial testing tool within an industrial environment, in *CIBSE 2014: Proceedings of the 17th Ibero-American Conference Software Engineering* (2014)
8. D.R. Kuhn, M.J. Reilly, An investigation of the applicability of design of experiments to software testing, in *Software Engineering Workshop, 2002. Proceedings. 27th Annual NASA Goddard/IEEE* (IEEE, Piscataway, 2002), pp. 91–95
9. D.R. Kuhn, D.R. Wallace, A.M. Gallo, Software fault interactions and implications for software testing. IEEE Trans. Softw. Eng. **30**(6), 418–421 (2004)
10. Y. Lei, R. Kacker, D.R. Kuhn, V. Okun, J. Lawrence, IPOG-IPOG-D: efficient test generation for multi-way combinatorial testing. Softw. Test. Verif. Reliab. **18**(3), 125–148 (2008)
11. D. Lübke, Unit testing bpel compositions, in *Test and Analysis of Service-Oriented Systems*, ed. by L. Baresi, E. Di Nitto (Springer, Berlin, 2007)
12. D. Lübke, Using metric time lines for identifying architecture shortcomings in process execution architectures, in *2015 IEEE/ACM 2nd International Workshop on Software Architecture and Metrics (SAM)* (IEEE, Piscataway, 2015), pp. 55–58
13. D. Lübke, Calculating test coverage for BPEL processes with process log analysis, in *Proceedings of the Eighth International Conference on Business Intelligence and Technology (BUSTECH 2018)* (2018, accepted)
14. D. Lübke, L. Singer, A. Salnikow, Calculating BPEL test coverage through instrumentation, in *Workshop on Automated Software Testing (AST 2009), ICSE 2009* (IEEE, Piscataway, 2009), pp. 115–122
15. D. Lübke, A. Ivanchikj, C. Pautasso, A template for sharing empirical business process metrics, in *Business Process Management Forum - BPM Forum 2017* (Springer, Cham, 2017), pp. 36–52
16. P. Mayer, D. Lübke, Towards a BPEL unit testing framework, in *TAV-WEB '06: Proceedings of the 2006 Workshop on Testing, Analysis, and Verification of Web Services and Applications, Portland* (ACM, New York, 2006), pp. 33–42

17. E. Puoskari, T.E.J. Vos, N. Condori-Fernandez, P.M. Kruse, Evaluating applicability of combinatorial testing in an industrial environment: a case study, in *Proceedings of the 2013 International Workshop on Joining AcadeMiA and Industry Contributions to Testing Automation, JAMAICA 2013* (ACM, New York, 2013), pp. 7–12
18. X.-F. Qi, Z.-Y. Wang, J.-Q. Mao, P. Wang, Automated testing of web applications using combinatorial strategies. J. Comput. Sci. Technol. **32**(1), 199–210 (2017)
19. T. Schnelle, D. Lübke, Towards the generation of test cases for executable business processes from classification trees, in *Proceedings of the 9th Central European Workshop on Services and their Composition (ZEUS) 2017* (2017), pp. 15–22
20. K.-C. Tai, Y. Lei, A test generation strategy for pairwise testing. IEEE Trans. Softw. Eng. **28**(1), 109–111 (2002)
21. K. Tatsumi, Test case design support system, in *Proceedings of International Conference on Quality Control, Tokyo* (1987), pp. 615–620
22. D. Vatlin, Generation of test suites for business processes based on combinatorial test design, Bachelor thesis, Leibniz University of Hanover, 2017
23. L. Yu, Y. Lei, M. Nourozborazjany, R.N. Kacker, D.R. Kuhn, An efficient algorithm for constraint handling in combinatorial test generation, in *2013 IEEE Sixth International Conference on Software Testing, Verification and Validation* (IEEE, Piscataway, 2013), pp. 242–251